PERSUASIVE COMMUNICATION

THE GUILFORD COMMUNICATION SERIES

Editors
Theodore L. Glasser
Department of Communication, Stanford University

Howard E. Sypher
Department of Communication Studies, Universitiy of Kansas

Advisory Board

Charles Berger	Peter Monge	Michael Schudson
James Carey	Barbara O'Keefe	Ellen Wartella

PERSUASIVE COMMUNICATION
James B. Stiff

REFORMING LIBEL LAW
John Soloski and Randall P. Bezanson, *Editors*

MESSAGE EFFECTS RESEARCH: PRINCIPLES OF DESIGN AND ANALYSIS
Sally Jackson

CRITICAL PERSPECTIVES ON MEDIA AND SOCIETY
Robert K. Avery and David Eason, *Editors*

THE JOURNALISM OF OUTRAGE: INVESTIGATIVE REPORTING
AND AGENDA BUILDING IN AMERICA
David L. Protess, Fay Lomax Cook, Jack C. Doppelt, James S. Ettema,
Margaret T. Gordon, Donna R. Leff, and Peter Miller

MASS MEDIA AND POLITICAL TRANSITION:
THE HONG KONG PRESS IN CHINA'S ORBIT
Joseph Man Chan and Chin-Chuan Lee

STUDYING INTERPERSONAL INTERACTION
Barbara M. Montgomery and Steve Duck, *Editors*

VOICES OF CHINA: THE INTERPLAY OF POLITICS AND JOURNALISM
Chin-Chuan Lee, *Editor*

COMMUNICATION AND CONTROL: NETWORKS
AND THE NEW ECONOMIES OF COMMUNICATION
G. J. Mulgan

PERSUASIVE
COMMUNICATION

James B. Stiff

THE GUILFORD PRESS
New York   London

*This book is dedicated to Gerald R. Miller,
a good friend and mentor.*

©1994 The Guilford Press
A Division of Guilford Publications, Inc.
72 Spring Street, New York, NY 10012

Printed in the United States of America

This book is printed on acid-free paper.

Last digit is print number: 9 8 7 6 5 4 3 2 1

Library of Congress Cataloging-in-Publication Data

Stiff, James B. (James Brian)
    Persuasive communication / James B. Stiff.
        p.   cm.—(The Guilford communication series)
    Includes bibliographical references and index.
    ISBN 0-89862-308-1
    1. Persuasion (Rhetoric)   2. Persuasion (Psychology)
3. Communication.   I. Title.   II. Series.
P301.5.P47S75   1993
808—dc20   93-23401
                                                                CIP

Acknowledgments

I would like to thank several friends who made important contributions to this project. I would like to acknowledge the contributions of Mike Allen, Jim Dillard, Jerry Hale, Paul Mongeau, Rodney Reynolds, Melanie Trost, Steve Wilson, Kim Witte, and an anonymous reviewer. They all provided much needed feedback and helpful recommendations on earlier drafts of the chapters that follow. I would like to thank Ellen Kussman who prepared the figures for publication and Lori Adler who provided valuable assistance in the preparation of the manuscript. Most important, I would like to thank Kathy Miller for her support throughout this project. She offered feedback about conceptual issues, spent hours in editorial support, and provided much needed encouragement and social support.

Preface

My primary motivation for writing this book was to have a textbook for my students that reflects the way I organize the persuasion literature in my persuasion courses. Instead of organizing the literature around classic theories, I prefer an organization that emphasizes important issues. Thus, unlike many persuasion textbooks, there are no chapters in this book that are devoted to the Theory of Reasoned Action, Cognitive Dissonance Theory, Social Judgment Theory, and the like. Instead, you'll find a review of essential characteristics of persuasion, and a discussion of how these characteristics are effectively used in persuasive transactions.

To be sure, there are thorough reviews of the classic theories of persuasion in the chapters that follow. However, I introduce these theories where they are informative about a particular substantive issue. For example, in Chapter 1, where the concept of an attitude is defined, I introduce the Theory of Reasoned Action because it provides some insights into the definition of an attitude. I revisit the Theory of Reasoned Action again in Chapter 3, where it also informs the discussion of the relationship between attitudes and behavioral intentions. Cognitive Dissonance Theory is introduced in Chapter 4 where I examine the influence of behavior on attitudes and attitude change. Thus, in the pages that follow, you'll find a discussion of many important theories of persuasion when they are relevant to the issue under consideration.

Two additional features of the book bear mentioning. First, the book is not intended to be an encyclopedic review of prior persuasion research. Such reviews are already available. Instead, I review enough research to clearly explain the issue under consideration, but not so much that the ideas under discussion become lost in a surfeit of studies. For most topics I describe a typical study in the research area and then summarize the important findings of studies in that area. Finally, where it was possible to summarize the findings of an area without becoming embroiled in a methodological debate, I avoid the

debate and focus on drawing substantive conclusions about the literature. Sometimes, however, substantive conclusions are affected by
researchers' methodological choices. In these cases, I examine the
methods and describe their influence on a study's findings.

There are three major sections in the book. The four chapters in
Part I discuss fundamental issues in persuasion research and lay the
foundation for the topics discussed later. Chapter 1 defines several essential concepts of persuasion and draws distinctions among several
types of persuasive activity. The broad definition of persuasion presented
in Chapter 1 reflects the diversity of the types of communicative activities that are examined in subsequent chapters. Chapter 2 reviews
the research methods that are most common to persuasion investigations. The book is written for students who have a basic knowledge
about social scientific research methods and Chapter 2 is meant as a
review of, rather than an introduction to, these methods. In my persuasion classes, I generally review fundamental issues in research
methods to ensure that students are informed consumers of the investigations we discuss. For students with an advanced understanding of
research methods, Chapter 2 may be the least valuable part of the book.
For students with more limited experience, Chapter 2 may be essential
to understanding the literature reviews that follow.

The next two chapters examine the relationship between attitudes
and behavior, which are the focus of many theories of persuasion. Consequently, researchers have devoted considerable effort to investigating
the relationship between them. In Chapter 3 I consider the conditions
under which attitudes predict behavior. In Chapter 4 I turn the table
and describe the conditions under which behaviors affect attitudes.

Having described the basic elements of persuasion research, I focus attention on the essential features of persuasive transactions in the
four chapters of Part II. Chapter 5 examines features of persuasive
sources, Chapter 6 describes persuasive message characteristics, Chapter
7 discusses important characteristics of message receivers, and Chapter 8 reviews persuasive settings.

Part III of the book examines three contemporary approaches to
persuasion theory. In these chapters I examine how the concepts and
research findings described in Parts I and II have been integrated into
theoretical perspectives for studying persuasive communication. Chapter
9 describes cognitive models of persuasion, Chapter 10 discusses models
of interpersonal compliance, and Chapter 11 examines models that have
been effectively applied in media influence campaigns. Each of these
three chapters reflects contemporary programs of persuasion research
that have evolved from knowledge of the basic elements of persuasion
that were examined in Part II of the book.

Contents

PART I

FUNDAMENTAL ISSUES IN PERSUASION RESEARCH

This section introduces the essential concepts of persuasive communication. Chapter 1 introduces and defines persuasive activity. Chapter 2 reviews the research methods that are common to persuasion research. Included in this review are criteria for evaluating the quality of research investigations. Chapter 3 investigates the relationship between attitudes and behavior and answers the question, "Under what conditions do attitudes predict behavior?" Chapter 4 concludes this part of the book by describing the conditions under which changes in behavior will produce attitude change.

CHAPTER ONE

Concepts, Definitions, and Basic Distinctions

LOOKING AHEAD . . .

This chapter introduces the concept of persuasion and provides a definition of the persuasion process. Following this, two related definitions of the attitude construct are discussed. The chapter concludes with a discussion of functional approaches to studying attitudes and the role of attitudes in the development of theories of persuasion.

As a connoisseur of late-night "junk TV" I routinely subject myself to the worst that television advertising has to offer. I am often amazed by the number and variety of advertisements that can be aired in a single commercial break. Not too long ago, I watched seven different messages during one break. One ad encouraged me to purchase a particular brand of batteries and another described the many household uses for baking soda. Of course, there were the obligatory late-night beer and pizza commercials. However, there was also an ad that promoted the virtues of labor unions, and, because it was an election year, there were two political advertisements. One campaign ad encouraged me to vote for a neighbor who was running for the U.S. House of Representatives, and another supported a proposition to create a state holiday in memory of civil rights leader Martin Luther King, Jr.

There were marked differences in the style, substance, and objectives of these advertisements, but they shared one important characteristic; they were all intended to persuade late-night television viewers like myself. The goals of these different television advertisements underscore the variety of functions that persuasive messages can serve.

For example, the baking soda commercial was designed to teach viewers about "new uses" for an old product. The beer and battery advertisements were intended to reinforce buying decisions and promote "brand loyalty." The pizza and political advertisements promoted a specific behavior, that is, voting for the candidate or proposition, or calling to order a late-night pizza. Finally, the union advertisement was designed to project a favorable image of organized labor.

The variety of goals and message characteristics apparent in these television commercials is evidence of the large number of communicative options available to people in everyday persuasive transactions. The diverse nature of this type of communication is also reflected in the variety of academic fields, ranging from communication and social psychology to political science and advertising, that study persuasive messages and their effects. Given the professional and intellectual diversity of people interested in this process, the term *persuasion* has taken on a number of different meanings. Thus, a clear definition of the concept of persuasion seems a logical way to begin a review of this literature. After describing the persuasion concept, I examine the concept of an attitude, which has been the conceptual cornerstone of many theories of persuasion. Finally, I integrate these concepts by examining the functions that attitudes serve in the persuasion process.

DEFINING PERSUASION

Miller (1980) recognized the breadth of communicative activities that are potentially persuasive. To reflect this range of persuasive activities, he advocated a definition of persuasion that is broader than the definitions reflected in prior reviews of the literature (Insko, 1967; Kiesler, Collins, & Miller, 1983; C. W. Sherif, M. Sherif, & Nebergall, 1965; Triandis, 1971). Specifically, G. R. Miller (1980) defined persuasive communication as *any message that is intended to shape, reinforce, or change the responses of another, or others.* This definition limits persuasive activity to intentional behavior. Though many activities might ultimately affect the responses of others, this discussion of persuasive activity will only consider communicative behaviors that are *intended* to affect the responses of others. Although one can argue that all communication is by its very nature persuasive, Miller identified three dimensions of persuasive activity; the processses of response shaping, response reinforcing, and response changing. A description of each process will provide a more complete understanding of this definition.

Response Shaping Processes

In the autumn of 1975, Jimmy Carter was virtually unknown to American voters. Because he was a newcomer to the national political scene, few people could correctly identify him as a former Governor of Georgia. In January 1976, a Gallup poll indicated that fewer than 5% of Democratic voters supported Jimmy Carter for their party's presidential nomination (Gallup, 1977). Ten months later he was elected President of the United States.

In the short time between the January Gallup poll and the November election, Americans witnessed one of the most remarkable persuasive campaigns in American politics. As a relative unknown and an outsider to Washington politics, Jimmy Carter enjoyed the advantages of anonymity while his advisors methodically introduced him to the American public. Together, they successfully created an image of Jimmy Carter as an intelligent, honest, and competent alternative to the Watergate-ravaged Republican party. Like many mass media campaigns, the Carter campaign was designed to foster positive responses to a new stimulus object. In this instance, the stimulus object was Jimmy Carter and the *response shaping process* was the creation of a favorable image.

G. R. Miller (1980) argued that this emphasis on response shaping processes is important because we are routinely exposed to new objects, people, and issues that require our evaluation. For example, the concept of nuclear safety did not exist in the early 1930s, but shortly after the advent of nuclear power, people began to develop favorable and unfavorable opinions about the use of nuclear energy. Today, fears of "meltdowns" and proper waste disposal are central features of most discussions about nuclear safety.

The Gulf War provided another example of the importance of response shaping processes. In January of 1990, few Americans had ever heard of Saddam Hussein. A year later, most Americans were convinced to support a war and destroy much of his country. This transformation was largely caused by the images created by President Bush and relayed through mass media. Hussein was characterized as an evil dictator and the second coming of Adolph Hitler. These images were so powerful that they motivated Americans to support a war in a region of the world that 12 months earlier was largely unknown to them.

Response shaping processes are also critical for people entering new professions. Large corporations develop extensive socialization and training programs that shape the desired values, goals, and objectives of new employees. Though less formally established, socialization processes are prevalent in smaller businesses and religious and social organizations as well.

Like socialization, many response shaping processes take place through social learning (cf. Bandura, 1977; J. K. Burgoon, M. Burgoon, G. R. Miller, & Sunnafrank, 1981). Social learning theories describe how people form responses to stimuli by modeling the behaviors of others and observing the positive and negative outcomes associated with a model's behavior (see Chapter 11, this volume).

Though notable situations provide the clearest examples, response shaping processes are typical of everyday persuasion. We routinely develop impressions about people we meet and form opinions about new consumer products. Although they are not considered in traditional, change-based definitions of persuasion, response shaping processes are a prominent feature of human social influence.

Response Reinforcing Processes

More than 500,000 self-help groups offer support to people who are coping with crises, role transitions, or problems (Naisbitt, 1982). Many of the 15 million Americans attending these self-help groups are recovering alcoholics and drug addicts who meet across the country in the basements of churches and community centers. For many people these weekly meetings provide the only meaningful encouragement they receive as they struggle to maintain their sobriety (Cline, 1990, p. 74).

Like many self-help groups, Alcoholics Anonymous reinforces the sobriety of alcoholics and assists them on the road to recovery. For most alcoholics, the decision to stop drinking is just the first step in the recovery process. Self-help groups provide social support and reinforce the decision to remain sober. These support activities reflect the *response reinforcing* dimension of G. R. Miller's (1980) definition of persuasive communication.

Response reinforcing processes are also the mainstay of the advertising industry. Although some advertising campaigns introduce new products and services, most advertising dollars are spent maintaining "brand loyalty." Findings of recent research suggest that advertising may be most effective in maintaining rather than creating brand loyalty. Tellis (1987) concluded "that advertising is more effective in increasing the volume purchased by loyal buyers than in winning new buyers" (p. 22). Recognizing that repeat customers are critical to their success, advertisers fill the mass media with jingles and slogans that increase the salience of products ranging from toothpaste to Cadillacs. Airline commercials promote frequent flyer programs that offer substantial rewards for returning customers. These commercials are an excellent example of the response reinforcement dimension of persuasion.

Likewise, politicians recognize the importance of reinforcing the opinions and values of their constituents. As political campaigns near election day, politicians spend a disproportionate amount of their time in precincts and districts where they enjoy widespread support. Returning home to friendly districts, political candidates reinforce existing political opinions and motivate people to go to the polls on election day.

Response reinforcing processes extend well beyond self-help groups and persuasive campaigns; they play a central role in the development of our social, political, and religious institutions. Most religious services, for example, are designed to reinforce belief in a prescribed doctrine and maintain lifestyles consistent with that doctrine. Elementary and high school curricula in the United States reinforce the positive attributes of capitalism while describing socialist and communist economic and political systems much less favorably.

Like the response shaping function, the response reinforcing dimension of persuasion has not been emphasized in traditional definitions of persuasion. However, G. R. Miller (1980) emphasized the importance of response reinforcing processes in his broad-based definition of persuasive communication.

Response Changing Processes

After breaking up with her boyfriend, Debbie left home on the East Coast to start summer school at a college in California. She was optimistic, if also a bit apprehensive, about her upcoming adventure. Her parents expected her to do well in the school environment, as she had dealt quite successfully with high school and the first year in a local college. Before summer school began, though, she was befriended by a group of youths who suggested that she get to know members of their informal organization dedicated to promoting "social ecology and world peace." Within a month she was spending all her spare time with the group. Only at this point was she told by them that the group was associated with a small religious cult with an elaborate and arcane theology. She was asked by the group's leader to adopt its idiosyncratic beliefs and leave school. Interestingly, she agreed to all of this without hesitation, and began to devote herself full time to raising funds for the cult. For the next three months her parents could not locate her. In the midst of their anxiety, they could offer no explanation as to why she "threw away" the family's values and her own stake in her future. Five years later Debbie described the period as a difficult but meaningful time, and the friends she made there as the best she ever had. (Galanter, 1989, pp. 4–5)

Debbie's story is just one illustration of the dramatic changes in personal and religious values that often coincide with cult indoctrination. Each year, thousands of adolescents and young adults abandon their traditional values, along with their family and friends, to become members of religious and political cults. In fact, recent estimates indicate that, in the United States, there may be as many as 5,000 cults and cult-like organizations involving more than 3,000,000 people (Allen & Metoyer, 1987).

The belief, value, and lifestyle changes that cult members experience clearly reflect the *response changing* dimension of persuasion. Though these changes are often extreme, marking a critical event in a person's life history, indoctrination into cults and cult-like organizations employs the same basic processes of attitude change underpinning many of our daily interactions.

Reliance on a charismatic leader, manipulation, and coercion are some of the persuasive characteristics that distinguish cults from other highly cohesive groups and organizations (MacHovec, 1989). Though perhaps more extreme, the persuasive strategies employed by cults are often reflected in mainstream political communication as well. For example, both politicians and cult leaders are often described as charismatic, and, like cult leaders, politicians have been known to use coercive strategies to achieve their goals. Although significant differences distinguish politicians from cult leaders, it is worth considering the similarities of many of their underlying influence strategies.

Although some response alteration experiences are sudden and extreme, as in the case of indoctrination into cults, most response changing processes evolve slowly over time. Consider, for example, two significant statements by Robert Kennedy about the United States' military involvement in Viet Nam: In 1964, he stated, "This kind of warfare can be long-drawn-out and costly, but if Communism is to be stopped, it is necessary. And we mean to see this job through to the finish " (Shannon, 1967, p. 101); whereas in 1966, Kennedy said, "A negotiated settlement means that each side must concede matters that are important in order to preserve positions that are essential" (Shannon, 1967, p. 101).

Because he helped shape America's Viet Nam policy as a member of the Kennedy Administration, his public opposition to the war in February of 1966 reflected a dramatic change in Robert Kennedy's position and signaled a clean break from the policies of the Johnson Administration. Johnson's open-ended commitment to ground troops in Viet Nam coincided with a growing number of casualties and a worsening of the conflict. Kennedy concluded that an American victory was not imminent and that our national interests would be best served by a negotiated settlement to the war (Shannon, 1967, pp. 101–109).

Like many response changing processes, Kennedy's shift on the United States' involvement in Viet Nam was motivated by new information and a reevaluation of previously held beliefs. Many persuasive theories, including Information Integration Theory (Anderson, 1971) and Social Judgment Theory (Sherif & Hovland, 1961) have helped to articulate these response changing processes that have been the central focus of traditional research in persuasion.

G. R. Miller's Definition of Persuasion

Miller's definition of persuasion expands the traditional boundaries of persuasion by emphasizing not only response changing processes, but response shaping and response reinforcing processes as well. Because all three of these dimensions are apparent in our everyday lives, a complete discussion of persuasive communication requires a definition that includes these three dimensions of social influence.

Two additional features of this definition bear mentioning. First, the term *response* underscores Miller's (1980) concern about approaches to studying persuasion that define persuasive outcomes solely in terms of attitudes and attitude change. Indeed, titles of traditional reviews of the persuasion literature such as *Theories of Attitude Change* (Insko, 1967), *Attitude and Attitude Change* (C. W. Sherif et al., 1965), *Attitudes and Attitude Change* (Triandis, 1971), and *Attitude Change* (Kiesler et al., 1983), reflect this emphasis. As discussed in Chapter 2, one overriding limitation of prior persuasion research stems from an emphasis on attitudes. However, G. R. Miller's (1980) use of the term *response* reflects an emphasis on other types of persuasive outcomes such as perceptions, emotions, beliefs, and behaviors.

The response shaping, reinforcing, and changing processes described above reflect the variety of outcomes that are consistent with Miller's definition of persuasion. For example, Jimmy Carter's presidential campaign reflected a concern with attitude and behavior formation. Voting behavior was the desired outcome of the campaign, but attitude formation was a critical intermediate step in that persuasion process. Organizational socialization, another response forming process, emphasizes the development of employee values. Response reinforcing processes apparent in self-help groups such as Alcoholics Anonymous often emphasize the maintenance of desirable behaviors. Advertising campaigns that promote brand loyalty are also geared toward the reinforcement of targeted behaviors. Finally, the example of Debbie's experience with a religious cult reflects a response changing process that targets a person's values and beliefs. In short, a broader definition of persuasion such as that offered by G. R. Miller (1980), is consistent with the wide range of cognitive, emotional, and behavioral outcomes that are routinely associated with persuasive communication.

Finally, although some scholars prefer to distinguish persuasion from the concepts of manipulation and coercion, this definition makes no attempt to draw conceptual distinctions among these related concepts. Though you might not consider the request of an armed robber to "hand over your wallet" as an instance of "persuasive communication," studies of interpersonal compliance examine similarly coercive messages that are generally considered under the umbrella of persuasive communication. As such, I examine manipulation and coercion as possible strategies for achieving persuasive outcomes. In summary, *any message that is intended to shape, reinforce, or change the responses of another, or others,* will be defined as *persuasive communication.*

DEFINING THE ATTITUDE CONSTRUCT

Many varied responses are consistent with G. R. Miller's definition of persuasion. Though affective and emotional responses are consistent with the definition of persuasion described above, attitudes, and, to a lesser extent, behaviors have been the focus of most prior studies of persuasion. The concept of a *behavioral response* is relatively concrete, and as such, behavioral responses are often accessible to direct observation by researchers. However, cognitive responses, such as *attitudes,* are more abstract and relatively difficult to observe directly. In this section of the chapter, I define the concept of an attitude and discuss the functions of attitudes in human interaction.

The attitude construct gained prominence through the writings of Gordon Allport (1935), who used it to help understand and explain human behavior. Over the past 60 years, attitudes have become a central component in many theories of persuasive communication. An attitude is a theoretical construction created by social scientists to explain the different reactions that people have toward similar objects or situations. Unlike behaviors, which are directly observable, attitudes are not directly observable and, hence, are more difficult to measure. Nevertheless, the explanatory power of the attitude construct has helped lay the foundation for contemporary persuasion research.

In its infancy, the attitude construct was defined as "a mental and neural state of readiness, organized through experience, exerting a directive or dynamic influence upon the individual's response to all objects and situations with which it is related" (Allport, 1935, p. 810). About this time, Thurstone (1928, 1931) identified methods for "measuring" people's attitudes. Since these early efforts, the evolution of the attitude construct is evidenced by the number of definitions that have been proposed to describe it and the variety of methods that have been developed to measure it.

Rokeach's Definition

One of the most parsimonious definitions of an attitude was provided by Rokeach, who defined it as *"a relatively enduring organization of beliefs around an object or situation predisposing one to respond in some preferential manner"* (1968, p. 112; italics added).

Rokeach (1968) offers several important considerations in this definition. First, *attitudes are relatively enduring.* Most scholars agree that attitudes represent more than a fleeting thought or evaluation about an object. Attitudes are developed over a long period of time and are frequently reinforced. As such, they are relatively stable and are difficult to change. This does not imply that attitudes are not susceptible to sudden and dramatic shifts, only that such changes are exceptional.

Second, *an attitude is an organization of beliefs.* Rather than being a single element within a person's cognitive or mental framework, Rokeach conceptualizes an attitude as a cluster or combination of several related cognitive elements. These cognitive elements are defined as beliefs that cluster around a central attitude object, and the entire cluster of beliefs is the attitude about the object.

A *belief* is a single predisposition about an object or a situation. The content of a belief usually describes the object as something that is correct or incorrect, good or bad, moral or immoral, and so forth. Rokeach identified two types of beliefs, descriptive beliefs and prescriptive beliefs.[1]

Descriptive beliefs are verifiable statements about people, objects, and situations. Like factual statements, descriptive beliefs are objective statements that, in principle, can be shown to be correct or incorrect. For example, the statement, "There are 260 million residents in the United States," is a descriptive belief because its validity can be established.

Prescriptive beliefs are statements about the appropriateness of a position or activity in a given situation. These subjective statements

---

[1] Actually, Rokeach distinguished between descriptive, prescriptive, and evaluative beliefs. However, it is difficult to distinguish conceptually the concept of an evaluative belief from the larger attitude construct. Hence, I restrict the discussion to descriptive and prescriptive beliefs.

reflect the values, morals, or ethics of the person or persons advocating them. For example, the statement, "The federal government should not interfere in a woman's decision to have an abortion," may reflect the degree to which a person values privacy and self-determination. It may also reflect a belief about the morality or ethics of abortion itself. Regardless, beliefs like these cannot be demonstrated to be incorrect, as they reflect subjective feelings about the attitude object.

Third, Rokeach's definition reflects the behavioral component of these individual beliefs. The attitude reflected in the combination of beliefs around an object or situation represents *a predisposition to respond*. Once established, this predisposition guides our behavior as we encounter similar attitude objects. For example, if you have a negative attitude toward drug use, you are likely to refuse a friend's offer of cocaine at a party. If this attitude is extremely negative, you might also be motivated to join a community organization and promote drug resistance among adolescents and young adults.

Fishbein and Ajzen's Definition

Adopting the perspective that an attitude is a combination of beliefs representing a predisposition to respond, Fishbein and Ajzen (1975) provided a more precise description of the influence of individual beliefs on people's attitudes and behavioral intentions. Fishbein and Ajzen argued that an attitude toward a particular behavior was a function of the perceived consequences of performing the behavior and an evaluation of those consequences. This relationship is represented in the equation:

$$A_B = \Sigma (b_i \times e_i) \tag{2.1}$$

where A_B is the attitude toward performing behavior B; b_i is the belief that performing behavior B leads to the outcome specified in belief statement i; e_i is the person's evaluation of outcome specified in belief statement i. To estimate a person's attitude toward performing a particular behavior, numbers are assigned to the belief value (b) and evaluation (e) components for each belief statement (i). The product of the belief and evaluation values ($b_i \times e_i$) for each belief statement (i) are summed (Σ) to produce a single value representing the attitude toward performing behavior B (Fishbein & Ajzen, 1975, p. 301).

To understand the contribution of beliefs and their evaluation to a person's attitude, consider the beliefs that an environmentalist and an industrialist might have about participating in a demonstration to prevent additional off-shore oil exploration along the California coastline (Table 1.1).[2]

TABLE 1.1. Hypothetical Beliefs about Participating in a Demonstration to Prevent Off-Shore Oil Exploration

Belief statement	Industrialist views		Environmentalist views	
	b	e	b	e
Coastal wildlife needs protection from oil companies.	+1	−1	+3	+3
Public demonstrations will cause politicians to vote against off-shore drilling.	0	−2	+3	+3
Prevention of off-shore drilling will increase development of alternative energy resources.	+1	−1	+2	+2
Prevention of off-shore drilling will decrease profits of oil companies.	+3	−3	+3	+2
	$\Sigma\,(b \times e) = -11$		$\Sigma\,(b \times e) = +28$	

Note. b represents belief in the statement (ranging from 0 to +3) and e represents evaluation of the belief statement (ranging from −3 to +3).

Our hypothetical industrialist and environmentalist share some beliefs, but differ on others about the merits of demonstrating against off-shore drilling. They also differ in their evaluation of these belief statements. For example, the two differ in their belief that coastal wildlife needs protection from oil companies. The industrialist believes this to be somewhat true (+1), but the environmentalist strongly believes this statement (+3). However, both agree that the prevention of off-shore drilling will decrease oil company profits. Notice, however, that although they share the same belief about oil company profits (+3), they differ in their evaluation of this belief. The industrialist has a negative evaluation of this statement (−3), whereas the environmentalist views the loss of company profits favorably (+2). Consequently, their attitudes about participating in the demonstration are likely to differ.

The attitude of the industrialist can be estimated with Fishbein and Ajzen's (1975) formula. To do this, first multiply the belief and evaluation score for each belief statement, then add these scores together. In this example, the products ($b \times e$) of the industrialist's views on the four belief statements are −1, 0, −1, and −9, respectively. The sum

---

[2]Fishbein and Ajzen (1975) provide more extensive discussion and examples of this expectancy-value model of attitude formation. Although only four beliefs are included in this example, Fishbein and Ajzen emphasize that attitudes are determined by all of the salient beliefs a person may hold about a particular attitude object.

of these products is −11, and this number represents the industrialist's attitude about participating in the demonstration against off-shore drilling along the California coast. Conversely, the products of the environmentalist's views on each of the four belief statements are +9, +9, +4, +6, respectively. Adding these four products produces an estimate of the environmentalist's attitude about participating in the demonstration (+28).

This definition permits a precise, quantitative estimate of a person's attitude about a particular object or situation. However, such estimates only become meaningful when they are compared with other attitude estimates. In the example, the industrialist's rating (−11) is difficult to interpret by itself. However, compared with the value for the environmentalist (+28), the industrialist's attitude is 37 units more negative than the attitude of the environmentalist. Indeed, this model provides an estimate of both the valence (positive or negative) and strength of a person's attitude.

When plotted over time, one can track changes in a person's attitude toward a particular object or situation through these attitude estimates. For example, if the public demonstration had little or no influence on the voting behavior of politicians, the environmentalist's belief regarding the effects of public demonstrations on political decisions might change, for example, from +3 to +1. This belief change would result in a less favorable attitude about participating in public demonstrations, that is, from +28 to +22.

In the example about off-shore drilling, the different attitudes held by the industrialist and environmentalist are due in large part to differences in their belief systems and how they value those beliefs. It is easy to understand the different attitudes of these hypothetical people given their beliefs about off-shore drilling and the utility of public demonstrations. However, it is possible for people to hold the *same* beliefs about a particular object or situation and yet maintain different attitudes toward it.

Americans often decide who they will vote for based on a single issue. For example, a pro-life activist may decide not to vote for a particular candidate who publicly supports abortion rights for women. This position may cause a pro-choice activist to support the candidate. It is possible that the different attitudes pro-choice and pro-life activists have toward a candidate may be based on similar beliefs about the candidate (Table 1.2). In this example, the hypothetical pro-choice and pro-life activists may hold identical beliefs about the likely effects of voting for the candidate; however, their evaluation of those beliefs differ. In the case of the pro-life activist, the negative evaluation assigned these beliefs results in a negative attitude (−24) about voting for the candidate. Conversely, the positive evaluations of these belief statements by the pro-choice activist lead to a positive attitude about voting for the candidate (+24).

Though it is unlikely that *all* of the salient beliefs of pro-choice and pro-life activists are identical, this example clarifies an important distinction between a person's belief in a particular statement and the evaluation of that statement. In so doing, it also highlights the important contributions of beliefs and evaluations to the formation of attitudes.

Comparing Rokeach's and Fishbein and Ajzen's Definitions

The definitions of attitude provided by Rokeach (1968) and Fishbein and Ajzen (1975) share a number of conceptual similarities. First, both definitions conceptualize an attitude as a combination of beliefs about a particular object or situation. Fishbein and Ajzen's definition is much more precise because it specifies how these beliefs and evaluations are combined to form an attitude.

Like Rokeach, Fishbein and Ajzen allow for some beliefs to be more influential than others in determining the overall attitude. Rokeach describes the most influential beliefs as being more centrally clustered around the attitude object, whereas Fishbein and Ajzen argue that highly

TABLE 1.2. Hypothetical Beliefs about Voting for a Political Candidate

Belief statement	Pro-life activist's views		Pro-choice activist's views	
	b	e	b	e
Candidate will support laws guaranteeing abortion rights.	+3	−3	+3	+3
Candidate will support federally funded abortions.	+2	−3	+2	+3
Abortion will increase if candidate is elected.	+2	−3	+2	+3
Teenage women will have more abortion rights if candidate is elected.	+1	−3	+1	+3
	$\Sigma\,(b \times e) = -24$		$\Sigma\,(b \times e) = +24$	

Note. b represents belief in the statement (ranging from 0 to +3) and e represents evaluation of the belief statement (ranging from −3 to +3).

influential beliefs receive more extreme evaluations than less influential ones. According to Fishbein and Ajzen, the multiplicative relationship between individual beliefs and their evaluation reflects the relative contribution of each belief to the overall attitude.

Finally, both definitions are consistent with Hovland, Janis, and Kelley's (1953) assertion that attitude change is dependent upon the addition to or alteration of a person's belief system. For Rokeach, attitude change is best accomplished by adding to or restructuring a person's system of beliefs clustered around the attitude object. Fishbein and Ajzen argue that attitude change is accomplished through the addition of new belief statements, or by altering a person's evaluation or belief in existing belief statements.

In summary, Fishbein and Ajzen provide a more precise definition of attitude that represents an extension of Rokeach's earlier thinking about the issue. Moreover, both definitions are consistent with the widely accepted position that an attitude reflects more than a single belief statement; it is a combination of all the salient beliefs a person may have about an attitude object.

THE ROLE OF ATTITUDE IN PERSUASION RESEARCH

Attitudes have become a central focus of many persuasion theories because social scientists believe that attitudes guide and direct human behavior. The attitude construct was originally introduced to explain why people respond differently to similar stimuli. One approach that emphasizes the predictive and explanatory power of an attitude is labeled the *functional approach.*

Functional Approaches to Studying Attitudes

Why do people form attitudes? What functions do attitudes serve? Questions like these led to the development of the functional approach to studying attitudes. The functional approach was developed in the 1950s, primarily through the work of Katz (1960) and Smith, Bruner, and White (1956). These researchers studied attitudes by examining the psychological functions they serve.

Katz (1960) identified four psychological functions that attitudes serve: (1) an *instrumental, adjustive,* or *utilitarian* function; (2) an *ego-defensive* function; (3) a *knowledge* function; and (4) a *value-expressive* function. Each of these functions is associated with a set of implicit goals that people have.

For example, people want a pleasant state of existence and are motivated to pursue pleasant states by maximizing rewarding experiences and minimizing negative ones. Consequently, Katz suggests that the instrumental, adjustive, or utilitarian function is reflected in the positive attitudes people develop toward objects or situations that are rewarding and the negative attitudes that are associated with situations that produce unfavorable outcomes. For example, college students usually develop an affinity for specialty courses in their chosen major, and they are less enthusiastic about general studies courses they perceive to be unrelated to their major field of study.

Developed from psychoanalytic theory, the ego-defensive function serves to protect people from basic truths about themselves and their environment that they don't want to face or deal with (Katz, 1960; Sarnoff, 1960). The attitudes people develop toward objects or situations allow them to insulate themselves from their insecurities or emotional conflicts. Prejudicial attitudes often serve this function. Negative evaluations of people from different ethnic and racial groups allow people to maintain the belief they are superior to "out-group" members who threaten their egos.

Attitudes also serve a knowledge function. They allow us to organize information and structure evaluations of novel stimuli. In situations where uncertainty is high, attitudes can bridge an information gap and permit the interpretation and categorization of new information into preestablished general categories. This process, referred to as *stimulus generalization,* involves the stereotyping of people or stimulus objects into categories based on the perceived similarities among them. For example, the knowledge function of attitudes is reflected in the generalizations people make about strangers during initial interactions. Automobile salespeople, for example, attempt to "size up" potential customers soon after meeting them in the showroom in an effort to determine how serious they are about purchasing a car. A well-dressed person with an automobile pricing guide book might be judged to be a prospective customer, whereas a person dressed in blue jeans and a sweatshirt might be thought of as merely a window shopper. In an effort to categorize people who enter their showroom, auto salespeople rely on well-established, but sometimes erroneous, attitudes about the appearance and behavior of potential customers. Salespeople who pay little attention to the person dressed in blue jeans and a sweatshirt may miss an opportunity to sell a car to a qualified, casually dressed potential customer.

Finally, the value-expressive function was conceptualized as a means for establishing and maintaining norms of social appropriateness. Katz argued that self-concepts are molded by social forces applied through interaction. Attitudes serve as reminders of the values and orientations of groups and organizations. When people identify with a reference group, they adopt the values and orientations of the group. For example, a devout member of the Catholic Church may hold attitudes about family planning that reflect the church's values about procreation and family development.

Also adopting a functional perspective, Smith et al. (1956) provided a list of attitude functions that parallel the list generated by Katz. Though important conceptual differences exist between the two lists, articulation of an exhaustive list of such functions is not the primary objective of functional theorists. Indeed, social scientists may never be able to present a truly exhaustive list of functions served by different attitudes. Instead, the functional approach seeks to understand the psychological foundations of attitudes and to identify specific strategies that may be effective for changing these cognitive structures.

Understanding the functions that attitudes serve is important for persuasion practitioners. For example, a politician may favor racial segregation because it expresses a value (value-expressive function) or because most of the politician's constituents live in racially segregated neighborhoods (utilitarian function). These two functions have very different implications for attitude change. If the politician's attitude expresses a value, then persuasive messages designed to change the politician's attitude must address prescriptive beliefs about segregation. If, on the other hand, the politician's attitude reflects a utilitarian function, then persuasive messages must convince the politician that although his or her constituents live in segregated neighborhoods, they would support programs that encourage racial integration. The functional nature of attitudes is apparent in the study of attitudes toward gay men and lesbians.

Functions of Attitudes
toward Gay Men and Lesbians

Many people maintain latent prejudicial attitudes toward people from different ethnic, religious, or racial backgrounds, people of the opposite sex, and people with different sexual orientations. Although some prejudicial attitudes remain subconscious and undetected, others surface in the form of discrimination and physical abuse. In a survey of 2,000 lesbians and gay men, more than 90% of the males and 75% of the females reported that they had been verbally abused because of their sexuality (National Gay Task Force, 1984). This violence has shown no signs of abatement, indeed "gay-bashing" is on the rise throughout America (J. D. Wilson, 1992).

The growing number of violent acts against lesbians and gay men has produced an increasing interest in homophobia, a colloquial term for negative attitudes toward gay men and lesbians. Adopting a functional framework, Herek (1984a, 1984b, 1987, 1988) has described the psychological functions served by experiential, ego-defensive, and symbolic attitudes and developed a measure of attitudes toward lesbians and gay men (Table 1.3).

TABLE 1.3. Herek's (1988) Measure of Attitudes toward Lesbians and Gay Men (ATLG Scale)

Attitudes Toward Lesbians (ATL) subscale

1. Lesbians just can't fit into our society. (Short-form item)
2. A women's homosexuality should *not* be a cause for job discrimination in any situation. (R)
3. Female homosexuality is detrimental to society because it breaks down the natural divisions between the sexes.
4. State laws regulating private, consenting lesbian behavior should be loosened. (R) (Short-form item)
5. Female homosexuality is a sin. (Short-form item)
6. The growing number of lesbians indicates a decline in American morals.
7. Female homosexuality in itself is no problem, but what society makes of it can be a problem. (R) (Short-form item)
8. Female homosexuality is a threat to many of our basic social institutions.
9. Female homosexuality is an inferior form of sexuality.
10. Lesbians are sick. (Short-form item)

Attitudes Toward Gay Men (ATG) subscale

11. Male homosexual couples should be allowed to adopt children the same as heterosexual couples. (R)
12. I think male homosexuals are disgusting. (Short-form item)
13. Male homosexuals should *not* be allowed to teach school.
14. Male homosexuality is a perversion. (Short-form item)
15. Just as in other species, male homosexuality is a natural expression of sexuality in human men. (R) (Short-form item)
16. If a man has homosexual feelings, he should do everything he can to overcome them.
17. I would *not* be too upset if I learned my son was a homosexual. (R)
18. Homosexual behavior between two men is just plain wrong. (Short-form item)
19. The idea of male homosexual marriages seems ridiculous to me.
20. Male homosexuality is merely a different kind of lifestyle that should *not* be condemned. (R) (Short-form item)

Note. Scoring for items followed by an (R) should be reversed. People's attitudes about lesbians often differ from their attitudes about gay men. Herek recommends using separate subscales for measuring attitudes about lesbians and gay men. Items used in the short version of each subscale are indicated. From "Heterosexuals' attitudes toward lesbians and gay men: Correlates and gender differences" by G. Herek, 1988, *Journal of Sex Research*, a publication of The Society for the Scientific Study of Sex, *25*, 451–477. Copyright 1988 by The Society for the Scientific Study of Sex, P.O. Box 208, Mount Vernon, IA 52314. Reprinted by permission.

The concept of an *experiential attitude* is consistent with the knowledge function identified by Katz (1960). According to Herek (1984a, 1987), experiential attitudes are formed whenever affects and cognitions associated with specific interpersonal interactions are generalized to all lesbians and gay men. People with mostly positive experiences will form positive attitudes, whereas those with mostly negative experiences will form negative attitudes. Because face-to-face interactions are more informative than stereotypical information, such interactions will serve to refute stereotypes and reduce ignorance (Herek, 1984a, p. 8). Consistent with this argument is the finding that heterosexuals with gay male and lesbian friends can more readily recognize inaccurate stereotypes and express more tolerant attitudes (Herek, 1984b). A recent poll indicated that only 43% of American adults know someone who is gay, and only 20% work with someone they know is gay (Wilson, 1992). Unfortunately, people with no gay male or lesbian friends may never experience the favorable interactions that are needed to eliminate their negative stereotypes.

Defensive attitudes are consistent with Katz's ego-defensive function. Defensive attitudes result from insecurity about one's sexual identity and sexual orientation. Herek (1984a, 1987) argues that protection of insecure sexual identities and the perceived threat of homosexuality is the primary function of defensive attitudes toward lesbians and gay men. Herek (1984a) argues that insecure heterosexuals should feel more threatened by similar homosexual men and hence be more negative toward them. Consistent with this argument, San Miguel and Millham (1976) reported that men with antigay attitudes were more punitive toward gay men who were described as being similar to themselves than they were to gay men who were described as being different from themselves.

Researchers often separate measures of attitudes about gay men from attitudes about lesbians. The reason for this is that heterosexual women tend to hold more negative attitudes toward lesbians than gay males, whereas heterosexual men tend hold more negative attitudes toward gay males than lesbians (Herek, 1988). This distinction is further evidence of the defensive function that attitudes toward gay men and lesbians serve.

Herek's *symbolic attitudes* are similar to Katz's (1960) value-expressive function because they represent values and beliefs that are reinforced by important reference groups. Herek (1984a, 1987) argues that sexual attitudes often symbolize a person's larger ideologies, a claim that is consistent with research findings that correlate negative attitudes toward gay men with positive attitudes toward authoritarianism and religiosity, and negative attitudes about pornography and erotic material (Herek, 1988). Not surprisingly, people with negative attitudes toward gay men and lesbians also tend to be less tolerant of other minority groups.

To reflect these experiential, defensive, and symbolic functions of attitudes toward gay men and lesbians, Herek (1987) developed and validated the Attitude Functions Inventory (AFI) to measure the psychological foundations of attitudes (Table 1.4). Three dimensions of the AFI, experiential-schematic, defensive, and value-expressive (symbolic), reflect Herek's three original functions of attitudes toward lesbians and gay men. An additional function, social-expressive, emphasizes the role of attitudes in the maintenance of social norms. Herek emphasizes that the AFI is a general measure of attitude functions and can be modified when used in different attitude domains.

TABLE 1.4. Herek's (1987) Attitude Functions Inventory (AFI)

Experiential-schematic function

1. My opinions about gay men and lesbians mainly are based on whether or not someone I care about is gay.
2. My opinions about gay men and lesbians mainly are based on my personal experiences with specific gay persons.
3. My opinions about gay men and lesbians mainly are based on my judgments of how likely it is that I will interact with gay people in a significant way.
4. My opinions about gay men and lesbians mainly are based on my personal experiences with people whose family members or friends are gay.

Defensive function

5. My opinions about gay men and lesbians mainly are based on the fact that I would rather not think about homosexuality or gay people.
6. My opinions about gay men and lesbians mainly are based on my personal feelings of discomfort or revulsion at homosexuality.

Value-expressive (symbolic) function

7. My opinions about gay men and lesbians mainly are based on my concern that we safeguard the civil liberties of all people in our society.
8. My opinions about gay men and lesbians mainly are based on my beliefs about how things should be.

Social-expressive function

9. My opinions about gay men and lesbians are based on my perceptions of how the people I care about have responded to gay people as a group.
10. My opinions about gay men and lesbians mainly are based on learning how gay people are viewed by the people whose opinions I most respect.

Note. The AFI is not a measure of attitude toward gay men and lesbians. Rather, it is a measure of the psychological functions served by such attitudes. The value-expressive dimension of the AFI is most similar to the symbolic function described by Herek. From "Can functions be measured?: A new perspective on the functional approach to attitudes" by G. Herek, 1987, *Social Psychology Quarterly, 50,* 285–303. Copyright 1987 by the American Sociological Association. Reprinted by permission.

A recent study examined the prominent influence of attitudes on learning about AIDS and HIV transmission. Using Herek's (1988) measure of attitudes toward lesbians and gay men, Stiff, McCormack, Zook, Stein, and Henry (1990) measured college student attitudes. Shortly after this pretest, these students received an extensive lecture on psychosocial issues related to the AIDS epidemic and methods of HIV transmission.

Because the AIDS epidemic was originally associated with gay men (mass media once referred to it as "The Gay Plague" and "Gay Cancer"), we hypothesized that attitudes toward gay men and lesbians might influence learning about AIDS and HIV transmission. We found that students with extreme positive attitudes about lesbians and gay men learned more about the psychosocial issues surrounding the AIDS epidemic than students with extreme negative attitudes. However, attitudes toward gay men and lesbians were unrelated to learning about HIV transmission. Presumably all students, including those with extreme negative attitudes, were motivated to learn about "protecting themselves from the virus," whereas only those with extreme positive attitudes were motivated to learn about psychosocial aspects of the disease itself. These findings suggest that the effects of prejudicial attitudes may extend beyond overt discrimination and violent behavior; they may also influence people's motivation to process information that has been associated with the attitude object.

SUMMARY

This chapter began with a definition of persuasion. Persuasion was defined as involving response shaping, response reinforcing, and response changing processes. Examples of each process were provided along with a discussion of their implications. Following this, attitudes were defined using definitions developed by Rokeach (1969) and Fishbein and Ajzen (1975). Rokeach defined an attitude as a combination of beliefs centered around an attitude object. Fishbein and Ajzen's definition was presented as an extension of Rokeach's definition. They provided a formula for defining an attitude, arguing that a person's attitude about performing a particular behavior is a function of his or her salient beliefs and evaluation of those beliefs. Finally, Katz's functional approach to studying attitudes was discussed. Herek's description of the psychological foundations of prejudicial attitudes toward lesbians and gay men exemplified the merits of this approach.

CHAPTER TWO

Investigating Persuasive Communication

LOOKING AHEAD . . .

This chapter examines the scientific approach to studying persuasive communication. The chapter begins by distinguishing social science and common sense observation. Following this is a discussion of scientific methods employed in individual investigations of persuasive communication. This discussion emphasizes design and observational procedures that are frequenty employed in persuasion research. The chapter ends with a discussion of narrative and meta-analytic procedures for cumulating the findings of individual investigations.

Students frequently challenge the role of academic research in understanding persuasion. They question the utility of investigations that draw common sense conclusions: "Why conduct an experiment that produces findings that everyone already knows to be true?" Responding to challenges like this is an excellent way to introduce the concept of scientific inquiry. This chapter discusses the superiority of scientific inquiry over common sense methods for generating knowledge about persuasion. Characteristics of scientific investigations of persuasion are introduced and criteria for evaluating and cumulating findings across research investigations are discussed.

COMMON SENSE VERSUS SOCIAL SCIENCE

Persuasion is the primary function of most communicative transactions. The social systems we live in are predicated on the development and maintenance of normative behavior. As participants in these social systems, we are routinely involved in the process of shaping, maintaining, and changing the thoughts and behaviors of those around us. Implicitly or explicitly, we communicate with one another in order to create, reinforce, or change behavior.

Through frequent involvement in persuasive transactions, we develop "implicit theories" about strategies and tactics that are useful to achieve desired outcomes. Children quickly learn that the timing of requests is essential to gaining compliance: Sensing that a parent's foul mood is likely to produce a negative response, a child may wait for a better opportunity to ask if a friend can spend the night. As children develop cognitively, they become more sophisticated managers of social interaction (Delia & Clark, 1977; Delia, Kline, & Burleson, 1979). Meanwhile, parents learn through trial and error which rewards and punishments are likely to influence a child's behavior, and parents with multiple children know that what is rewarding for one child may not be rewarding for another.

Over time, we come to view ourselves as experts in social influence. Armed with years of personal experience and countless opportunities for testing and validating these implicit theories, we gain confidence in our understanding of the process of persuasion. Indeed, we become so strongly attached to these implicit theories that we develop routine patterns of social influence. Salespeople, for example, can precisely describe the sequence and timing of specific compliance strategies that are most likely to result in a sale. Expert teachers know when to apply sanctions for noncompliance and when to provide rewards that reinforce behavior. Politicians have discovered that "10-second sound bites" are more persuasive than 30-minute speeches. However, although they are often insightful and frequently correct, these implicit theories are often inadequate representations of human behavior. Compared to the explanations derived from social scientific inquiry, implicit theories of persuasion have several important deficiencies.

First, because people have different experiences, they are likely to differ in their interpretation and explanation of human behavior. For example, a woman who has been sexually harassed by a previous employer might respond suspiciously to her current supervisor's request to stay after business hours in order to help him complete a project. However, this same request might not arouse the suspicions of a women who had never experienced sexual harassment. Clearly, individual biases and predispositions can affect interpretation of another's behavior. These differing interpretations are likely to result in the development of competing implicit theories to explain behavior. In this example, one implicit theory may be that the supervisor is interested in exploring the possibility of an amorous relationship. However, a competing implicit theory might be that the supervisor's request to work late reflects confidence in the subordinate's ability to work effectively under the pressure of a deadline. Additional implicit theories are possible. Indeed, it is not hard to imagine how every person in the work situation could evoke a separate implicit theory to explain the meaning of the supervisor's request. Thus, while this hypothetical example demonstrates how the separate experiences of two people can lead them to draw different inferences about the same overt behavior, it also underscores the possibility that an infinite number of equally valid implicit theories may exist to explain the same phenomenon.

Second, implicit theories of human interaction are not objective. Because they are derived from personal experience, common sense observations are inextricably woven with the biases of the observer. Thus, an implicit theory is likely to reflect the biases of the person who developed it. Unlike implicit theories, social science strives to make objective observations about phenomena that are not encumbered by the people making them.

Third, implicit theories are not derived from systematic observation. Instead, they rely on common sense observation that is less likely to recognize or explore counterintuitive explanations of human interaction. Though many useful theories are intuitively obvious, some are not. For example, Dissonance Theory (Festinger, 1957) offered a counterintuitive prediction about the amount of attitude change people experience after advocating a position they do not believe (see Chapter 4, this volume). Over the years, Dissonance Theory has been one of the most influential and provocative theories of attitude change. However, without systematic observation it is unlikely that Dissonance Theory would have ever been developed.

Finally, though common sense and social science explanations are both fallible, only science has a built-in self-correcting function (Cohen, 1949, p. 51; Kerlinger, 1973, p. 6). Through replication by different investigators, social science explanations are frequently reexamined. Over time, errors are detected, and when necessary theories are modified, even discarded. On the other hand, as common sense explanations become reified through experience, errors in reasoning become more difficult to change. Although many common sense observations may be accurate, people often cling tenaciously to beliefs derived from common sense observations that are incorrect. For example, for over 120 years it was wrongly believed that 98.6° Fahrenheit was the normal body temperature of healthy adults. Recently, however, medical researchers reexamined this long-held belief and found that the normal body temperature of humans is actually 98.2° Fahrenheit (Mackowiak, Wasserman, & Levine, 1992). Although this finding appears to be of little

practical importance for lay people, physicians and medical researchers routinely use the normal body temperature as a comparative bench-
mark for diagnosis and treatment evaluation. For our purposes, this
finding reflects the self-correcting nature of scientific research. Although
there was an incorrect definition of normal body temperature for over
120 years, this error was eventually corrected through the scientific
process.   .

Formal distinctions between science and common sense observation are often based on Pierce's discussion of the scientific method. Pierce
wrote:

> . . . it is necessary that a method should be found by which our beliefs
> may be determined by nothing human, but by some external
> permanency—by something upon which our thinking has no effect. . . .
> The method must be such that the ultimate conclusion of every man [sic]
> shall be the same. Such is the method of science. Its fundamental hypothe-
> sis . . . is this: There are real things whose characters are entirely indepen-
> dent of our opinions about them. . . . (Kerlinger, 1973, p. 6)

Pierce's definition allows for only one approach to scientific inquiry. However, there are a variety of methods consistent with this approach that scientists employ to avoid the deficiencies of common sense
observation (Kerlinger, 1973, p. 6). At the level of the individual investigation, the scientific approach provides specific standards for making systematic and objective observations that are capable of producing
counterintuitive findings. However, scientific discovery involves more
than careful attention to the design and conduct of specific investigations. It also suggests that scientists work within a community of scholars
replicating and cumulating findings over time. This self-correcting function requires different methods than those used to generate primary
research findings.

The next section describes several scientific methods that are frequently used in persuasion research. For individual studies, methods
of observing persuasive phenomena are presented along with criteria
for evaluating the quality of those observations. Following this, two
procedures for reviewing and cumulating the findings of individual
studies are discussed.

SCIENTIFIC METHODS OF PERSUASIVE COMMUNICATION INQUIRY

Designing Scientific Investigations

Over the past 50 years, a variety of experimental, quasi-experimental,
and nonexperimental research designs have been employed to test the-

oretical hypotheses about persuasive communication. Regardless of their nature, research designs serve three scientific functions: (1) structuring the observations of investigators, (2) providing a logical rationale for making comparisons among observations, and (3) establishing a procedural record for other scholars who wish to examine or replicate a study's findings.

Research Design Categories

Two design characteristics distinguish experimental, quasi-experimental, and nonexperimental investigations. Experimental and quasi-experimental investigations control at least one independent variable (hypothesized to be the cause) and measure its influence on one or more dependent variables (hypothesized to be caused by the independent variables). These controls are also called experimental manipulations or treatments. Nonexperimental designs involve no such control. Instead, investigators measure one or more independent variables and assess their influence on one or more dependent variables. In short, if a study involves the *experimental control* of a variable, then it is classified as an experimental or quasi-experimental investigation.

The difference between an experiment and a quasi-experiment rests on the use of *random assignment* of research participants to experimental conditions. Random assignment means that every research participant has an equal chance of being placed in each of the experimental conditions. In some investigations, it is possible to randomly assign participants to experimental treatments. This procedure allows investigators to assume that participants assigned to different experimental conditions are similar.[1] This assumption is useful in assessing the effects of experimental treatments (manipulations) on research participants. If there are no systematic differences among participants assigned to different experimental conditions before the experiment, then any differences arising after the experiment can be attributed to the experimental treatment (manipulation) because everything else besides the independent variable is assumed to be held constant across conditions.[2]

[1]It should be emphasized that random assignment does not guarantee equivalence among participants in different experimental conditions. Random assignment reduces systematic differences among the participants in experimental conditions but it cannot eliminate them. In addition, the procedures used for random assignment in many experiments are not truly random. As a result, random and nonrandom differences may exist in many investigations that are labeled experiments.

[2]Such conclusions should not be taken lightly, however. To assume that there are no threats to the validity of a design or research procedure is akin to assuming a perfect world. In almost any experiment there are several issues that can be raised to challenge the internal or external validity of the findings. Given this, researchers strive to minimize

In many investigations, however, random assignment is not possible. Participants are often assigned to treatment conditions on the basis of their membership in some predetermined group. For example, a field experiment on the effectiveness of two different television advertising campaigns may be conducted in two separate, but similar cities. Although the communities may be randomly assigned to the treatment conditions, there are likely to be important differences in the characteristics of people in these two conditions. Thus, the effectiveness of the two campaigns can only be compared after differences between the two treatment groups are measured and *statistically controlled*. For example, if socioeconomic status (SES) is considered to be an important factor in the campaign's effectiveness, then comparisons must statistically control for differences in SES across the two communities. In this case, statistical control replaces random assignment as a means of equating the two treatment groups.

Thus, experimental control and random assignment of research participants are two factors that determine the nature of a research design. These factors are summarized in the decision tree in Figure 2.1.

In addition to the differences among experimental, quasi-experimental, and nonexperimental designs, there are also important variations in design characteristics within each of these general categories. The studies described below underscore these differences and reflect the variety of procedures employed to investigate persuasive communication. Three experimental studies help distinguish between single factor, factorial, and repeated measures designs. Following this discussion, two investigations are presented as examples of quasi-experimental and nonexperimental research designs.

Single Factor Experimental Designs. The most basic experimental design involves the control (manipulation) of a single independent variable (factor) and the assessment of its influence on a dependent variable. One of the first fear-appeal experiments employed this design. Janis and Feshbach (1953) were interested in the effects of a single independent variable, *fear-arousing content*, on a dependent variable, *adherence to message recommendations*.

To study this relationship, Janis and Feshbach varied the amount of fear-arousing content in three persuasive messages. High school students were randomly assigned to one of three message (experimental) conditions or a control group. In the strong fear condition, students

---

such threats and replicate their findings by conducting multiple investigations with different samples and procedures. Only after repeated replication with various methods should researchers become confident of the findings they observe. Campbell and Stanley (1966) and Cook and Campbell (1979) provide an excellent discussion of these issues.

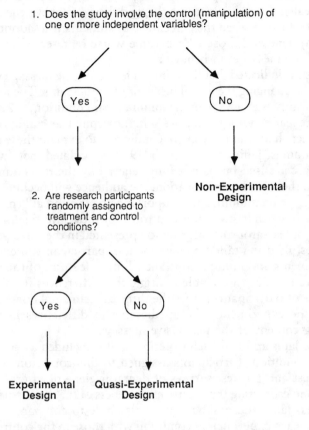

FIGURE 2.1. Decision tree for categorizing study designs.

heard a lecture, that emphasized "the painful consequences of tooth decay, diseased gums, and other dangers that can result from improper dental hygiene." The moderate fear-arousing message contained a milder and more factual presentation of these issues, and the minimal fear message contained a minimal fear appeal that "rarely alluded to the consequences of tooth neglect" (Janis & Feshbach, 1953, p. 79). Participants in the no-treatment control group heard a factual lecture about the functions of the eye that was similar in intensity to the low fear message.

One week prior to the experiment, every student completed a survey of personal dental hygiene practices, such as the type of brushing strokes they used and the amount of time they spent brushing their teeth. A week following the experiment, students once again reported on these practices. Comparison of the premessage and postmessage surveys revealed that some students changed their dental hygiene practices. The difference between the percentage of students who adopted better dental hygiene and those who became worse represented the "net effect" of the message on behavior.

Results indicated that the minimal fear-arousing message was most effective in changing the actual behavior of participants. The net change in conformity was +36% in the minimal fear condition, +22% in the moderate fear condition, and +8% in the strong fear condition. There was no net change in the control condition. To explain these unanticipated findings, Janis and Feshbach (1953) speculated that "when fear is strongly aroused but is not fully relieved by the reassurances contained in the mass communication, the audience will become motivated to ignore or minimize the importance of the threat" (p. 90).

The independent variable controlled by these investigators was the amount of fear-arousing information presented in the three persuasive messages. By using random assignment of participants to experimental treatments and holding constant all other features of the message, Janis and Feshbach were able to argue that differences in the hygiene practices of participants across the three experimental conditions following the experiment were attributable to differences in the fear-arousing content of the persuasive messages.

The Janis and Feshbach experiment also included a no-treatment control condition. Participants assigned to this condition completed the pretest and posttest surveys of dental hygiene practices. Thus, in addition to estimating the relative effectiveness of the three experimental messages, Janis and Feshbach were also able to compare the survey results in each experimental condition with those in the control condition and estimate the absolute effectiveness of the three experimental messages. It should be noted that although many single factor experiments contain a no-treatment control condition, this feature is not a requirement of the design. Investigators who are only concerned with the relative effects of various experimental treatments need only to include the various treatment groups in the design.

Janis and Feshbach employed a single factor experimental design because they were only concerned with assessing the persuasive effect of a single independent variable. However, researchers soon became interested in estimating the separate and combined effects of two or more independent variables on a dependent variable, and factorial designs were developed to accomplish this objective. For example, if one wanted to determine if fear appeals are more persuasive when they come from highly credible sources, a factorial design that manipulates both the amount of fear-arousing information and the credibility of the source would be useful. Factorial designs were first employed by agricultural researchers of the 1930s and 1940s; by the 1960s they had become a prominent tool of persuasion scholars as well.

Factorial Experimental Designs. Often researchers are interested in investigating the separate and joint effects of two or more independent variables in a single study. Factorial designs satisfy the demands of such an investigation.

The basic requirement of a factorial design is that two or more of the independent variables must be crossed with one another. An experimental design is said to be "completely crossed" when a separate condition is created for every possible combination of the levels of the independent variables. For example, if one independent variable (A) has three levels (A_1, A_2, and A_3) and another (B) has two levels (B_1 and B_2), then a completely crossed design will have six experimental conditions or cells (A_1B_1, A_2B_1, A_3B_1, A_1B_2, A_2B_2, and A_3B_2).

Petty, Cacioppo, and Goldman (1981) employed a factorial experimental design to test the combined effects of source credibility, argument quality, and involvement on attitude change. They argued that when messages are highly involving (i.e., personally relevant), message receivers are motivated to scrutinize the quality of message arguments. However, when message topics have little personal relevance, message receivers are unwilling to think carefully about the issue and instead base their attitudes on more superficial cues such as a source's expertise. Thus, Petty et al. hypothesized that when persuasive messages are personally relevant for receivers, argument quality should have an important influence on attitudes. Conversely, when persuasive messages lack personal relevance for receivers, the source's expertise should be more important in changing attitudes. Stated differently, they hypothesized two interaction effects: one specified that the level of personal relevance would "interact" with argument quality to influence attitudes and the other specified that personal relevance would "interact" with source credibility to influence attitudes.

| | | Factor A | | |
		A_1	A_2	A_3
Factor B	B_1	A_1B_2	A_2B_1	A_3B_1
	B_2	A_1B_2	A_2B_2	A_3B_2

FIGURE 2.2. Diagram for a 3 × 2 factorial design.

These hypotheses specified that certain combinations of involvement and argument quality or involvement and source credibility would produce attitude change and that other combinations would produce little or no attitude change. Hence, a three-way factorial design, which completely crossed high and low levels of involvement, argument quality, and source credibility, was employed to test these hypotheses.

Two levels of message relevance (high, low), two levels of argument quality (strong, weak), and two levels of source expertise (expert, inexpert) were completely crossed to create an eight-condition experimental design (Table 2.1). Petty et al. then created eight experimental messages on the topic of comprehensive exams, one for each condition. For example, students in one condition heard a high involvement message containing strong arguments that was attributed to an expert source. Students in another condition heard a high involvement message containing strong arguments that was attributed to a inexpert source, and so on.

Participants were randomly assigned to one of the eight experimental conditions and listened to a recorded message. Participants then completed an attitude questionnaire. The use of random assignment permitted the assumption that the attitudes of participants across the eight experimental conditions were similar prior to hearing the message. Hence, any differences across conditions after the message presentation could be attributed to the message presentation.

Petty et al. observed their hypothesized effects. As Table 2.2 reveals, participants hearing the high involvement message were influenced primarily by the quality of the message arguments and not by the source's expertise. Participants hearing the low involvement message were influenced primarily by the source's expertise and were relatively unaffected by the quality of message arguments.

The factorial design was critical for the Petty et al. experiment. The design systematically controlled the levels of involvement, argument quality, and source expertise, and it assessed the separate and

TABLE 2.1. Three-Way Factorial Design from Petty, Cacioppo, and Goldman (1981)

	High involvement		Low involvement	
	Expert source	Nonexpert source	Expert source	Nonexpert source
Strong arguments				
Weak arguments				

TABLE 2.2. Findings from the Petty, Cacioppo, and Goldman (1981) Study

	High involvement		Low involvement	
	Expert source	Nonexpert source	Expert source	Nonexpert source
Strong arguments	.64	.61	.40	−.12
Weak arguments	−.38	−.58	.25	−.64

Note. Numbers are standardized attitude scores for participants in the experimental conditions. The score for participants in a no-message control condition was −.18. From "Personal involvement as a determinant of argument-based persuasion" by R. E. Petty, J. T. Cacioppo, & R. Goldman, 1981, *Journal of Personality and Social Psychology, 41,* 847–855. Copyright 1981 by the American Psychological Association. Reprinted by permission.

combined influence of these independent variables on the attitudes of message receivers. Without a factorial design, it would have been very difficult to assess the combined (interaction) effects of these variables. Because researchers are frequently interested in both the separate and combined effects of two or more independent variables, factorial designs have become a critical tool of experimental persuasion research.

Though research designs have become more sophisticated over the past 40 years, one important feature of many early persuasion experiments has been lost in contemporary persuasion research. Early researchers were frequently interested in both the immediate and delayed effects of persuasive communication, however, present-day theorists demonstrate relatively little concern for the persistence of persuasive effects. As a result, designs that assess persuasive effects over time are rarely employed in contemporary persuasion research. Nevertheless, repeated measures designs remain an important, though underutilized, tool of persuasion research.

Repeated Measures Experimental Designs. The critical feature of repeated measures designs is the use of multiple assessments of the dependent variable. Repeated measures can be used in conjunction with both single factor and factorial designs. Whereas the terms "single factor" and "factorial" describe the structure of the experimental treatments (controls), the term "repeated measures" refers to the assessment of a dependent variable at multiple points in time. Thus, both single factor experiments and factorial designs can incorporate repeated measures of the dependent variable. For example, if Janis and Feshbach (1953) had been interested in the persisting effects of high, moderate, and minimal fear appeals, they would have measured the dental hygiene behaviors of students after 1 week and again a few weeks later to see if the changes in behavior remained over time.

Investigations of the "sleeper effect" have traditionally relied on repeated measures designs. The sleeper effect was first observed by Hovland, Lumsdaine, and Sheffield (1949), when they found that messages presented by low-credible sources were not immediately accepted, but became more influential over time. Hovland and his colleagues speculated that the positive effects of a persuasive message may be initially offset by the negative effects of the source's credibility, but that over time the source becomes disassociated with the message. That is, people remember the message content, but not its source. Because the message content is persuasive, attitude change at a later point in time is more positive than immediately following the message presentation.

As part of a larger study, Kelman and Hovland (1953) tested this hypothesis. They exposed students to a persuasive message from a positive or negative communicator. The message advocated lenient treatment of juvenile delinquents. The positive communicator was described as a judge who had authored several books on juvenile delinquency and was well known for his views on the integration of the delinquent into society. The negative communicator was described as a "man on the street" who gave the impression of being obnoxious and self-centered and indicated he got into several "scrapes" as a youngster.

Before the experiment, participants in both groups had similar opinions about the treatment of juvenile delinquents. Immediately following the message presentation, participants listening to the positive communicator demonstrated significantly more agreement with the communicator ($M = 46.70$) than participants exposed to the same message attributed to a negative communicator ($M = 42.75$, $t(186) = 4.11$, $p < .001$). After 3 weeks, participants were once again asked to indicate their opinions about the treatment of juvenile delinquents. Posttest opinions had decreased significantly ($M = -3.22$) among participants exposed to the positive communicator, while the posttest opinions of participants exposed to the negative communicator became slightly more positive ($M = +0.65$). Together, these changes represented a convergence of opinions once the effects of the positive and negative communicators had been disassociated from the message. This finding is consistent with the general pattern predicted by the sleeper effect. Over time, attitude change produced by the positive communicator decreased considerably while attitude change produced by the negative communicator increased slightly.

Relatively few studies have focused on the immediate and delayed effects of persuasive messages on attitudes and behaviors. Nevertheless, investigators who are interested in the persistence of change in attitudes and behaviors over time typically employ a repeated measures design.

Quasi-Experimental Designs. For many investigations, it is possible to experimentally control one or more of the independent variables under consideration but impossible to randomly assign participants to experimental conditions. Field studies, for example, often involve the use of intact groups. Reliance on intact groups negates the advantages of random assignment and results in reliance on quasi-experimental designs. Because quasi-experiments do not involve random assignment of participants to treatment conditions, they preclude the assumption that participants in different treatment groups are relatively similar to one another. To alleviate this problem, statistical techniques (i.e., analysis of covariance), permit researchers to control statistically for preexisting differences between treatment groups.

With the exception of assigning participants to treatment conditions, quasi-experimental and experimental designs are identical. Hence, one could conduct a quasi-experiment using a single factor or factorial design with single or repeated measures of the dependent variables. Though random assignment of participants to treatment conditions is desirable, field investigations do not always afford researchers this luxury. For example, a study of the effectiveness of a drug resistance programs for high school students would be difficult to conduct with an experimental design. Most likely, a quasi-experimental design would be used and intact classes (or high schools) would be assigned to the treatment and control conditions. In this instance, it would be impractical, and perhaps undesirable, to randomly assign students within the same classes (or high school) to different conditions. Nevertheless, because field settings often prove to be more realistic arenas for persuasion research, quasi-experimental designs are an attractive alternative for scholars of persuasion.

Though experimental and quasi-experimental designs have several desirable features, in many situations it is impossible or impractical for investigators to control or manipulate theoretical variables of interest. In these situations, researchers rely on nonexperimental procedures for estimating relationships among variables and testing hypotheses. Though a variety of procedures exist, the study described below illustrates the utility of nonexperimental procedures for persuasion research.

Nonexperimental Designs. For over 50 years, persuasion scholars have devoted considerable effort to understanding the relationship between attitudes and behaviors. Recently, researchers have become interested in identifying factors that influence the strength of the attitude–behavior relationship. For example, Sivacek and Crano (1982) hypothesized that vested interest would moderate the strength of this relationship. They argued that when people had a vested interest in a topic, their attitude about the issue would correspond with their behavior about the issue. Conversely, when people had no vested interest in a topic, Sivacek and Crano predicted a weak attitude–behavior relationship.

To test this hypothesis, Sivacek and Crano (1982, Study 1) asked college students to complete an attitude survey that included questions about a proposal to raise the legal drinking age from 18 to 21 years. After 7 to 10 days, students were contacted by a different person and asked if they were willing to work to defeat the proposal to raise the drinking age. The amount of time students volunteered to work was the measure of their behavior (actually their behavioral intention, as students did not actually participate in the campaign against the proposal).

Most of the students (80%) reported a negative attitude toward the proposal. Demographic information allowed students to be classified into three groups. Students who would be unaffected by the proposal (i.e., those who would be 21 when the law was enacted) were placed in the low vested-interest group. Students who would be legally prevented from drinking for at least 2 years (i.e., 18- and 19-year olds) were placed in a high vested-interest group. Finally, a few students were placed in a moderate vested-interest group because the new law would affect them for less than 2 years. Notice that this categorization scheme produced three groups of participants who were analytically equivalent to participants in three experimental conditions.

Sivacek and Crano reported that the attitude–behavioral intention relationship was strongest for students in the high vested-interest group ($r = .61$), followed by those in the moderate vested-interest group ($r = .40$), and by those in the low vested-interest group ($r = .16$). Thus, without the use of an experimental treatment, Sivacek and Crano were able to statistically create three groups that represented varying levels of vested interest and estimate the effect of vested interest on the relationship between attitude and behavior. Although these procedures may appear similar to those used in experimental investigations, the Sivacek and Crano study did not involve the experimental control or manipulation of independent variables. Nevertheless, the statistical controls employed by Sivacek and Crano permitted a scientific examination of the relationship between attitudes and behaviors.

Critics of nonexperimental investigations sometimes engage in fallacious reasoning. These critics have argued that one cannot draw causal inferences with correlational data. Causal inferences, they argue, can only be derived from experimental investigations. Such claims reflect a basic misunderstanding of causal inference and experimental design.

John Stuart Mill identified three requirements for inferring causation; time ordering, covariation, and elimination of alternative interpretations for the relationship. That is, before *A* can be inferred to cause *B, A* must precede *B* in time, *A* and *B* must be conceptually and empirically related, and all alternative explanations for the relationship between *A* and *B* must be examined (Cook & Campbell, 1979, pp. 18–19). For example, if attitudes are hypothesized to cause behaviors, then attitudes must be formed before the behavior occurs, attitudes must be conceptually and empirically related to behaviors, and the rival explanations for the attitude–behavior relationship must be examined.

Notice, however, that Mill's criteria suggest nothing about the method of observation to be used in gathering the necessary information for causal inference. Individual experiments or quasi-experiments are helpful in meeting the first two criteria, time ordering and covariation, but alone they cannot rule out all rival explanations for the hypothesized causal relationship. Nonexperimental observations can also be used to establish temporal ordering and covariation. Statistical procedures such as causal modeling and time-series analyses are effective substitutes for experimental control. Once again, however, the application of these techniques in a single investigation is inadequate for eliminating rival explanations. Thus, regardless of its design, no single investigation is capable of meeting Mill's criteria for inferring a causal relationship. Instead, the process of causal inference occurs over time and with converging evidence generated from many different observations. Clearly, the observation of correlation between two variables is inadequate for drawing a causal inference. Instead, careful procedures must be employed to meet all three of Mill's criteria.

Many additional designs have been employed in prior persuasion research and could have been included this review. However, the purpose of this section was to describe the basic designs that have contributed to our understanding of persuasive communication. The designs discussed in this chapter reflect a variety of analytical problems investigators face when structuring observations of persuasive phenomena. Although they provide the structure necessary to make systematic and objective observations, these designs provide only a partial picture of the observation process. The next section reviews methods of observation frequently employed in persuasion research and identifies criteria for evaluating these methods.

Evaluating Observational Procedures

A variety of observational procedures are frequently employed by persuasion researchers and each can be placed on a direct–indirect continuum. Direct observational procedures typically involve the coding of actual behavior by trained observers. For example, an investigation of the nonverbal correlates of high- and low-credible speakers might involve the videotaped recording of message presentations by speakers who are judged to have high or low credibility. These videotaped messages could then be coded (evaluated) by trained raters who identify the frequency and/or duration of various nonverbal behaviors. Such coding procedures are relatively direct because there are few opportunities for slippage between the actual and measured behavior.

Less direct procedures involve self-reports of prior behavior. For example, memory recall procedures may ask participants to remember a time when they persuaded a friend to do a favor for them and describe the strategies they used. Though they focus on actual behavior, these procedures depend on accurate memories and can be biased by memory lapses and willful distortion. Hence, the opportunity for measurement error is greater with self-report and recall procedures than with observation of actual behavior.

Because attitudes are constructs that cannot be directly observed, assessment of their existence is often based on the indirect self-reports of research participants. The Gallup poll, for example, routinely assesses the opinions and attitudes of Americans about a variety of topics. Because self-reports of attitudes or opinions cannot be verified, this measurement technique is placed at the indirect end of the continuum.

Regardless of its placement along the direct–indirect continuum, the utility of any observational procedure is determined by its *reliability* and *validity*. The application of these criteria is discussed below.

Reliability

An observational procedure is said to be reliable if it produces consistent and stable estimates of the phenomenon under investigation. For direct observation procedures, reliability is typically assessed by having at least two people observe the behavior of interest and then comparing their ratings. If there is considerable agreement among the coder's ratings (generally 85% or more is acceptable), the coding is considered reliable. However, the amount of agreement among coders depends in part on the number of categories in the coding scheme. If a coding scheme includes only three categories, then 33% agreement among coders should be expected by chance alone. If a coding scheme has only two categories, chance agreement is 50%. Cohen's kappa, a more sophisticated reliability statistic, was developed to account for chance probabilities in agreement percentages. Kappa values never exceed 1.00. Typically, coding procedures that produce kappa values above .75 are considered to be sufficiently reliable, though higher values are always desirable.

When self-report procedures are used, researchers often assess reliability by comparing the responses among two or more items (questions or opinion statements) that were designed to measure the same construct, that is, an attitude or behavioral intention. If a measurement scale is reliable, then a person's responses to one item measuring the construct will be similar to his or her responses to all other items in the scale. For example, a correlation of .80 between two items reflects a high degree of association between peoples' responses to the two items. Coefficient alpha is a statistic that represents the proportion of measurement error in a scale and is a function of the degree of association among all the items in a scale or measure. Alpha values range from .00 to 1.00. Typically, self-report measures that produce alpha levels exceeding .70 are considered to be sufficiently reliable, though once again, higher alpha values are desirable.

Validity

An observational procedure is said to have validity if it precisely measures the phenomenon of interest. Though there are few statistical procedures for assessing the validity of a measure, four criteria—face validity, content validity, pragmatic validity, and construct validity—are frequently employed to evaluate the validity of an observational procedure (Kerlinger, 1973).

Face validity is a "common sense" criterion. Most often, checks for face validity consist of reviewing the questions contained in a measure to determine if they seem to be measuring the construct they are intended to measure. Although it is the least important of the four criteria, a check for face validity is an important step in the validation process. If a measure lacks face validity, it will probably fail to meet the other checks for validity as well.

Content validity reflects the extent to which the measure or observational procedure fully represents the phenomenon under consideration. For example, the content validity of a midterm exam depends on the extent to which questions on the exam reflect the scope and depth of issues covered in the course. When students complain that an exam "did not cover the material discussed in class," they are essentially criticizing the content validity of the exam.

Pragmatic validity refers to the utility of a measure or observational procedure. Measures that discriminate between groups of people at the present time are said to have concurrent pragmatic validity. For example, a final exam in a persuasion course has concurrent pragmatic validity if it discriminates between students who understand the course material and those who do not. A measure is said to have predictive pragmatic validity if it helps predict or forecast differences among people at some point in the future. Standardized exams such as the Scholastic Aptitude Test are part of the entrance requirements to many universities and colleges because they help predict how students will perform in university settings.

Construct validity refers to the relationship between the measure under consideration and measures of other variables. A measure has construct validity if it is positively correlated with measures of variables that are conceptually similar, negatively correlated with measures of conceptually opposite variables, and unrelated to measures of variables that are conceptually independent. For example, responses to a valid measure of attitudes toward Barry Goldwater should be positively related to a measure of political conservatism, negatively related to a measure of attitudes toward Marxism, and unrelated to a measure of intelligence.

Unfortunately, most persuasion studies fail to document the validity of the measures used. Though it is common practice to discuss the reliability of measures, most studies provide little or no evidence to establish the validity of the measurement instrument. Nevertheless, validity and reliability are essential features of effective observation and, consequently, the quality of the investigation.

Evaluating Experimental and Quasi-Experimental Treatments

Validity and reliability concerns are not limited to the observation of independent and dependent variables. Experimental controls (manipulations) also vary in the degree to which they produce their intended effects. Reports of experimental and quasi-experimental studies typically include information regarding the effectiveness of the manipulations.

Manipulation checks are often used to evaluate the quality of the treatment. Frequently, manipulation checks involve asking research participants to evaluate the effects of the treatment. For example, a study of fear appeals may manipulate the amount of fear-arousing content in persuasive messages. To check the quality of the manipulation, a researcher might ask participants to indicate how fearful the message made them feel. If participants exposed to the high fear message treatment perceived significantly more fear than those exposed to the low fear message, evidence exists for the quality of the treatment.

A prevalent limitation of persuasion research stems from the weak correlation between the intended and actual effects of experimental treatments. The pervasiveness of this problem is apparent in several quantitative literature reviews. For example, a review of the fear-appeal literature found only a moderate average correlation ($r = .36$) between manipulated and perceived fear (Boster & Mongeau, 1984). Though manipulation checks in most fear-appeal experiments were statistically significant, a correlation of $r = .36$ means that the average manipulation accounted for less than 13% of the variance in participant reports of aroused fear.

Findings such as these raise two essential concerns about experimental treatments. First, when ineffective treatments are employed, it is very difficult to examine the hypothesis in question. For example, if fear-appeal experiments fail to create messages that differ considerably in the amount of fear they arouse, then it is difficult to determine whether differences in fear-arousing content account for observed changes in attitudes and behaviors. Second, the use of ineffective treatments raises questions about the conceptual development of the variable or construct under consideration. Perhaps researchers have difficulty creating effective fear-appeal treatments because they do not clearly understand what makes a message arouse fear in message receivers.

Together, these issues underscore a point raised earlier in this chapter: Though experimental treatments are often referred to as manipulations, we rarely "manipulate" people in our research. Instead, we manipulate levels of the independent variable and assess the effects of these treatments on relevant attitudes and behaviors. The fact that our treatments are always less than perfect in creating their intended effect (e.g., the arousal of fear) underscores the importance of viewing a treatment as the manipulation of a variable rather than the manipulation of research participants.

Even when they achieve their intended effects, experimental treatments may fail because they also produce unanticipated effects. This problem arises most frequently in experiments that cross two or more treatments in a factorial design. Treatments in factorial designs are usually intended to be independent of one another. However, when used in combination, they may produce perceptions that are highly related. For example, in the seminal investigation of the Elaboration Likelihood Model (ELM) of persuasion (Petty, Cacioppo, & Goldman, 1981), the argument quality treatment had a stronger effect on perceived source expertise than the source expertise treatment! Clearly the perceptions created by the source expertise and argument quality treatments were confounded, so that the strength of the arguments had more influence on perceived source expertise than the source's credentials did. These problems are not limited to investigations of the ELM, but are prevalent throughout the persuasion literature.

Up to this point, the issues discussed in this chapter have focused on the generation and interpretation of scientific data in single study investigations. However, the generation of effects is only part of the scientific process. Once numerous studies have investigated a particular phenomenon, scholars face the task of combining findings from individual studies and integrating them with a larger body of persuasion literature. The next section discusses two methods for combining or cumulating findings of individual investigations.

Cumulating Findings of Individual Investigations

The most difficult requirement for drawing causal inferences is the elimination of rival explanations for the findings of an individual investigation. Many rival explanations can be routinely discounted through careful design and analysis of observations. However, rival explanations that are derived from alternative theoretical perspectives often require researchers to develop and conduct several investigations before they can confidently choose among competing explanations. Examination of self-perception and dissonance explanations for attitude change following counterattitudinal advocacy provides a clear account of this process. As discussed in Chapter 4, Bem's (1972) Self-Perception Theory provided a plausible rival account for the findings from many tests of Dissonance Theory conducted during the 1960s. After a decade of investigations pitting the two competing explanations against one another, researchers concluded that both explanations may be correct, but that each is applicable in certain circumstances (Fazio, Zanna, & Cooper, 1977).

The process of testing rival explanations exemplifies the continuous nature of scientific inquiry. Through replication and extension of prior investigations, scientists accumulate knowledge about phenomena of interest. The knowledge generated by individual investigations is then codified in reviews of the literature. Two types of reviews — narrative summaries and meta-analysis — appear frequently in the persuasion literature, and both are described below.

Narrative Summaries

Traditional reviews of the persuasion literature consist of narrative descriptions of studies investigating the same phenomenon. These summaries critically evaluate the quality of individual investigations, high-light conceptual differences among them, and organize their findings along unifying dimensions.

Ajzen and Fishbein's (1977) review of the attitude–behavior liter-ature exemplifies the narrative review. They attempted to reconcile the contradictory conclusions of studies investigating the relationship be-tween people's attitudes and behaviors. As discussed in Chapter 3, Ajzen and Fishbein developed several conceptual and empirical explanations for the apparent discrepancies among the findings of studies in their review.

Eagly's (1978) review of studies investigating the effects of gender on persuasibility (see Chapter 7, this volume) is another example of a narrative review. In addition to evaluating the conceptual and methodo-logical characteristics of studies in her review, Eagly counted the num-ber of investigations that found women to be more easily persuaded, less easily persuaded, and no more or less persuasible than men. This counting procedure allowed her to draw inferences about the relation-ship between gender and influenceability based on a large number of investigations.

Although such counting procedures can be insightful, they represent only rough approximations of the actual relationship among variables of interest. As such, narrative reviews can result in more erroneous con-clusions than reviews employing meta-analytic procedures.

Meta-Analytic Summaries

During the 1980s, meta-analytic procedures were developed to provide more quantitative literature reviews (Glass, McGaw, & Smith, 1981; Hunter, Schmitt, & Jackson, 1982). Meta-analytic reviews begin with a critical assessment of the quality of individual investigations and the conceptual differences among them. This leads to a more complete un-derstanding of the relationship between the independent and depen-dent variables. Once the important study features have been identified, the empirical review takes place in two stages. The first stage of this review involves the estimation of the relationship among variables of interest for each study. This estimation is called a *study effect size*. Af-ter the effect sizes have been computed for each study in the review, they are averaged into a set of statistics that summarizes the entire body of literature.

Meta-analysis has a number of empirical advantages over tradi-tional counting procedures. Counting procedures rarely consider the strength of the relationship among variables of interest. Hence, a small, but significant, effect is counted the same as a very strong effect. However, meta-analysis is predicated on estimating the strength of relationships among variables. In addition, Hunter et al. (1982) provide formulas for correcting these estimates for measurement error. Measures used in persuasion research are never perfect and the presence of measurement error always reduces the size of the observed relationship among variables. Correcting individual study estimates for measurement error produces a more accurate estimate of the relationship between variables. Finally, although counting procedures weigh all studies equally, the procedures developed by Hunter et al. correct for sampling error. By weighing each estimate by the study sample size, meta-analysis places more emphasis on findings of studies with large samples than those with smaller samples.

In addition to its statistical prowess, meta-analysis has the added advantage of giving equal consideration to every study included in the review. Narrative reviews are sometimes biased by the findings of one or two studies published in prominent journals. To correct this problem, meta-analysis requires the analysis of every investigation that meets conceptual criteria for inclusion in the review. With meta-analysis, an investigation conducted by the most prominent persuasion scholar receives the same attention as one that appears in a more obscure journal.

Because they do not always concur with prevailing wisdom, or the conclusions of prior narrative reviews, meta-analytic reviews are sometimes controversial. Two recent reviews (Johnson & Eagly, 1989; Stiff, 1986) produced findings that questioned the validity of the ELM of persuasion (see Chapter 9, this volume), and these reviews were met with intense criticism from the authors of the model (Petty & Cacioppo, 1990; Petty, Kasmer, Haugtvedt, & Cacioppo, 1987). Critiques such as the latter often focus on the appropriateness and utility of various meta-analytic techniques. As these exchanges indicate, meta-analytic reviews are subject to the same reinterpretation and scrutiny as original investigations of persuasive communication. Moreover, as with any narrative review, the validity of a meta-analytic review is dependent on the quality of the individual investigations included in the review. Though procedures for correcting measurement and sampling error exist, other limitations of primary research are often reflected in the quality of conclusions emerging from these reviews.

SUMMARY

This chapter began with a discussion of the differences between scientific and common sense observation. It was argued that scientific observations are a superior method for generating knowledge because they are systematic and strive for objectivity, are capable of producing counterintuitive findings, and have a self-correcting function. Consistent with the scientific method, several experimental, quasi-experimental, and nonexperimental research designs were described. These designs reflect strategies for structuring observations about persuasive phenomena. Following this was a discussion of several procedures for observing persuasive phenomena along with criteria and procedures for assessing the reliability and validity of these observations. The chapter concluded with a discussion of narrative and meta-analytic methods for cumulating the findings of individual investigations in a review of the literature.

CHAPTER THREE

Examining the Attitude–Behavior Relationship

LOOKING AHEAD . . .

This chapter examines the attitude–behavior literature with an eye toward establishing the boundary conditions under which attitudes predict behavior. The chapter begins with a description of the first classic investigation of the relationship between attitudes and behaviors. Next comes a discussion of Ajzen and Fishbein's (1977) review of this literature as a framework for assessing this relationship. Following this, Fishbein and Ajzen's (1980) Theory of Reasoned Action is presented to describe factors that attenuate the attitude–behavior relationship. Finally, the chapter closes with a discussion of several factors that moderate the strength of the attitude–behavior relationship.

Persuasion scholars have traditionally focused attention on predicting attitudes and attitude change and have exhibited relatively little concern for assessing persuasive effects via behavioral measures. "So pervasive has been the tendency of persuasion researchers to employ attitude change as their principle measure of persuasive effect that the terms 'persuasion' and 'attitude change' are virtually synonymous" (Miller & Burgoon, 1978, p. 34). As was discussed in Chapter 1, the attitude construct was created by social scientists who sought an intervening process to explain behavioral reactions to stimuli. Conceptually, the utility of the attitude construct rests largely on its contribution to the explanation of behavior. Consequently, the utility of any persuasive theory emphasizing attitudes as the key dependent measure is dependent on the predictive strength of the corresponding attitude–behavior relationship.

If the relationship between attitudes and behaviors is consistently strong, then reliance on attitudes as a sole measure of persuasive effect permits the prediction of consequent behaviors. Unfortunately, the relationship between attitudes and behaviors has been difficult to establish. Since the early 1930s, investigations of this relationship have produced mixed findings and stimulated considerable debate about the utility of the attitude construct.

THE LaPIERE STUDY

One of the first investigations of the relationship between people's attitudes and their corresponding behavior was conducted by LaPiere (1934). LaPiere was intrigued by earlier research suggesting that people's attitudes on racial issues were not closely related to their behaviors. To investigate these issues, LaPiere traveled the West Coast for an entire summer with a Chinese couple. During their travels, they stayed in hotels and roadside campgrounds that varied in quality. They also ate at cafés and restaurants, some of which were much nicer than others. On some occasions, LaPiere entered the service establishments with the Chinese couple and asked for service. On other occasions, he asked the Chinese couple to enter establishments on their own and ask for service. Sometimes the trio was well dressed, and other times they dressed casually.

LaPiere kept a diary of the group's interactions with people they encountered. He noted that of the 251 hotels, campgrounds, restaurants, and cáfes they entered, they were only refused service once. Moreover, LaPiere found no pattern of discriminatory service in the establishments they visited.

Several months after they completed their travels, LaPiere sent questionnaires to many of the establishments they visited and several that they did not visit. The questionnaires asked whether the establishment would provide service to a Chinese couple. Of the responses 92% from the restaurants and cafes and 91% from hotels and campgrounds indicated that the establishment would *not* provide service to Chinese.

Clearly, the attitudes reflected in the questionnaire responses were incompatible with the pattern of behavior LaPiere observed when traveling with the Chinese couple. Though this investigation is not without its methodological limitations, the findings are incontrovertible: The attitudes reflected in the questionnaire responses were inconsistent with, indeed the opposite of, the behaviors LaPiere observed.

The LaPiere investigation raised questions about the validity of self-report attitude measures and about the relationship between attitudes and behavior. Investigations that followed contributed to the controversy over the utility of the attitude construct. Early optimistic assessments of the importance of attitudes (e.g., Allport, 1935) faded into critical evaluations of the attitude construct. By the 1960s, contradictory findings from many investigations caused some scholars to seriously question the viability of the attitude construct for predicting behavior (Festinger, 1964; Wicker, 1969).

Partly because of the confusion surrounding the predictability of the attitude construct, and partly because of the heuristic qualities of the construct itself, several scholars began investigating factors that affected the strength of the attitude–behavior relationship. Early efforts (Ajzen & Fishbein, 1977; Fishbein & Ajzen, 1975) emphasized methodological explanations for the contradictory findings of prior investigations. Later, researchers began to investigate conceptually related factors that affect the strength of the attitude–behavior relationship (Fazio & Zanna, 1981; O'Keefe & Delia, 1981; Sivacek & Crano, 1982). These efforts are examined in the following sections.

CHARACTERISTICS OF ATTITUDES AND BEHAVIORS

Ajzen and Fishbein's (1977) review of the attitude–behavior literature emphasized the conceptual and operational characteristics of attitudes and behaviors. Essentially, Ajzen and Fishbein argued that the weak attitude–behavior relationship found in prior research was due to a lack of specificity in both the conceptual definitions and measures of attitudes and behaviors.

Ajzen and Fishbein described attitudes and behaviors in terms of their action and target entities. The action component of an attitude is the activity implied or specified by the attitude. The target component of an attitude is the object toward which the action is directed. For example, if an undergraduate student expresses a dislike for taking comprehensive exams, the action component of the attitude is "taking the exam" and the target of this activity is a "comprehensive exam." Similarly, behaviors can be described in terms of their action and target components. If concern about the exam causes the student to study for the exam, then the action component of the behavior is "studying" and the target toward which the activity is directed is the "comprehensive exam."

Ajzen and Fishbein argued that a strong attitude–behavior relationship should only be expected when there is a high degree of correspondence between the action component of an attitude and the action component of a behavior, as well as between the target component of an attitude and the target component of a behavior. As depicted in Figure 3.1, an attitude is said to correspond to the behavior to the extent that the action which is the object of the attitude is similar to the action which is the object of the behavior *and* the target which is the object of the attitude is similar to the target of the behavior. Thus, there is a high degree of attitude–behavior correspondence in the above example of comprehensive exams; the action of the attitude and behavior is "taking an exam" and "studying for an exam" respectively, and the target of both the attitude and behavior is a "comprehensive exam."

Relying on this conceptual framework, Ajzen and Fishbein reviewed prior studies investigating the relationship between attitudes and behaviors. They categorized each study as having low, moderate, or high correspondence between the attitude–behavior entities. Low correspondence studies were defined as those that lacked correspondence on both the action and target components of the attitude and behavior. Moderate correspondence studies exhibited correspondence on either the action or the target components, but not both. Finally, studies in the high correspondence group had correspondence on both the action and target components of the attitude and behavior.

If Fishbein and Ajzen's explanation is correct, then studies with low correspondence should exhibit a weak attitude–behavior relationship, studies with moderate correspondence should exhibit a moderate attitude–behavior relationship, and studies with high correspondence should exhibit a strong attitude–behavior relationship. Ajzen and Fishbein's (1977) findings were consistent with this analysis (Table 3.1). Of the 27 studies classified as having low correspondence, 26 produced

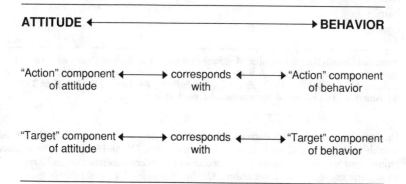

FIGURE 3.1. A diagram of attitude–behavior correspondence.

an attitude-behavior correlation that was not significantly different from zero. One study produced a small attitude–behavior correlation. Among the 71 studies in the partial correspondence category, 20 found non-significant attitude–behavior correlations, 47 found small to moderate attitude–behavior correlations, and 4 studies exhibited a strong attitude–behavior relationship. Finally, among the 44 studies with high correspondence, 9 found a small to moderate attitude–behavior correlations, and 35 found strong attitude–behavior correlations.[1] The pattern that emerged from this analysis was clear and supported the importance of correspondence in assessing the relationship between attitudes and behaviors.

In addition to these findings, a recent meta-analytic review of the attitude–behavior literature found a pattern of effects consistent with the Ajzen and Fishbein analysis (Kim & Hunter, 1993). In a review of over 100 studies, the strength of the attitude–behavior relationship was a function of the relevance of the attitude measure to the corresponding behavioral intention measures. Studies that had a high degree of relevance (correspondence) exhibited an average attitude–behavioral intention correlation that was larger ($r = .69$) than studies in which the relevance (correspondence) was moderate ($r = .62$), or low ($r = .46$). In addition, this review underscored the effects of measurement problems

TABLE 3.1. Studies Exhibiting the Relationship between Attitude–Behavior Correspondence and the Strength of the Attitude–Behavior Relationship

Degree of correspondence	Size of the attitude–behavior relationship		
	Strong	Small to moderate	Nonsignificant
High	35	9	0
Partial	4	47	20
Low	0	1	26

Note. Numbers reflect the number of studies that fell within each of these categories. From "Attitude–behavior relations: A theoretical analysis and review of empirical research" by I. Ajzen & M. Fishbein, 1977, *Psychological Bulletin, 84,* 888–918. Copyright 1977 by the American Psychological Assocation. Adapted by permission.

[1]Actually, studies with high correspondence divided into two groups, those which used reliable measures and those without reliable measures. Of the 18 studies with suspect attitude and behavior measures, 9 reported small to moderate correlations and 9 reported strong attitude–behavior correlations. Of the 26 studies that used reliable measures, all 26 found a strong attitude–behavior correlation. This finding emphasizes the importance of measurement qualities discussed in Chapter 2 of this volume.

(described in Chapter 2, this volume) on the estimation of the attitude–behavior relationship. Once statistical corrections were applied, the corrected correlations for the high, moderate, and low relevance studies increased dramatically ($r = .90$, $r = .82$, and $r = .70$, respectively) (Kim & Hunter, 1993).

In summary, the findings of these reviews (Ajzen & Fishbein, 1977; Kim & Hunter, 1993) are consistent with earlier speculation that the weak attitude–behavior relationship found in many studies is due in part to conceptual ambiguity in the attitude and behavior measures (Miller, 1967; Wicker, 1969). Many prior studies lacked correspondence because they measured general attitudes and used them to predict behaviors toward specific people or situations, for example, using a measure of religiosity to predict attendance at Sunday church services. Essentially, these reviews argued that conceptual and measurement problems attenuated the strength of the attitude–behavior relationship in prior research.

The viability of the attitude–behavior relationship was reasserted in the Ajzen and Fishbein review. However, the specific nature of this relationship remained to be examined. The next section reviews a mathematical model of the attitude–behavior relationship. Following this is a discussion of several factors that affect the size of this relationship.

AJZEN AND FISHBEIN'S THEORY OF REASONED ACTION

By the late 1960s, researchers had focused considerable attention on understanding the specific nature of the relationship between attitudes and behaviors. Perhaps the most widely investigated model to emerge from these efforts became known as the Theory of Reasoned Action (Ajzen & Fishbein, 1980; Fishbein, 1967). Examination of this model and the research that tested it provides a clearer understanding of the relationship of attitudes to behaviors.

Examining the Ajzen and Fishbein Model

Extending Dulany's Theory of Propositional Control (1961, 1968) to examine social behavior, Fishbein (1967) argued that the best predictor of behavior (B) was an individual's intention (I) to perform a particular behavior. Hence, the Theory of Reasoned Action (Ajzen & Fishbein, 1980) was designed to predict behavioral intentions toward specific objects or situations. To understand this theory, I begin by examining the specific components that affect behavioral intentions, then

applying them to the example from Chapter 1 of this volume regarding voting for a pro-choice politician.

The model specifies that two theoretical components, the individual's attitude toward performing the particular behavior (A) and the existing subjective norms (SN), combine additively to determine a person's
behavioral intention (I). Specifically, the model holds that a behavioral
intention (I) is a function (f) of the importance (W₁) of an individual's attitude (A) plus the importance (W₂) of the subjective norms (SN).
The model is represented in the following mathematical equation:

$$I = f(W_1 A + W_2 SN) \tag{3.1}$$

A person's attitude (A) toward performing a particular behavior
is determined by the sum of particular beliefs about performing the
behavior and the evaluations those beliefs receive. This is the same definition as presented in Chapter 1. Recall the examples used to describe
attitudes about demonstrating to prevent off-shore oil exploration (see
Table 1.1) and voting for a political candidate (see Table 1.2). Both examples described how beliefs about the consequences of performing
particular behaviors and evaluations assigned to those beliefs combine
to determine an individual's attitude toward performing a behavior. This
relationship is represented in the following equation:

$$A = \Sigma (b_i \, e_i) \tag{3.2}$$

The concept of a subjective norm (SN) has not been previously
introduced, and it can be defined as the influences of the social environment on a person's behavioral intentions. Although it is likely that
attitudes guide behavioral intentions, Ajzen and Fishbein (1980) argued
that the opinions and attitudes of a person's reference group (i.e., friends,
family, coworkers, religious and political leaders) can influence behavioral intentions as well. Hence, the subjective norm represents an
individual's perceptions of the social appropriateness of performing a
particular behavior. Mathematically, the subjective norm is defined by
the following equation:

$$SN = \Sigma (b_i \, m_i) \tag{3.3}$$

The subjective norm (SN) is a sum of the products of normative
beliefs (b) and one's motivation to comply (m) with those beliefs. The
normative beliefs (b) are simply the beliefs reference group members
have about the consequences of performing the behavior, whereas the
motivation to comply (m) represents the likelihood a person will accept influence from the reference group member in question.

Consider the example from Chapter 1 that described a person's attitude about voting for a political candidate who supported abortion rights for women. Voting intentions are likely to be influenced by the person's individual attitude and by the beliefs of his or her reference group. Who is likely to have an influence on voting decisions? Assume that the relevant reference group contains four people: a minister, a parent, a coworker, and a relational partner. Table 3.2 reflects the hypothetical beliefs (b) each of these reference group members may have about the consequences of voting for the pro-choice candidate. Because these beliefs are from members of one's reference group, they set a standard or norm for beliefs about the candidate. The beliefs of some reference group members are more influential than those of others. Thus, the importance of each reference group member's belief is reflected in the motivation to comply (m).

Referring to the hypothetical reference group in Table 3.2, the normative belief of the minister (-3) is more negative than the relational partner's belief ($+2$). However, the person in our example feels less motivation to comply with the minister's position ($+1$) than with the relational partner's position ($+3$). The normative influence of each reference group member is determined by multiplying the value for the normative belief (b) by the value for the motivation to comply (m). The resulting value (bm) reveals that the influence of the minister's belief is somewhat negative (-3), but the influence of the relational partner's belief is more positive ($+6$). These products (bm) can then be added across reference group members to obtain the subjective norm (SN) for the entire reference group ($+2$).

Included in the equation of the entire model (Equation 3.1) are two weights (W_1 and W_2) that reflect the relative importance of the

TABLE 3.2. Subjective Norm (SN) of a Hypothetical Reference Group

Reference group member	Belief about voting for pro-choice candidate (b)	Motivation to comply (m)	Normative influence (bm)
Minister	-3	1	-3
Parent	-1	2	-2
Coworker	$+1$	1	$+1$
Relational partner	$+2$	3	$+6$
		$SN = \Sigma (bm) =$	$+2$

Note. Belief about voting for the candidate (b) scores range from -3 to $+3$ and motivation to comply (m) scores range from 0 to $+3$.

attitude (A) and subjective norm (SN) in determining the behavioral intention (I). In situations where a person's own attitude is the primary determinant of the behavior intention, the weight assigned to the attitude component is larger than the weight assigned to the subjective norm component. In these instances, a person is more concerned with acting in accordance with personal beliefs than with conforming to the beliefs of others. When the subjective norm is more influential than the attitude, the weight assigned to the subjective norm is larger than the weight assigned to the attitude. In such instances, behavioral intentions are affected more by the influence of others than by one's personal beliefs. When the two components contribute equally to the behavioral intention, their weights are equal.

Evaluating the Theory of Reasoned Action

Ajzen and Fishbein (1980) described several investigations that successfully employed their model to predict behavior. Since then, the model has been tested extensively across a variety of behavioral situations. A recent meta-analytic review of these investigations found that the attitude and subjective norm components explained much of the variance in behavioral intentions $(R^2 = .44)$ and behavioral intentions explained much of the variance in actual behavior $(R^2 = .27)$ (Sheppard, Hartwick, & Warshaw, 1988). These findings suggest that the model is an excellent device for predicting and understanding behavior. However, in many of these investigations, the attitude component was a much stronger predictor of behavioral intentions than the subjective norm component. Combined with the fact that these two components tend to be positively correlated with one another, this finding has caused some researchers (Mindred & Cohen, 1979, 1981) to question the predictive utility of the subjective norm component of the model.

There are theoretical reasons to anticipate a strong relationship between the attitude and subjective norm components of the model. Researchers of interpersonal attraction have consistently found that people like others who share similar attitudes and values (Byrne, 1971). If it is true that "birds of a feather flock together" in many personal and social relationships, then one should anticipate a correspondence between personal attitudes and the attitudes of one's friends and family. Does this mean that the subjective norm is a redundant, thus unnecessary, component of the model? Probably not. Although the attitude and subjective norm components are often strongly associated, there are many situations in which personal attitudes are incompatible with social norms. For example, research on adolescent smoking indicates that although many teenagers have negative attitudes about smoking, they engage in smoking behavior as a result of actual or perceived peer pressure. To combat these influences, researchers have begun to employ peer pressure to help teenagers resist smoking and alcohol and drug use (McAlister, Perry, & Maccoby, 1979).

Unfortunately, tests of the Theory of Reasoned Action have traditionally focused on predicting individual behaviors in relatively private settings. Some studies have focused on attitudes about abortion (Smetana & Adler, 1980), minor consumer decisions (Ryan, 1982; Warshaw, 1980), and voting decisions (Bowman & Fishbein, 1978; Fishbein & Coombs, 1974; Jaccard, Knox, & Brinberg, 1979). Given the circumstances of these tests, it is not surprising that personal attitudes have been found to be stronger predictors of behavioral intentions than subjective norms. Had more investigations examined behavioral intentions in group or public settings, findings may well have indicated a more important role for subjective norms.

Indeed, normative theories of social influence (Aronson, 1984; Deutsch & Gerard, 1955; Kelley, 1952) describe the effects of social norms on conformity to group behavior. People often find themselves performing certain behaviors in order to get along with group members and avoid group conflict. In addition, people rely on social norms to interpret ambiguous situations. Such influences stimulated research on *bystander intervention* (Latane & Darley, 1968, 1970; Latane & Rodin, 1969). In several investigations, Latane and his colleagues observed people's reactions to a variety of emergency situations. They consistently found that when others were around to observe the situation, people were unlikely to offer assistance. However, if the situation was observed by a single person, assistance was frequently offered. One explanation for this curious finding is the hypothesis that when others do not respond immediately to an apparent emergency, a nonintervention norm is established. People look to the behaviors of others to determine whether assistance is necessary and appropriate. In situations like these, the influence of subjective norms on behavioral intentions may be considerably stronger than the influence of individual attitudes. This norm decreases the likelihood that anyone will offer assistance. Given the potential for normative influences on individual and group behavior, it would be unwise to underestimate the importance of the subjective norm component of the Theory of Reasoned Action.

Furthermore, it is possible that normative influences dictated personal behavior in LaPiere's (1934) investigation of attitudes and behavior toward a Chinese couple. Recall that respondents to the questionnaire reported strong prejudicial attitudes, but LaPiere found no evidence of prejudicial behavior. Although the influence of social norms was not measured in this investigation, it is possible that had they been assessed,

LaPiere would have concluded that social norms prevented people from behaving in accordance with their personal attitudes.

In summary, existing evidence supports the Theory of Reasoned Action as a valid representation of the role of attitudes and normative influences in the formation of behavioral intentions. In addition, the model points to opportunities for behavior change. By specifying the effects of attitude and normative influences, the model provides a framework for persuasion practitioners. For example, in Chapter 11 of this volume I review persuasive campaigns, derived from Social Learning Theory (Bandura, 1977), that use individual attitudes and social norms to mold the behaviors of adolescents. Due to its theoretical precision and easy application across a variety of persuasive situations, the Theory of Reasoned Action remains a popular description of the relationship between attitudes and behavior.

In an effort to improve the predictability of attitudes and normative beliefs, Ajzen (1985) extended the Theory of Reasoned Action by arguing that *perceived behavioral control,* or the belief that one can perform the behavior in question, is sometimes an important predictor of behavioral intentions and subsequent behavior. Consistent with earlier research on *self-efficacy* (Bandura, 1982; Bandura, Adams, Hardy, & Howells, 1980), Ajzen argued that people's intentions to perform a behavior are often thwarted by a lack of confidence in their ability to perform the behavior. For example, people may perceive more behavioral control over taking daily vitamins than they do over getting a good night's sleep (see Madden, Ellen, & Ajzen, 1992). Thus, the Theory of Planned Behavior (Ajzen, 1985) posits that perceived behavioral control combines with the attitude and subjective norm components to predict behavioral intention. In addition, this theory hypothesizes a direct effect of perceived behavioral control on behavior. The conceptual differences between these two models are reflected in Figure 3.2.

A recent comparison of these two theories (Madden et al., 1992) found strong support for the perceived behavioral control component. The Theory of Planned Behavior explained significantly more of the variation in behavioral intentions and behavior than did the Theory of Reasoned Action. In addition, the predictive value of perceived behavioral control was greater for behaviors that lacked predictive control than it was for behaviors where predictive control was high. In other words, when people are certain that they can perform the behavior in question (e.g., taking daily vitamins), perceived behavioral control is not related to behavior. However, when people question their ability to perform the behavior in question (e.g., getting a good night's sleep), perceived behavioral control is an important predictor of their behavior.

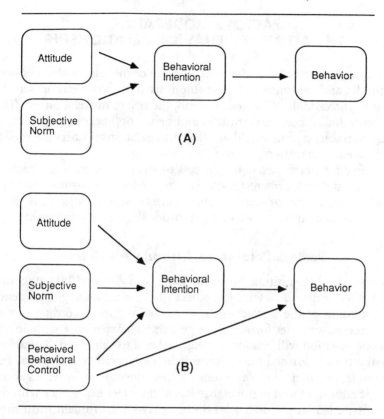

FIGURE 3.2. Comparison of the Theory of Reasoned Action (A) and the Theory of Planned Behavior (B). From "A comparison of the theory of planned behavior and the theory of reasoned action" by T. J. Madden, P. S. Ellen, & I. Ajzen, 1992, *Personality and Social Psychology Bulletin, 18,* 3–9. Copyright 1992 by Sage Publications. Reprinted by permission.

Together, these two theories provide strong support for the position that attitudes, subjective norms, and perceived behavioral control are important predictors of a person's behavior. Although the subjective norm and perceived behavioral control components are not always essential, the theories of Reasoned Action and Planned Behavior established an important role for attitudes in the prediction of behavior. Indeed, by the mid-1980s, these theories replaced speculation about the existence of an attitude–behavior relationship. Confident that attitudes predict behavior, researchers focused their efforts on identifying factors that affect the strength of the attitude–behavior relationship. Several of these factors are described in the next section.

FACTORS MODERATING
THE ATTITUDE–BEHAVIOR RELATIONSHIP

Investigating factors that affect the strength of the relationship between attitudes and behaviors shifts the emphasis away from behaviors as the dependent variable of interest. Instead, the *size* of the relationship (i.e., the correlation between attitudes and behaviors) becomes the dependent variable, and factors that affect this relationship become the independent variables of interest.

Two factors related to the process of attitude formation, *direct experience* and *vested interest* and two factors related to cognitive processing, *cognitive differentiation* and *attitude accessibility*, have been investigated as moderators of the attitude–behavior relationship.

Factors Related to Attitude Formation

In a review of the attitude literature, Fazio and Zanna (1981) suggested that *direct experience* with the object of the attitude might influence the strength of the attitude–behavior relationship. According to this hypothesis, attitudes formed through personal experience with an object or situation will be more strongly related to subsequent behaviors than attitudes formed through the indirect experiences of others. For example, children who play a musical instrument form attitudes about music education and performance based on direct experience with the activity, whereas children who do not play an instrument form their attitudes indirectly, through discussions with others, or perhaps by MTV. Consequently, Fazio and Zanna hypothesized that children with favorable or unfavorable attitudes formed through direct experience are more likely to act in accordance with those attitudes than children whose attitudes are formed through indirect experience.

Support for this proposition came from a study of college student attitudes about a campus housing shortage (Fazio & Zanna, 1981). Participants in this study were Cornell University students who were experiencing an acute housing shortage. As a result, many freshmen spent the first few weeks of the Fall semester sleeping on cots in the lounge and common areas of campus dormitories. Questionnaires were sent to students who received permanent housing accommodations and to those who were assigned temporary accommodations. Almost every student was aware of the housing shortage, and most had formed negative attitudes about the university's response to the crisis. However, the manner in which these attitudes were formed differed between students assigned immediately to permanent housing and those assigned to temporary housing accommodations. Students assigned to the temporary housing accommodations formed their attitudes through direct personal experience, whereas those assigned to permanent housing accommodations formed their attitudes after talking with friends and reading articles in the student newspaper.

In addition to measuring attitudes, Regan and Fazio invited students to take a series of actions in response to the crisis. Students were given a list of six behavioral options:

1. Sign a petition urging the university to solve the problem.
2. Encourage other students to sign the petition.
3. Agree to attend a future meeting to discuss potential solutions.
4. Indicate interest in joining a committee to investigate the problem.
5. Develop a written list of recommendations for solving the problem.
6. Write a letter expressing opinions about the shortage that would be forwarded to the campus housing office.

Regan and Fazio calculated the relationship between student attitudes and behavioral intentions toward the housing crisis. As anticipated, they found that students whose attitudes were formed through direct experience exhibited significantly stronger attitude–behavior correlations than those whose attitudes were formed through indirect experience. In other words, students who formed negative attitudes because they were living in the lounge area were more willing to act on their attitudes than students who formed negative attitudes based on a friend's experience or by reading articles in the newspaper.

Though the Regan and Fazio (1977) findings are consistent with the argument that direct experience moderates the size of the attitude–behavior correlation, the method employed by Regan and Fazio to assign students to the direct and indirect experience conditions confounded the concept of direct experience with a number of related variables. For example, students in these two groups may have also differed in the amount of vested interest and ego-involvement with the situation. Most likely, students assigned to the temporary housing conditions also had more of a vested interest, or personal stake, in potential solutions to the housing shortage than students assigned to the permanent housing conditions. Thus, it is difficult to determine whether direct experience, vested interest, or both factors accounted for differences in the strength of the attitude–behavior relationship.

To test the hypothesis that vested interest moderates the attitude–behavior relationship, Sivacek and Crano (1982) assessed attitudes of college students about proposed changes in the legal drinking age (also see Chapter 2, this volume). During the course of the investigation, residents of the state of Michigan were considering a ballot proposition to increase the age for legal consumption of alcohol from 18 years to 21 years. As part of a large attitude survey, students at Michigan State University were asked to provide their opinions about the proposition. Students were contacted by phone 7 to 10 days after completing the opinion survey, and they were asked if they would like to volunteer time to campaign against passage of the proposition. Willingness to participate and the number of phone calls they were willing to make served as measures of students' behavioral intentions.

Sivacek and Crano reasoned that all students formed attitudes about drinking through direct experiences that were similar. After all, most students were at least 18 and had direct experience with alcohol consumption. Thus, the topic selected for investigation provided a natural control for direct experience. Vested interest, however, was higher among students who were between the ages of 18 and 21 than among students who were at least 21 years old. As a result, the proposition to increase the legal drinking age provided two natural levels of vested interest while controlling for the effects of direct experience.

Findings were consistent with the vested interest hypothesis. Students who had the greatest vested interest in the proposal volunteered more time and exhibited a stronger attitude–behavior correlation than students who were relatively unaffected by the proposal.

Sivacek and Crano conducted a second study in which they assessed attitudes and behaviors toward a proposal to institute comprehensive exams as a graduation requirement for undergraduate students. Students who expected to graduate before the proposal was enacted were placed in the low vested-interest group, whereas those who would be required to complete the exams were placed in the high vested-interest group. Once again, the attitude–behavior correlation was significantly higher among students with a high vested interest ($r = .82$) than among students with limited vested interest ($r = .52$).

Together, the housing shortage, drinking age, and comprehensive examination studies reveal that the method of attitude formation influences the relationship between attitudes and behaviors. These studies are not without their limitations. In the housing study, the concept of direct experience was confounded with the concept of vested interest. Moreover, the effect of direct experience was held constant in the drinking age and comprehensive examination studies. Thus, although Sivacek and Crano (1982) documented the importance of vested interest, they were unable to estimate effects due to direct experience. Notwithstanding their limitations, these investigations suggest that vested interest and perhaps direct experience influence the extent to which people act in accordance with their attitudes.

Factors Related to Cognitive Processes

A number of cognitive style constructs have been developed over the years to describe differences in the ways people process information. One recently developed measure of cognitive style, *construct differentiation,* has been investigated as a moderator of the attitude–behavior relationship.

Delia and his colleagues (Delia & Crockett, 1973; B. J. O'Keefe & Delia, 1978; D. J. O'Keefe & Delia, 1981) have argued that construct differentiation is an important characteristic of a person's cognitive style. Construct differentiation refers to the number of different dimensions along which people judge objects and situations. People with highly sophisticated construct systems employ a greater variety of attributes when describing a person, object, event, or situation, while those with less developed construct systems use fewer traits and characteristics.

Construct differentiation is typically measured by asking respondents to write a short paragraph describing a positive and negative event, object, or situation. For example, respondents may be asked to describe someone they like and then to describe someone they dislike. These descriptions are then analyzed for the number of different dimensions the person used to describe the liked and disliked persons. Though other coding procedures are available, evaluation of these descriptions usually consists of counting the number of different constructs included in the paragraph. Constructs are typically reflected in the use of adjectives and adverbs. The greater the number of unique constructs, the more differentiated the construct system.[2] For example, a person with a less differentiated construct system might describe a well-liked friend as someone who was "fun" and "easy to talk with." Conversely, a person with a highly developed construct category system might describe the same well-liked person as a "thoughtful, compassionate, and empathic" person who is "quite entertaining" and "fun to be with."

D. J. O'Keefe and Delia (1981) argued that people with more developed construct systems should demonstrate lower attitude–behavior intention correlations than those with less developed systems. They rea-

[2]There has been considerable controversy surrounding the cognitive measures employed by Delia and his colleagues. Some critics have argued that the cognitive differentiation measure is confounded with a person's verbosity and lexical diversity; the greater a person's command of the language, the more constructs he or she is likely to include in a description (Allen, Mabry, Banski, Stoneman, & Carter, 1990; Beatty, 1987; Beatty & Payne, 1984, 1985; Powers, Jordan, & Street, 1979). Such criticisms have not gone unnoticed by constructivist researchers who attempted to demonstrate that lexical diversity and verbosity are unrelated to the measure of cognitive differentiation (Burleson, Applegate, & Newwirth, 1981; Burleson, Waltman, & Samter, 1987).

soned that people with less developed systems are more likely to be guided by a concern for cognitive consistency. Hence, they are more likely to demonstrate a strong relationship between attitudes and behavioral intentions. People with well-developed construct systems, on the other hand, are more likely to tolerate apparent discrepancies between attitudes and behavioral intentions, because they are able to more precisely differentiate the characteristics of an attitude object from the characteristics of related behavior. By drawing precise conceptual distinctions, people with highly differentiated construct systems are able to logically behave in a manner that is not consistent with the related attitude.

To test their hypotheses, D. J. O'Keefe and Delia (1981) asked students to write a short paragraph describing a person they liked and another paragraph describing someone they disliked. These descriptions were coded for the measure of construct differentiation. After 3 months, they asked these participants to write a description of a classmate with whom they had become acquainted. There were about 15 people in the class and students got to know several other classmates.

Students then completed an attitude measure about this classmate and responded to a series of hypothetical social and work situations in which they might find themselves interacting with another person. They were asked to indicate, for each context, the extent to which they would choose the classmate they earlier described for their "social partner in that situation." Responses to this measure constituted the measure of behavioral intentions.

Results of this investigation were consistent with D. J. O'Keefe and Delia's predictions regarding the moderating role of construct differentiation on attitude and behavior consistency. First, low-differentiation participants showed more consistency in the description of their classmate (either mostly positive or mostly negative), whereas high-differentiation participants tended to provide a mixture of positive and negative characteristics in their descriptions. Compared to the high-differentiation participants, low-differentiation participants also exhibited more consistency between the attitude rankings on the survey and the attitudes reflected in their written descriptions.

Low-differentiation participants also demonstrated more consistency between the attitude and behavioral intention rankings than high-differentiation participants. On eight of the nine hypothetical situations, and for the composite measure of behavioral intentions, correlations between attitudes and behavioral intentions were higher for low-differentiation subjects ($r = .88$) than high-differentiation subjects ($r = .65$).[3]

These findings are consistent with D. J. O'Keefe and Delia's reasoning and suggest that cognitive style may influence individual concerns about attitude–behavior consistency. Though it may be reasonable to conclude that people desire consistency in their attitudes and actions, these findings suggest that people with highly developed cognitive systems are better equipped to tolerate apparent cognitive inconsistencies than people whose cognitive systems are less complex.

Attitude accessibility is another cognitive variable that has been hypothesized to moderate the relationship between attitudes and behaviors. Attitude accessibility refers to the extent to which an attitude is activated automatically from memory. Fazio and his colleagues (Fazio, Chen, McDonel, & Sherman, 1982; Powell & Fazio, 1984) have demonstrated that when a person repeatedly expresses an attitude toward an object or situation, it becomes chronically accessible. Once an attitude has become chronically accessible, it can be activated automatically from memory in response to future encounters with the object or situation (Fazio, Sanbonmatsu, Powell, & Kardes, 1986). Thus, the more frequently an attitude is expressed, the more readily it is recalled from memory. For example, a person who actively works to promote legislation about abortion rights is likely to express pro-choice or pro-life opinions more frequently than someone who holds an identical attitude, but is less actively involved on the topic. Though both people may possess similar attitudes about abortion rights, the person who frequently expresses his or her opinion will have a more accessible attitude and respond more rapidly to abortion-relevant stimuli.

To test the influence of attitude accessibility on the attitude–behavior relationship, Fazio and Williams (1986) examined attitudes toward Reagan and Mondale during the 1984 presidential campaign. Attitude accessibility was assessed by measuring the response latency (the amount of time that elapses between the end of a question and the beginning of a response) associated with attitudes toward Reagan and Mondale. Later, Fazio and Williams measured perceptions of candidate performance in the presidential debates and conducted a postelection interview to assess voting behavior.

Consistent with their hypothesis, Fazio and Williams found that people with highly accessible attitudes toward either Reagan or Mon-

---

[3]One limitation of this study stems from the measure of behavior intention, which may be little more than another measure of the participant's attitude toward his or her classmate. If this criticism is valid, then analysis of the situational, descriptive, and questionnaire measures of attitude demonstrated that attitudinal consistency was greater among subjects with lower cognitive differentiation scores. Though consistent with their reasoning, such a conclusion is not informative about the relationship between attitudes and behaviors.

dale exhibited more bias in their perceptions of the presidential debates than people with less accessible attitudes. Independent of attitude intensity, they also found that people in the high attitude-accessibility group were more likely to vote in accordance with their attitudes than those with less accessible attitudes.

A study of attitudes toward the environment produced similar results. Kallgren and Wood (1986) found that attitude accessibility was a strong predictor of the strength of the attitude–behavior relationship; participants with highly accessible beliefs showed the strongest attitude–behavior relationship whereas those with relatively inaccessible beliefs exhibited the weakest attitude–behavior relationship.

These findings suggest that attitude accessibility affects the extent to which attitudes predict behavior. For example, two people may hold similar attitudes on a political issue such as gun control, but differ in their expression of this attitude. For example, one person might frequently discuss the need for gun control legislation, whereas another person with the same attitude may rarely discuss the issue. Research on attitude accessibility suggests that, although these two hypothetical people share the same attitude, the person who routinely discusses the merits of gun control is likely to have the more accessible attitude, and thus be more likely to act (e.g., vote or circulate a petition to promote gun control legislation).

It bears mentioning that attitude accessibility is conceptually distinct from attitude extremity. Though the two have been statistically related in prior research (Powell & Fazio, 1984) they remain separate constructs. That is, attitudes can vary along an extremity dimension and along an accessibility dimension. The findings of Fazio and his colleagues suggest that highly accessible attitudes affect the perception of attitude relevant information and moderate the strength of the attitude–behavior relationship.

Together, construct differentiation and attitude accessibility appear to be two important cognitive factors that influence the relationship between attitudes and behaviors. Given the cognitive nature of the attitude definition presented in Chapter 1 of this volume, it is not surprising that cognitive processes can influence the predictive utility of the attitude construct.

SUMMARY

Several conclusions emerge from prior investigations of the attitude–behavior relationship. First, the attitude–behavior controversy, which emerged in the early 1960s, appears to have been created by sloppy conceptual definitions and poor investigative procedures. Though regarded as a theoretical review of the literature, Ajzen and Fishbein (1977) focused primarily on conceptual and operational limitations of prior investigations. By the late 1970s, this controversy had been laid to rest. Assuming that precise conceptual and operational definitions are employed, most scholars agree that attitudes are predictive of related behavior.

Having resolved the controversy that had persisted for nearly two decades, researchers turned their attention to examining factors that influence the strength of the relationship between attitudes and behaviors. Research on attitude formation suggests that two factors, direct experience and vested interest, may affect the strength of this relationship. Given the quantity of attitudes people hold about a variety of issues, it is unrealistic to expect that people always behave in accordance with their attitudes. Instead, people are most likely to act in accordance with their attitudes when the issue is central to their lives.

Investigations of cognitive processing revealed two additional factors that influence the predictive utility of attitudes. Delia and O'Keefe's investigation of construct differentiation found that people possessing complex cognitive systems tolerate apparent inconsistencies by drawing precise distinctions between attitudes and related behavior. In addition, research by Fazio and his colleagues demonstrated the importance of attitude accessibility in determining the extent to which attitudes guide behavior.

Thus, although we can safely conclude that attitudes predict behaviors, Allport's (1935) assertion that attitudes exert a directive influence on all objects with which they come in contact (p. 810) is perhaps overstated. Over the past 50 years we have learned that, when properly defined and measured, personal attitudes guide individual behavior, but that the strength of this directive influence varies across people and situations.

CHAPTER FOUR

The Effects of Behavior on Attitudes

Looking AHEAD . . .

Though attitudes were viewed as the causal antecedents to behavior in the previous chapter, it is equally plausible that behaviors influence people's attitudes. This chapter investigates the causal influences of behavior on subsequent attitude change. This discussion begins with a review of Cognitive Dissonance Theory and the counterattitudinal advocacy research paradigm. Following this, several modifications to the original theory and alternative explanations for research findings are discussed. One rival explanation, Self-Perception Theory, has been particularly troublesome for Dissonance Theory advocates. Theoretical differences between these rival explanations and corresponding investigations of these explanations are reviewed.

Can changes in behavior affect subsequent attitudes? The answer is most definitely yes, under certain circumstances. Advertisers have long recognized the role of behavior in the formation and reinforcement of attitudes. Automobile salespeople encourage potential customers to "test drive" a particular car early in the sales process. A 1970s advertising jingle for a breakfast cereal, "Try it, you'll like it," echoed similar convictions. Religious leaders encourage regular participation in organized religious ceremonies to reinforce beliefs and strengthen commitments. Few persuasion scholars would quarrel with the claim that behavior influences the formation and reinforcement of attitudes. However, the causal influence of behavior on subsequent *attitude change* is less straightforward.

Investigations of this issue have traditionally employed counterattitudinal advocacy (CAA) procedures to investigate the effects of behavior on attitude change. CAA requires people to advocate a position that is inconsistent with their existing attitude. This research paradigm was initially developed in the early 1950s and was employed in several investigations of active and passive persuasive message processing (Janis & King, 1954; King & Janis, 1956). A decade later it became a staple in attitude change research.

THE CAA RESEARCH PARADIGM

The CAA research procedure is relatively straightforward. It requires investigator knowledge of research participants' attitudes toward a particular issue, object, or situation. Sometimes investigators will conduct attitude pretests several weeks prior to the experiment in order to assess participant attitudes. More frequently, a topic is selected because most participants hold similar known attitudes about the issue. For example, most Americans are opposed to tax increases. Though not everyone opposes them, few people openly advocate tax increases. Similarly, college students are almost uniformly opposed to tuition increases. Thus, for most students, advocating a tuition increase represents CAA.

Once a topic has been selected, investigators ask research participants to advocate a position that is opposite to the attitude they hold. Participants are usually asked to write an essay, present a speech, or talk with another person in order to advocate the counterattitudinal position. Thus, for the topic of tax increases, CAA might involve writing an essay supporting a tax increase.

CAA poses an interesting dilemma. People engaging in CAA knowingly articulate a position that is inconsistent with their personal beliefs and convictions. They believe "x" but they advocate "not-x." What effect does such advocacy have on a person's attitude toward an issue? For example, if the president of a local chapter of student Republicans was opposed to tax increases, but advocated an income tax increase to reduce the budget deficit, would this CAA influence his or her attitude toward tax increases?

The answer to such questions is somewhat complicated, but a qualified generalization can be offered. Provided that certain situational conditions are present, CAA will produce attitude change in the advocate. It bears mentioning that CAA emphasizes attitude change in the advocate, not an audience or target person. That is, CAA is a technique for inducing self-persuasion, not for persuading target audiences. The amount of attitude change that advocates experience following CAA is dependent on several situational factors including perceived justification, freedom of choice, and the consequences of the CAA.

It is relatively uncommon for people in natural communicative interactions to freely engage in CAA without sufficient external justification. Thus, the pragmatic utility of CAA to induce attitude change may be limited. Nevertheless, the CAA paradigm has important theoretical implications for persuasion as it allows researchers to distinguish attitude reinforcement and attitude formation processes from attitude change processes.

There has been little disagreement about the effectiveness of CAA for changing an advocate's position. However, considerable controversy has surrounded several theoretical explanations of this effect. The most extensively investigated explanation is Cognitive Dissonance Theory (Festinger, 1957). The original theory, along with its subsequent modifications and extensions, is discussed in the next section of this chapter. Following this is a discussion of several alternative explanations of the CAA effect.

A THEORY OF COGNITIVE DISSONANCE

In 1957, Leon Festinger described his Theory of Cognitive Dissonance, which became the most widely investigated social psychological theory of its era. Evolving from basic consistency principles (Heider, 1946; Newcomb, 1953), Dissonance Theory postulated three basic assumptions about human cognition: (1) people have a need for cognitive consistency; (2) when cognitive inconsistency exists, people experience psychological discomfort; and (3) psychological discomfort motivates people to resolve the inconsistency and restore cognitive balance. Though it can be situated in a larger family of consistency theories, Dissonance Theory differs from other consistency models in that it is a postdecisional theory. Festinger was interested in explaining how people resolve the internal psychological conflict they often experience after making an important decision.

Basic Components of Dissonance Theory

Festinger argued that not all cognitive elements (e.g., thoughts, ideas, values, etc.) are relevant to one another. For example, the belief that one is an honest person is probably unrelated to a preference for the color blue. Hence, Festinger stipulated that his theory only explained cognitions that were perceived to be relevant, or related to one another, by the attitude holder.

Festinger then proposed two cognitive states to describe the relations among relevant cognitive elements. Though he employed somewhat different language, Festinger argued that a state of *consonance* was said to exist when two or more cognitions were consistent with one another and a state of *dissonance* was said to exist when two or more cognitions were inconsistent with one another.

Dissonance occurs in varying degrees. Some cognitive elements may be inconsistent with one another, yet produce a negligible amount of dissonance. For example, if a person believes in the merits of recycling, but disposes of a soft drink can in a waste basket instead of recycling the can, cognitive dissonance should result. However, the extent of this dissonance and the subsequent motivation to reduce it will likely be quite small. However, if this same person failed to vote for a proposition to institute a local recycling program and the proposition was defeated by a single vote, the magnitude of the resulting cognitive dissonance would be considerably larger.

Festinger stated that the greater the dissonance, the greater the motivation to reduce it. The magnitude of dissonance is determined by two factors: (1) the importance of the dissonant elements, and (2) the proportion of consonant to dissonant relations among relevant elements in the cognitive system.

Implications of Cognitive Dissonance

Dissonance is an inevitable consequence of making decisions. When people choose among two or more competing alternatives, the amount of dissonance experienced is dependent on the importance of the decision and the relative attractiveness of the unchosen alternative.

Each year, college seniors interview for jobs in their chosen fields of interest. The fortunate ones receive multiple offers and are placed in the enviable position of having to choose among alternative employment opportunities. If the alternatives are relatively dissimilar—for example, a choice between a $18,000-a-year job in Otis, Kansas and a $40,000-a-year job in Minneapolis—the amount of dissonance produced by the decision should be minimal. However, if the alternatives are equally attractive—for example, a choice between a $40,000-a-year job in Minneapolis and a $37,000-a-year job in Chicago, the amount of dissonance experienced may be substantial, and the decision maker will attempt to reduce it.

Festinger (1957) described three ways a person can reduce cognitive dissonance following a decision. First, the person can change the *cognitive element related to the behavior.* Thus, if our college senior's decision to accept a job in Minneapolis instead of Chicago produces cognitive dissonance, dissonance can be reduced by changing the cognitive elements related to the decision. One might attempt to change the decision, but more likely a change in the cognitive element related to the decision will involve distorting information about the decision or denying that there was much of a choice to begin with.

A second method of reducing dissonance is to change the *cognitive element related to the attitude*. That is, if the decision is inconsistent with the person's existing attitude, a common method of dissonance reduction is modification of the attitude. Indeed, most investigations of the theory have employed measures of attitude change to document the existence and reduction of cognitive dissonance. Thus, another way to reduce dissonance stemming from the decision to accept the job in Minneapolis is to form a more negative attitude about living or working in Chicago, a more positive attitude about Minneapolis, or both.

Finally, Festinger specified that dissonance may be reduced by *adding new cognitive elements*. Selective exposure to new information (Freedman & Sears, 1965) often occurs after a decision has been made. People expose themselves to information that will reinforce the merits of their decision, and they avoid information that may be critical of the decision. This new information can force a realignment of the cognitions and reduce dissonance. Extending the example about accepting the job in Minneapolis, the college senior might reduce dissonance after making the decision by paying special attention to reports that favorably compare Minneapolis to Chicago.

The Festinger and Carlsmith Study

The initial test of Dissonance Theory was conducted by Festinger and Carlsmith (1959). In this study, participants arrived one at a time at the experimental laboratory and were asked to turn pegs on a board for a long period of time. This task was unmistakably dull. After completing this task, participants were told that the experiment was designed to examine the effects of expectations on performance. Participants were told that they were in a control condition where there were no prior expectations and that other participants would be in a condition where they would be told that the task was very exciting and interesting. Then the experimenter indicated that the assistant who was hired tó provide positive expectations for subjects in expectancy condition had just called and indicated he would be unable to work that day. The experimenter then asked the subject if he or she would be willing to introduce the experiment to the next research participant. The experimenter indicated that this procedure required the participant to indicate that the study was fun and exciting, and that the participant would be paid ($1 or $20) for this assistance.

Once the participant agreed to serve as the assistant he or she was asked to introduce the experiment to the next subject (actually a confederate of the experimenter, who played the role of a subject). The participant introduced the task and described it as fun and exciting.

After introducing the experiment, the participant attended in a previously arranged interview with another person in the psychology department who was conducting a separate survey on departmental research. Respondents were told that the survey was being administered to students who had participated in any type of research project sponsored by the department. Participants were asked how much they liked the experiment, how much they felt they had learned by participating in the experiment, and how likely they would be to participate in similar research projects. Actually, this interview was created to assess participant reactions to the experimental task.

The Creation of Cognitive Dissonance

Because the procedure was dull and uninteresting, Festinger and Carlsmith (1959) hypothesized that people would experience dissonance after introducing the study as interesting and exciting. Because participants had clearly been deceptive when introducing the study, it was difficult for them to deny or distort the CAA behavior. Moreover, it was unlikely that participants could anticipate seeing the confederate again to alter the consequences of their decision or provide an explanation for their behavior. There were also no sources of external information about the experiment readily available to participants. Hence, selective exposure to information was unlikely.

Thus, these procedures restricted two of the three methods outlined by Festinger (1957) for reducing dissonance; that is, changing the cognitive element related to the behavior or adding new cognitive elements. Hence, the easiest method for reducing dissonance created by the CAA was attitude change.

Effects of Cognitive Dissonance

To the extent that their procedures induced cognitive dissonance, Festinger and Carlsmith (1959) hypothesized that participants would change their attitudes, because other methods of reducing dissonance had been controlled. Recall that there were two payment conditions in the investigation. Some participants received $1 and others were paid $20 for their CAA introduction of the experiment.[1] The payment

---

[1] It bears mentioning that due to inflation, the purchasing power of values of $1 and $20 in 1959 are roughly equivalent to $5 and $100 today.

served as a source of justification for the CAA. Participants receiving $1 had little external justification for their behavior whereas those receiving $20 could easily justify their CAA. Participants receiving $20 could easily say to themselves, "Why did I say the task was interesting? Because I received $20 for it." Because the CAA of participants in the $20 condition was easily justified, the possibility of cognitive dissonance and subsequent attitude change was reduced. In the $1 condition, however, participants had less external justification for their behavior and, hence, would experience more cognitive dissonance. Thus, Festinger and Carlsmith hypothesized that to reduce their dissonance, participants who received $1 (low justification) would change their attitudes more than participants who were paid $20 (high justification).

Findings were consistent with these expectations. Participants in the $1 condition reported attitudes toward the experimental task that were significantly more enjoyable than participants in the $20 condition. However, there were no differences between these two groups on three additional questions regarding "desire to participate in a similar experiment," "the scientific importance of the experiment," and "the educational value of the experiment." Nevertheless, Festinger and Carlsmith concluded that difference between the attitudes of participants in the low and the high justification conditions "strongly corroborated the theory that was tested."

Though there was reason to question the strength of their convictions at the time they drew this conclusion, the pattern of attitudes emerging from the Festinger and Carlsmith (1959) study has been replicated in many subsequent investigations of Dissonance Theory (for reviews, see Cooper & Fazio, 1984; Greenwald & Ronis, 1978; Miller, 1973). Today, there remains little doubt about the persuasive effects of CAA. However, the "correct" theoretical explanation of these effects remains a source of considerable controversy.

Limitations of Cognitive Dissonance Theory

Although many investigations provided support for Dissonance Theory, it is difficult to imagine a set of research findings that could not be explained by Festinger's original explication of Dissonance Theory. Festinger's writing was conceptually vague and sufficiently general to prevent falsification of the theory. For example, Dissonance Theory fails to articulate when people will use each of the three methods for reducing cognitive dissonance. Instead, Festinger stated that dissonance is reduced by modifying the cognitive element that is least resistant to change. Because no suggestions are provided about how one might assess the resistance of various cognitive elements, it is difficult to predict a priori whether dissonance will produce behavior change, attitude change, or selective exposure to new information. In particular, the notion of adding new cognitive elements is vague and nearly impossible to assess.

Following CAA, a person may exhibit no observable signs of psychological discomfort or dissonance reduction, yet dissonance and its subsequent reduction may have occurred. Because thinking fulfills the requirement of adding new cognitive elements, a person may reduce dissonance by generating new thoughts or recalling information stored in memory. Consider the earlier example of a student Republican who had publicly supported a "no new taxes" position, only to find herself advocating a tax increase to reduce an unexpected deficit. Though no observable signs of dissonance reduction may occur, our young Republican may internally rationalize her counterattitudinal behavior by recalling a similar move by President Bush. Though investigators may never have access to this private internal rationalization, dissonance and its subsequent reduction may nevertheless have occurred.

Because two of the three methods for reducing dissonance, attitude change and adding new cognitive elements, are not directly observable, the original version of Dissonance Theory was virtually impossible to disprove. If observable changes follow CAA, Dissonance Theory may account for these changes. However, the absence of observable change does not mean that dissonance did not occur and was not reduced internally. It simply means that researchers did not observe dissonance reduction if it occurred. In an effort to resolve this limitation, researchers have suggested several modifications and extensions of the original theory. For the most part, these suggestions were intended to limit the scope of the theory.

Modifications and Extensions of Dissonance Theory

The evolution of Dissonance Theory has been impressive. Greenwald and Ronis (1978) summarize several modifications that have been suggested to clarify Festinger's original articulation of the theory. Two of the earliest modifications were suggested by Brehm and Cohen (1962) who conducted a series of investigations testing the theory. Brehm and Cohen introduced the notion of *commitment* to Dissonance Theory. Though Festinger originally argued that dissonance resulted from decision making, Brehm and Cohen argued that dissonance will only occur when people experience a state of psychological commitment to the decision they have made. In essence, if a decision can be easily reversed, then the decision-maker should experience little dissonance. If the decision is not reversible, then cognitive dissonance should occur and the extent of this dissonance will be a function of the importance of the decision and the relative attractiveness of the unchosen alternative.

The importance of Brehm and Cohen's suggestion is apparent in consumer purchasing decisions. If you go to a shopping mall and buy $800 worth of clothes for your wardrobe, should you experience cognitive dissonance? According to Festinger's version of the theory, the answer is yes, and the amount of dissonance will be a function of the importance of the $800 and your evaluation of alternative uses you might have for the $800. If we consider Brehm and Cohen's notion of commitment, however, dissonance will only occur if you feel psychologically committed to your purchase. Because most clothing stores permit shoppers to return unwanted merchandise, often there is no legal commitment to the purchase. However, the act of returning clothes is psychologically easier for some people than it is for others. While I was growing up, one of my sisters made a hobby out of purchasing clothes and returning them a week later. She was rarely committed to her purchasing decisions. On the other hand, I often feel uncomfortable returning unwanted merchandise. Consequently, there is more psychological commitment associated with my purchasing decisions. Indeed, marketing experts understand the force of psychological commitment. Television ads routinely promise a 30-day, money-back guarantee for their products. Such guarantees serve to temporarily reduce the commitment consumers experience when they call to purchase a product. Such guarantees underscore the importance of psychological commitment in the postdecision dissonance reduction process.

In addition to commitment, Brehm and Cohen (1962) argued that *volition* (free choice) is essential to the onset of cognitive dissonance. If people perceive their options were limited, or that their decision was heavily influenced by someone else, then they may feel as though they had little choice in the decision they made. If people do not feel personal responsibility for a decision, then dissonance should not occur (Wicklund & Brehm, 1976).

The concept of volition highlights a major criticism of the *forced-compliance* research paradigm. If research participants engage in CAA in the course of fulfilling a research requirement, or to assist an experimenter, they may perceive limited choice in their behavior and, hence, experience limited dissonance. Thus, one explanation for the limited effects of earlier research may be the lack of free choice associated with the counterattitudinal behaviors of participants.

In addition to the stipulations offered by Brehm and Cohen, Aronson (1968) offered another modification of the original theory. Aronson's version of the theory argued that the source of dissonance following

CAA was not the knowledge that cognitions were inconsistent with one another, but rather the belief that a person is sensible combined with the knowledge that he or she behaved in a nonsensible manner.

Sometimes referred to as Later Dissonance Theory, this modification casts the inconsistency at a higher level of abstraction and this modification underscores the role of personality factors on cognitive dissonance. Aronson argued that people with high self-concepts should experience greater dissonance following willful CAA than those with lower self-concepts. Presumably, people with higher self-concepts can tolerate fewer inconsistencies than those with low self-concepts. People with low self-concepts do not have the expectation that they will always be sensible, therefore limited dissonance may result when their behavior is inconsistent with their attitude, for example, when they write a CAA essay. The key to Aronson's modification is the realization that not all people experience the same levels of dissonance.

Together, the modifications suggested by Brehm and Cohen (1962) and Aronson (1968) produced versions of Dissonance Theory that had greater precision and were more limited in scope. Although additional modifications have been suggested, the issues discussed above represent the types of concerns dissonance theorists raised about the original version of the theory.

ALTERNATIVE THEORETICAL EXPLANATIONS

In addition to these modifications, two rival theoretical explanations have been developed to account for the findings produced by many dissonance experiments. Both Self-Perception Theory (Bem, 1967, 1972) and Impression Management Theory (Tedeschi, Schlenker, & Bonoma, 1971) questioned the viability of the cognitive dissonance construct. Bem's self-perception process represented a serious challenge for dissonance theorists and received considerable conceptual and empirical scrutiny (Cooper & Fazio, 1984). However, considerably less attention has been focused on the impression management explanation and it is no longer considered a viable explanation for the findings emerging from dissonance experiments (Cooper & Fazio, 1984). Thus, only Self-Perception Theory is examined below.

Self-Perception Theory

From 1957 to 1965, most Dissonance Theory experiments served to provide empirical support for the theory or clarify the scope of the theory. In 1965, and later 1967, Bem introduced Self-Perception Theory, which refuted the major assumptions of Dissonance Theory while accounting for the findings of prior dissonance experiments. In a short time, Self-Perception Theory emerged as a major theoretical roadblock for dissonance theorists, and in the decade that followed an intense rivalry evolved between the proponents of these two competing theories.

The basic assumption of Self-Perception Theory is that:

> Individuals come to know their own attitudes, emotions, and other internal states partially from inferring them from observations of their own overt behavior and/or circumstances in which this behavior occurs. Thus, to the extent that external cues are weak, ambiguous, or uninterpretable, the individual is functionally in the same position as an outside observer, an observer who must rely upon those same external cues to infer the individual's internal states. (Bem, 1972, p. 2).

Bem (1972) reported findings from several investigations that corroborated his assumptions about the inference-making process. In each of these investigations, people's evaluations of experimental stimuli were guided by their overt behavior toward the stimuli.

Explaining Attitude Change

Bem employed this self-perception process to explain attitude change following CAA. Absent any external justification, Bem argued, people modify their attitudes following CAA because they have observed a change in their own overt behavior. Applied to the Festinger and Carlsmith (1959) experiment, Bem's explanation holds that participants receiving $1 for their CAA changed their attitudes because they observed a change in their overt behavior, the advocacy itself. Participants who received $20 for their CAA exhibited less attitude change because the monetary reward served to justify their behavior. The $20 payment invalidated the inference-making process and provided a compelling explanation for their change in behavior. In short, Bem's alternative explanation accounted for the findings of Festinger and Carlsmith's (1959) seminal investigation.

The concepts of volition and justification are equally important to Bem's explanation of attitude change. According to Self-Perception Theory, CAA will not produce attitude change when people perceive that their behavior was not volitional, or that some external justification caused their behavior. In these instances, people conclude that observation of their own behavior is not a valid indicator of the underlying attitude.

Self-Perception versus Dissonance Theory

The most compelling aspect of Bem's argument is his ability to account for the findings of most prior dissonance experiments. Because the amount of attitude change predicted by the two theories is almost identical, Dissonance Theory and Self-Perception Theory are extremely difficult to separate empirically.

Nevertheless, the theoretical differences between Self-Perception and Dissonance Theory are significant. The fundamental disagreement between these two explanations stems from assumptions about the underlying causes of attitude change. According to Dissonance Theory, CAA creates a feeling of psychological discomfort, which motivates people to reduce the cognitive inconsistency, often by changing their attitudes. Bem makes no mention of internal motivational pressures. Instead, Self-Perception Theory postulates that attitude change following CAA is produced by observation of overt behavior. When behavior is counter to prior attitudes, people conclude that the underlying attitude that produced the behavior must have also changed.

Because the fundamental difference between these two theoretical processes is not directly observable, early tests of the relative merits of these theories produced equivocal findings (Greenwald, 1975). By the mid-1970s, most dissonance theorists had redefined Festinger's concept psychological discomfort to mean *physiological arousal*. As a result, subsequent critical tests between these two competing explanations focused on the emergence of arousal following CAA.

AROUSAL, CAA, AND ATTITUDE CHANGE

Several studies have investigated the precise role of arousal in the attitude change process. For the most part, studies investigating the effects of CAA on arousal and subsequent attitude change have employed a *misattribution* research procedure developed by Schachter and Singer (1962). This procedure does not involve the direct measurement of arousal, but it provides research participants with an external cue to explain any arousal they might experience. Though the external cue is not the cause of the arousal, its presence allows people to misattribute their arousal to the external cue.

Applied in dissonance experiments, an external cue provides a clear explanation for the arousal that participants experience following CAA. If arousal is misattributed to the external cue, instead of being attributed to the CAA, then little or no attitude change should result. On the other hand, participants who experience arousal in the absence of an external cue should attribute their arousal to the CAA and subsequently change their attitude in order to reduce it.

The Zanna and Cooper Study

Zanna and Cooper (1974) used a misattribution procedure to determine whether arousal associated with CAA was sufficient to produce attitude change. Participants in the study either volunteered (free choice, dissonance arousal condition) or were induced to comply (forced choice, no dissonance arousal condition) with a request to write a counter-attitudinal essay. Recall that Brehm and Cohen (1962) argued that free choice (volition) was necessary to produce dissonance following CAA.

In addition to the free-choice versus forced-choice manipulation, Zanna and Cooper gave all participants in their study a placebo. Half of the participants in the free-choice and forced-choice conditions were told that the placebo was a mild tranquilizer and that it would have a relaxing effect on them. The remaining participants in each condition were told that the placebo was a stimulant that would lead to physiological arousal.

As expected, participants in the forced-choice (no dissonance) conditions exhibited little attitude change after writing their CAA essay. Among participants who freely chose to write the CAA essay (dissonance condition), those who were told the placebo was a stimulant exhibited little attitude change. Presumably, these participants attributed their arousal to the drug, not to the CAA. Thus, attitude change was unnecessary to reduce their arousal. Conversely, participants in the free-choice condition who were told they had received a tranquilizer exhibited significant attitude change. These participants had no external cue to explain their arousal. Presumably, these participants attributed their arousal to the CAA and changed their attitude in an effort to reduce arousal.

Thus, in conditions where the arousal following CAA can be misattributed to an external cue, no attitude change is necessary to reduce arousal. When arousal is attributed to CAA, attitude change occurs to reduce arousal. In sum, this study suggests that arousal attributed to CAA is sufficient to produce attitude change.

The Cooper, Zanna, and Taves Study

The conclusion that arousal is sufficient for attitude change does not imply that arousal is necessary for attitude change following CAA. To investigate this latter issue, Cooper, Zanna, and Taves (1978) conducted another study using the misattribution research procedure.

In this study, however, all participants were told they had been placed in the placebo condition and that the pill they were to ingest would have no effect on them. Although this was true for one-third of the participants, one-third were actually given a tranquilizer that had a relaxing effect, and one-third were given an amphetamine that heightened their physiological arousal. Participants wrote CAA essays about Richard Nixon. Half of the participants were in the high-choice (dissonance) condition and half were in the low-choice (no dissonance) condition.

By manipulating arousal physiologically, the experimenters were able to hold constant participants' attributions for their physiological arousal. Participants experiencing heightened arousal had no external cue to explain their arousal and would be likely to attribute it to the CAA. Moreover, participants in the high-choice, tranquilizer condition probably did not experience the arousal that they normally would because the drug physiologically relaxed them.

The attitudes of research participants after writing the counterattitudinal essay are summarized in Table 4.1. Inspection of this table reveals a number of interesting findings. First, attitudes toward Nixon were more favorable in the high-choice, placebo condition than in the low-choice, placebo condition. This difference represents the classic dissonance effect found in prior research. Moreover, the attitudes of participants in the three high-choice (dissonance) conditions suggests that as arousal increases, attitude change increases. This finding is consistent with Dissonance Theory's assertion that arousal motivates attitude change following CAA.

TABLE 4.1. Summary of Attitudes in the Cooper, Zanna, and Taves (1978) Study

	Type of drug administered		
	Tranquilizer	Placebo	Amphetamine
High-choice CAA (dissonance)	8.6	14.7	20.2
Low-choice CAA (no dissonance)	8.0	8.3	13.9

Note. Numbers reflect favorable attitudes toward Richard Nixon after writing the counterattitudinal essay. From "Arousal as a necessary condition for attitude change following induced compliance" by J. Cooper, M. P. Zanna, & P. A. Taves, 1978, *Journal of Personality and Social Psychology, 36,* 1101–1106. Copyright 1978 by the American Psychological Association. Reprinted by permission.

There was no difference in attitudes between the high- and low-choice, tranquilizer conditions. Heightened arousal that might have been associated with volitional CAA was most likely offset by the relaxing effects of the tranquilizer. As a result, participants in the high-choice, tranquilizer condition exhibited little attitude change. Thus, volitional CAA was not sufficient to produce attitude change; it must be associated with a heightened level of arousal. This finding suggests that arousal may be necessary for attitude change following CAA.

The difference between the attitudes of the low-choice, placebo and amphetamine conditions suggests that physiological arousal is sufficient to produce attitude change if it is misattributed. In the low-choice, amphetamine condition, individuals probably misattributed the cause of their arousal to the CAA. Individuals in this condition, after experiencing an unexplained high level of arousal, may have perceived that they had more of a free choice than they actually did when they wrote the CAA essay. In fact, analysis of the measures of *perceived choice* in writing the CAA revealed that participants in the low-choice, amphetamine condition reported significantly higher perceived choice than participants in the other two low-choice conditions and had perceptions of choice similar to participants in the three high-choice conditions. If individuals in the low-choice, amphetamine condition attributed their arousal to the CAA, and there is good evidence to suggest that they did, then we should expect the same levels of attitude change as we observed in the high-choice, placebo condition. This, in fact, was the case. After feeling aroused, the participants apparently deduced that they were in some way responsible for writing the CAA essay.

The Croyle and Cooper Studies

One limitation of the Zanna and Cooper (1974) and the Cooper, Zanna, and Taves (1978) experiments is their reliance on misattribution procedures to make inferences about arousal. Although these studies provided compelling support for Dissonance Theory explanations of attitude change, they employed indirect assessments of physiological arousal.

To address this limitation, Croyle and Cooper (1983) conducted two experiments that demonstrated the effects of CAA on attitudes and measured the physiological level of arousal induced by CAA. In the first experiment they found the traditional pattern of attitude change predicted by Dissonance Theory. Participants in the high-choice condition reported significantly more attitude change after writing a counterattitudinal essay than participants in the low-choice condition.

The second experiment employed the same design and used physiological measures to directly record participants' arousal after they wrote the counterattitudinal essay. Consistent with Dissonance Theory, participants in the high-choice CAA condition exhibited significantly greater levels of physiological arousal than participants in the low-choice CAA condition.[2] Taken together, these studies provide strong support for the dissonance arousal explanation for attitude change following CAA; the first study demonstrated the effects of CAA on attitude change and the second study demonstrated that willful CAA heightened physiological arousal, which is the hypothesized cause of the attitude change.

Summary of Arousal Studies

Findings from the arousal studies provide clear and compelling evidence for recent Dissonance Theory explanations of attitude change following CAA. Investigations using either the misattribution research procedure or direct measurement of arousal provide consistent evidence linking arousal to attitude change. Two specific conclusions can be drawn from this research.

First, CAA is not sufficient to produce attitude change. For attitude change to occur, CAA must be associated with physiological arousal. Cooper and Fazio (1984) argued that people must perceive that their counterattitudinal behavior will produce aversive consequences before they experience physiological arousal. If no aversive consequences are perceived, then dissonance arousal will not occur. Zanna and Cooper (1974) and Cooper et al. (1978) provided support for this conclusion when they demonstrated that arousal attributed to CAA is necessary for attitude change. When arousal following CAA was misattributed, attitude change did not occur.

Second, the amount of physiological arousal experienced following CAA appears to determine the extent of attitude change. Croyle and Cooper (1983) provided a direct link between physiological arousal and attitude change, while Cooper et al. (1978) found that the amount of arousal attributed to CAA was positively related to the amount of attitude change exhibited by participants.

[2]There was no difference across conditions in the amount of attitude change in Study 2, but Croyle and Cooper attributed this finding to a misattribution of arousal. Participants in the high-choice condition could easily have attributed their heightened arousal to the devices that were used to measure arousal. If this misattribution occurred, then attitude change would be unlikely for these participants.

INTEGRATION OF DISSONANCE
AND SELF-PERCEPTION THEORIES

Research examining the physiological arousal associated with CAA provides strong support for dissonance explanations of attitude change. Clearly research establishing a link between arousal and attitude change is incompatible with Self-Perception Theory. But does this research invalidate the self-perception explanation?

In an effort to reconcile the different theoretical positions advanced by self-perception and dissonance theorists, Fazio and his colleagues proposed that perhaps both theories were correct explanations of attitude change following CAA, but that each theory had its own domain (Fazio, Zanna, & Cooper, 1977). That is, Fazio and his colleagues suggested that once the "scope" of each theory is clearly defined by specifying its boundary conditions, the apparent contradiction between dissonance and self-perception explanations of attitude change following CAA can be resolved.

Fazio and his colleagues argued that attitudes and behaviors are neither consistent nor inconsistent, but consistent or inconsistent to some degree. That is, some behaviors can be counterattitudinal, but only marginally discrepant from a person's attitude, whereas other counterattitudinal behaviors are largely discrepant from the relevant attitude. For example, if a student who was opposed to tuition increases wrote an essay advocating a 20% increase in tuition, the CAA would be greatly discrepant from the student's position on the issue. However, if the student wrote an essay advocating only a 5% increase in tuition, the CAA would be slightly discrepant from the student's position.

Fazio et al. (1977) argued that when the discrepancy between a person's attitude and a counterattitudinal behavior is relatively small, there should be little physiological arousal. However, when the discrepancy is quite large, physiological arousal should occur. In short, they proposed that because there is little or no arousal with mildly discrepant CAA, Self-Perception Theory can explain the subsequent attitude change. However, when the attitude–behavior discrepancy is quite large, physiological arousal is likely to occur and Dissonance Theory is needed to explain the subsequent attitude change (Fazio et al., 1977). In other words, Fazio and his colleagues proposed *boundary conditions* to limit the scope of each theory: Self-Perception Theory explains attitude change following mildly discrepant CAA and Cognitive Dissonance Theory explains attitude change following highly discrepant CAA.

To test this explanation, Fazio et al. (1977) conducted an experiment in which participants were given the option to write a counterattitudinal essay (high-choice condition) or were told to write the essay (low-choice condition). Based on the results of an attitude pretest, the counterattitudinal position was slightly discrepant or greatly discrepant from their position on the issue. In addition, the high-choice participants were asked to write their essays in a small soundproof booth during the experiment. They were told that the booths were new and that the psychology department was interested in people's reactions to them. Half of the high-choice participants were then asked if the booth made them feel tense or uncomfortable. This induction provided them with an external cue to misattribute any arousal they might have experienced to the booth, instead of attributing it to writing the counterattitudinal essay. The other half of the high-choice participants were not asked about their reactions to the booth, and thus were not provided with a misattribution cue.

Both Self-Perception Theory and Dissonance Theory predict no attitude change in the low-choice conditions (Table 4.2). In the high-choice, no-misattribution-cue conditions, attitude change was expected to occur. In fact, attitudes in these two conditions were predicted to be significantly more favorable than attitudes in the two no-choice conditions. Thus far, the hypotheses were consistent with traditional dissonance and self-perception experiments.

The high-choice, misattribution-cue conditions provided the critical test of the study. According to the theoretical integration proposed by Fazio and his colleagues, participants in the high-choice, misattribution-cue condition who wrote a highly discrepant counterattitudinal essay were likely to experience dissonance-induced arousal. However, the presence of the misattribution cue would lead these participants to attribute their arousal to the booth and not to writing the counterattitudinal essay. Because their arousal would not be associated with the CAA, Dissonance Theory would predict no attitude change. Conversely, participants in the high-choice, misattribution-cue condition who wrote counterattitudinal essays that were less discrepant should

TABLE 4.2. Predicted Pattern of Attitude Change in the Fazio, Zanna, and Cooper (1978) Study

Discrepancy level of CAA	Low-choice	High-choice, no misattribution-cue	High-choice, misattribution-cue
Small	No attitude change	Attitude change	Attitude change
Large	No attitude change	Attitude change	No attitude change

not have experienced arousal, and would not have used the booth as a misattribution cue. Nevertheless, these participants should have observed a discrepancy between their behavior and attitude, and according to Self-Perception Theory, adjusted their attitudes to match their behavior. If this occurred, then attitude change of participants who wrote the slightly discrepant counterattitudinal essays in the high-choice, misattribution-cue condition would mirror the attitude change of participants writing slightly discrepant counterattitudinal essay in the high-choice, no misattribution-cue condition. Moreover, attitude change of participants who wrote the mildly discrepant essays in the misattribution-cue condition would be greater than the attitude change of participants who wrote the highly discrepant essays in the misattribution-cue condition. This predicted pattern of attitude change in this study is reflected in Table 4.2.

Findings of this study were generally consistent with the predicted pattern of attitudes and hence consistent with the boundary conditions that Fazio and his colleagues proposed for limiting the scope of these two theories. Given their proposed boundaries, both Self-Perception Theory and Dissonance Theory are viable accounts of attitude change following CAA. When CAA is only mildly discrepant and does not heighten arousal, Self-Perception Theory can explain subsequent attitude change. When CAA is highly discrepant and heightens a person's physiological arousal, Dissonance Theory can explain subsequent attitude change.

Although the Fazio et al. (1977) integration of dissonance and self-perception processes is compelling, it remains at odds with research finding that arousal is both necessary and sufficient for attitude change to occur following CAA (Cooper et al., 1978; Zanna & Cooper, 1974). However, neither of these studies examined the effect of the level of discrepancy in the counterattitudinal message and measured its influence on arousal. Thus, although arousal remains an important factor in the explanation of attitude change following CAA, it is possible that many of the counterattitudinal behaviors we engage in are only minimally discrepant from our position on an issue and unlikely to induce arousal. In these cases, Self-Perception Theory appears to be the better theoretical explanation for attitude change.

SUMMARY

Chapter 3 examined the attitude–behavior relationship, and concluded that, under certain circumstances, attitude change will result in behavior change. The present chapter examined the effects of behavior change on attitude change. Most studies investigating the behavior–attitude relationship employed a CAA research paradigm. Though few people willfully engage in CAA without some external justification for doing so, the CAA research paradigm has proven effective for investigating the effects of behavior change on subsequent attitude change.

Several theories have been proposed to explain the effects of CAA on subsequent attitudes. Among them, Dissonance Theory has received the most attention. Though the original version of Dissonance Theory (Festinger, 1957) was sufficiently vague to prevent falsification, the theory has undergone a remarkable evolution (Greenwald & Ronis, 1978; Ronis & Greenwald, 1979). Instead of its original description as "psychological discomfort," cognitive dissonance is presently defined as a state of "physiological arousal." Recently, physiological arousal associated with CAA has been linked to attitude change in several investigations.

Self-Perception Theory (Bem, 1967) posed a serious challenge to Dissonance Theory and many studies attempted to examine the relative merits of each theory. Although research linking physiological arousal to highly discrepant, counterattitudinal behavior is incompatible with Self-Perception Theory, other research has shown that minimally discrepant, counterattitudinal behaviors are likely to produce little arousal. In these cases, Self-Perception Theory remains a viable explanation for attitude change.

Together, the studies reviewed in this chapter provide strong evidence that behavior change can produce attitude change. Although there is some debate about the best theoretical explanation for this effect, the relationship between behaviors and subsequent attitudes is clear. Although the scope of Dissonance Theory has been narrowed over the years, the theory remains a viable tool for persuasion in a variety of influence situations (Wicklund & Brehm, 1976).

PART II

COMPONENTS OF PERSUASIVE TRANSACTIONS

This section explores essential characteristics of persuasive transactions. Chapter 5 reviews research on characteristics of persuasive sources. Chapter 6 summarizes research on persuasive message characteristics. Chapter 7 identifies features of message receivers that affect the effectiveness of a persuasive appeal. Finally, Chapter 8 describes characteristics of persuasive situations that influence the persuasion process.

CHAPTER FIVE

Source Characteristics in Persuasive Communication

L OOKING AHEAD . . .

This chapter examines characteristics of message sources that enhance the effectiveness of persuasive messages. I begin by identifying two dimensions of source credibility—expertise and trustworthiness. I examine how people form judgments about these factors and how these judgments affect attitudes and behavior. The chapter concludes with a discussion of two related source characteristics, perceived similarity and physical attractiveness, and the effects of these factors on persuasion.

Are characteristics of message sources important factors in persuasive communication? Is the credibility or attractiveness of a message source more persuasive than the content of the message itself? Although there are no simple answers to these questions, source characteristics are often critical, and sometimes they are the most important features of persuasive communication. Public hearings, courtroom testimony, and political campaigns are situations in which effective communication skills and personal demeanor are essential for persuasive communication.

The Senate confirmation hearings of Supreme Court Justice Clarence Thomas underscore the persuasive effects of source credibility. During the hearings, a national television audience was confronted with conflicting accounts of personal behavior, and there was scant physical evidence to directly substantiate these accounts. Ultimately, judgments about the validity of Anita Hill's complaint of sexual harassment and the suitability of Clarence Thomas as a Supreme Court Justice were based on the assessments of the believability of Professor Hill and Judge Thomas.

Shortly thereafter, a televised court case presented viewers with a similar set of judgments. Patricia Bowman accused William Kennedy Smith of sexual battery on the grounds of the Kennedy estate in West Palm Beach. There was little direct evidence to substantiate Ms. Bowman's accusation. Instead, judgments made by jurors and television viewers were based largely on the credibility of testimony provided by Ms. Bowman and Mr. Smith.

These high-profile examples provide compelling evidence for the importance of source features in persuasion. However, source factors are equally important in mundane persuasive transactions. Consumers prefer honest and likeable salespeople and voters often cast their ballots for candidates who demonstrate competence and trustworthiness.

This chapter examines the influence of source characteristics in persuasive communication. Because much of the prior research investigating source characteristics has focused on source credibility, much of the chapter will be devoted to this issue. Following this, the persuasive influence of additional source characteristics, such as likeability and perceived similarity, will be examined.

SOURCE CREDIBILITY

Dimensions of Credibility

One of the early empirical debates in the scientific study of communication surrounded the definition and operationalization of the construct *source credibility*. Hovland et al., (1953) initially defined source credibility as a combination of two factors, *source expertise* and *source trustworthiness*.

Later, Berlo, Lemert, and Mertz (1969) conducted two studies that examined the dimensions people used to make judgments about a source's credibility. Using factor-analytic procedures, they found three dimensions—safety, qualification, and dynamism—that explained most of the variance in people's ratings of a source's credibility. The qualification dimension found by Berlo et al. (1969) was similar to the expertise dimension identified by Hovland et al. (1953). However, the safety dimension identified by Berlo and his colleagues was much broader in scope than the trustworthiness dimension identified by Hovland and his colleagues. The third dimension identified by Berlo and his colleagues, dynamism, was previously unidentified in the literature.

The Berlo et al. paper had been circulated in unpublished form for nearly a decade before it appeared in print in 1969 (Cronkhite & Liska, 1980). During that period, McCroskey (1966) examined the dimensions of source credibility in a series of investigations. Though he included items to measure the dynamism dimension, McCroskey consistently found only two dimensions of source credibility, authoritativeness and character, that corresponded to the dimensions found in prior research. McCroskey's authoritativeness dimension (Table 5.1) accounted for a large amount of the variation (47%) in people's responses, whereas the character dimension (Table 5.2) accounted for a smaller amount of the variation (29%) in responses to items in the credibility measure.

In summary, these three reports suggest that two factors, trustworthiness and expertise, adequately represent people's judgments about a source's credibility. Though the factor-analytic procedures employed in these investigations have been criticized and other dimensions of

TABLE 5.1. McCroskey's (1966) Authoritativeness Scale

1. I respect this person's opinion on the topic.
2. The speaker is *not* of very high intelligence.
3. This speaker is a reliable source of information on the topic.
4. I have confidence in this speaker.
5. This speaker lacks information on the subject.
6. This speaker has high status in our society.
7. I would consider this speaker to be an expert on the topic.
8. This speaker's opinion on the topic is of little value.
9. I believe that the speaker is quite intelligent.
10. The speaker is an unreliable source of information on the topic.
11. I have little confidence in this speaker.
12. The speaker is well-informed on this subject.
13. The speaker has low status in our society.
14. I would *not* consider this speaker to be an expert on this topic.
15. This speaker is an authority on the topic.
16. This speaker has very little experience with this subject.
17. This speaker has considerable knowledge of the factors involved with this subject.
18. Few speakers are as qualified to speak on this topic as the speaker.
19. This speaker is *not* an authority on the topic.
20. This speaker has very little knowledge of the factors involved with the subject.
21. The speaker has had substantial experience with this subject.
22. Many people are much more qualified to speak on this topic than this speaker.

Note. Recommended response options are Strongly Agree, Agree, Undecided, Disagree, and Strongly Disagree. From "Scales for the measurement of ethos" by J. C. McCroskey, 1966, *Speech Monographs, 33,* 65–72. Copyright 1966 by the Speech Communication Association. Reprinted by permission.

TABLE 5.2. McCroskey's (1966) Character Scale

1. I deplore this speaker's background.
2. This speaker is basically honest.
3. I would consider it desirable to be like this speaker.
4. This speaker is *not* an honorable person.
5. This speaker is a reputable person.
6. This speaker is not concerned with my well-being.
7. I trust this speaker to tell the truth about the topic.
8. This speaker is a scoundrel.
9. I would prefer to have nothing at all to do with this speaker.
10. Under most circumstances I would be likely to believe what this speaker says about the topic.
11. I admire the speaker's background.
12. This speaker is basically honest.
13. The reputation of this speaker is low.
14. I believe that this speaker is concerned with my well-being.
15. The speaker is an honorable person.
16. I would *not* prefer to be like this person.
17. I *do not* trust the speaker to tell the truth on this topic.
18. Under most circumstances I would *not* be likely to believe what this speaker says about the topic.
19. I would like to have this speaker as a personal friend.
20. The character of this speaker is good.

Note. Recommended response options are Strongly Agree, Agree, Undecided, Disagree, and Strongly Disagree. From "Scales for the measurement of ethos" by J. C. McCroskey, 1966, *Speech Monographs, 33,* 65–72. Copyright 1966 by the Speech Communication Association. Reprinted by permission.

credibility have been suggested (Cronkhite & Liska, 1976, 1980), most persuasion scholars now describe credibility as a combination of a source's perceived expertise and trustworthiness.

Defining Credibility as a Receiver Perception

Perhaps the greatest source of agreement about the credibility construct lies in the definition of credibility as a perception held by message recipients. Eschewing a source-oriented approach to credibility, Hovland and his colleagues defined credibility as a perceptual state, not a characteristic of message sources (Hovland et al., 1953). Cronkhite and Liska echoed this sentiment when they wrote that, "it is not merely the needs/goals of sources which must be assessed" (1980, p. 105). Instead, assessments of source credibility must focus on the attributions made by targets of persuasive messages. This receiver-oriented focus has lead persuasion scholars to define credibility in terms of the perceptions message recipients hold about a source's expertise and trustworthiness. Thus, credibility is not a commodity that message sources possess. Rather, it is the perception of trustworthiness and expertise that sources are able to engender in a target audience.

The perceived trustworthiness and expertise dimensions are generally considered to be separate, but related, constructs. Although these perceptions are often related to one another, it is possible for a message source to engender the perception of expertise without creating the perception of trustworthiness. For example, Richard Nixon was generally believed to possess considerable expertise in foreign policy. However, in the aftermath of Watergate, most Americans no longer thought him to be worthy of their trust. Conversely, message sources can create the perception of trustworthiness without the perception of expertise. At the end of his political career, Jimmy Carter was regarded as highly trustworthy, but many voters no longer believed he possessed the expertise to run the country. As a result, the general factor, credibility, lacks the precision necessary for effective persuasion research. Instead of describing a source's credibility, persuasion scholars have relied on the more precise constructs of expertise and trustworthiness.

Variations in Perceived Expertise and Trustworthiness

Because trustworthiness and expertise are perceptions held by message recipients, judgments made about a message source's expertise or trustworthiness are likely to be influenced by the message recipients' views of their own expertise or trustworthiness. As a result, a nuclear physicist may be perceived as highly expert when talking to students in a college physics class, but may lack this same level of perceived expertise when presenting a paper at an international conference on nuclear physics. Similarly, an inmate at a federal prison may be perceived as relatively trustworthy by other inmates, yet relatively untrustworthy by nonincarcerated members of the population. Thus, it is likely that perceptions of credibility will vary considerably from one target audience to another.

In addition, the perceived expertise and trustworthiness of a message source can change over time. During the 1980s, this fact was evident throughout international politics. In the Philippines, the Marcos regime was toppled when citizens lost trust in the leaders. At the same time, Gorbachov was rapidly gaining the confidence of the Russian people. In the span of only a few years, he rose from relative obscurity to become the leader of the Soviet Union. However, by 1991, it became clear that his economic reforms were unsuccessful, and soon thereafter, his popularity declined and his political career was over.

In much the same fashion, perceived expertise may change from topic to topic. Although perceptions of trustworthiness are likely to be relatively stable across topics, an audience's judgment of a source's expertise may be topic dependent. It makes sense that a known economist will be perceived by many people to have expertise when talking about deficit reduction options. However, the same person may lack expertise to speak persuasively about child development.

The emphasis on receiver perceptions, central to the definition of source expertise and trustworthiness, highlights the importance of factors that affect the perceptual judgments people make about message sources. The next section examines this perceptual process.

Attributions about Message Sources

After reaching agreement on the definition and measurement of credibility, researchers turned their attention to understanding how people make judgments about a source's expertise and trustworthiness. Because message sources rarely enter a persuasive situation with a blank slate, the expectations message recipients have about the source and the positions the source might advocate are essential to understanding perceptions of source expertise and trustworthiness.

Indeed, the notion of "creating expectations" was a hallmark of George Bush's presidential campaign in 1988. Before his debate with Michael Dukakis, Bush's media specialists indicated that although Dukakis was a polished debater, Bush lacked formal debate experience. The media specialists created the expectation that Dukakis would perform well during the debates, whereas expectations of George Bush's performance were significantly lower. Though both candidates performed well during the debates, Bush's performance was a "surprise" and received considerable media attention, while the Dukakis performance simply met expectations and was less newsworthy.

The influence of receiver expectancies on perceptions of source expertise and trustworthiness were examined in a series of studies by Eagly and her colleagues (Eagly & Chaiken, 1976; Eagly, Chaiken, & Wood, 1981; Eagly, Wood, & Chaiken, 1978). These investigations employed Kelley's (1967) Attribution Theory to explain how message recipients draw causal inferences about message sources.

Attribution Theory

Kelley argued that people behave as naive psychologists as they attempt to form explanations for events that occur around them. Kelley was particularly concerned with inferences people draw about the behaviors of others. Two major categories of causal inferences exist. A person's behavior can be attributed to dispositional (personal) characteristics or to environmental (situational) characteristics.

When dispositional attributions are invoked, the inference is that the behavior is due to some characteristic of the person him- or herself. For example, if a friend is always late for class, appointments, and work, you might well conclude that the person is not punctual. That is, some characteristic of the person him- or herself has led to the tardiness. Contrast this with a friend who is always punctual, but is late on a single occasion. In this instance, you are much more likely to infer that a situational factor led to the person's tardiness.

When we invoke a situational attribution for someone's behavior, we suggest that situational constraints caused the behavior. For example, if your relational partner is irritable during final examination week, you might easily attribute the irritability to the stress associated with final exams.

Expectancies and Credibility Assessments

Eagly et al. (1981) argued that message recipients initiate this type of causal analysis when they evaluate the credibility of a message source. By using existing information about the source, message recipients generate expectations about the position the speaker will advocate. For example, during the 1960s, Americans heard a great number of political speeches about civil rights. Audiences anticipating speeches by Hubert Humphrey or Martin Luther King Jr. used information available to them to form expectations about the position these speakers were most likely to advocate. Indeed, people may have gone to hear Senator Humphrey or Reverend King speak at a political rally *because* they wanted to hear someone speak in favor of civil rights.

These expectations can be characterized by two types of biases that people form about the positions a speaker will advocate. *Knowledge bias* refers to the judgment, based on available information about the source, that the source does not possess accurate information about the message topic. *Reporting bias* reflects the belief that the source is unwilling to report accurate, or full, information about the message topic (Eagly et al., 1978). Although Eagly and her colleagues distinguish between knowledge bias and source expertise (Eagly et al., 1978, p. 426), the two concepts are quite similar. In addition, reporting bias corresponds with perceived trustworthiness.

Expectancy Violations and Attitude Change

The premessage expectations of message receivers are based on available information about the source's personal preferences and the situational pressures. These "mini-theories" are either confirmed or disconfirmed by the position the communicator takes in the message (Eagly et al., 1981). When premessage expectations are confirmed, receivers may attribute the views advocated by the speaker to personal preferences of the speaker, the speaker's background, or to pressures of the situation. These causal attributions lead to the perception that the speaker is biased. Because communicator bias compromises the validity of the message as an accurate representation of the issue being discussed, the message has little persuasive impact (Eagly et al., 1978, 1981).

When a source disconfirms premessage expectations, message recipients generate a new mini-theory to explain why the speaker advocated the position he or she did. Generally, this new mini-theory suggests that especially compelling evidence made the communicator overcome the bias that was expected to influence the message content. Such explanations lead to perceptions that the source is unbiased and enhance the persuasive effect of the message. This disconfirmation process was evident in a public service message from former President Reagan. Although he displayed little concern about the AIDS crisis during his Presidency, once he returned to private life, Reagan appeared in a public service announcement advocating greater compassion for children with AIDS. This public service announcement received considerable attention in the news media because it violated expectations of the position he advocated.

Several investigations by Eagly and her colleagues (Eagly & Chaiken, 1976; Eagly et al., 1978; Wood & Eagly, 1981) examined the persuasive effects of expectancy disconfirmations. In one study, participants were exposed to a proenvironment message that was attributed to a source described as having either a probusiness or proenvironment background (Eagly et al., 1978). The background attributed to the source created knowledge bias, the perception that the source would possess either probusiness or proenvironment information. Participants exposed to the message advocating a proenvironment position and attributed to the proenvironment source had their premessage expectancies confirmed. Those exposed to the proenvironment message attributed to a probusiness source experienced a disconfirmation of their premessage expectancies.

Reporting bias expectancies were created by telling participants that the message (proenvironment) was presented to either a proenvironment audience or a probusiness audience. When presented to the proenvironment audience, the message confirmed the reporting bias expectancy. However, when the audience was probusiness, the proenvironment message disconfirmed the reporting bias expectancy.

When an audience's premessage expectancies were disconfirmed by the position advocated in the message, the message source was judged to be less biased and was more persuasive. Apparently, following expectancy disconfirmation, audience members concluded that factual evidence must have been overwhelming to cause the message source to advocate a new position. When premessage expectancies were confirmed, message recipients attributed the position advocated to the source's background characteristics or to situational constraints. Such attributions led to a perception of source bias and limited the persuasive effect of the message (Eagly et al., 1978). This process is depicted in the model in Figure 5.1.

These findings are consistent with the attribution analysis advanced by Eagly and her colleagues and suggest that the expectancies that message recipients bring to persuasive situations influence their judgment

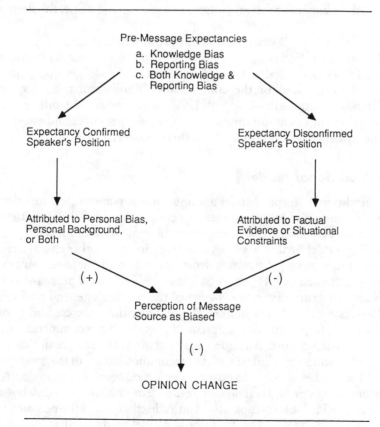

FIGURE 5.1. An expectancy model of opinion change.

about the message source. This psychological approach to studying source characteristics is consistent with the definition of credibility as a perception held by message recipients that can change over time.

Persistence of Credibility Effects

The long-term persuasive effects of source credibility factors have been of interest to persuasion scholars since the early 1950s. Although most scholars agree that the expertise and trustworthiness dimensions of source credibility are persuasive, the persistence of these persuasive effects has been questioned. In 1949, Hovland et al., published the findings of several investigations of persuasive effects of source credibility. In one investigation, they found that a persuasive message attributed to a source lacking credibility was more persuasive after some time had passed than immediately following the message presentation. This unexpected finding was given an unusual but appropriate name, the sleeper effect.

Over the past 50 years, a number of researchers attempted to replicate these early findings, but they met with limited success (Gruder et al., 1978). Several alternative definitions of the sleeper effect have emerged to account for the contradictory findings in this body of research. Recently, Allen and Stiff (1989) summarized the differences among three different interpretations of the sleeper effect and evaluated the evidence to support each of these models.

The Traditional Model

The Traditional Sleeper Model assumes that persuasion is a function of both source credibility and message content and that the evaluation of a source's credibility is separate from the evaluation of message content. The model further assumes that attention to speaker characteristics distracts message receivers from attending to message content (Hovland et al., 1949; Hovland & Weiss, 1951). Hence, persuasive effects are due primarily to knowledge of the speaker's general position and assessments of his or her credibility. Over time, the credibility of the source is forgotten, and recipients are left with a recommendation that has little support. Attitude decay occurs when the credibility of the source is no longer linked with the recommendations of the message.

Most studies of this effect used a single message that was attributed to either a low- or high-credibility source. An immediate and delayed posttest provided information about attitude change and the persistence of the attitude change. The Traditional Model predicted that immediately following message presentation, the message attributed to a highly credible source would be more persuasive than one attributed to a less credible source. Over time, however, the persuasive effects of the highly credible source and the inhibiting effects of the less credible source are not remembered. Initial attitude change produced by the highly credible source decays, or becomes smaller. Meanwhile, the removal of the inhibiting effects of the low-credibility source causes an increase in attitude change over time. At the delayed posttest, the Traditional Model predicts that attitude change produced by the low-credibility source will exceed attitude change produced by the highly credible source (Matice, 1978).

It bears mentioning that the Traditional Model was developed as a post-hoc explanation for the findings in the Hovland et al. (1949) study. Thus, although this model is consistent with their findings, there is no theoretical explanation for the prediction that a low-credibility source will produce more attitude change over time than a high-credibility source. Indeed, our meta-analytic review of this literature found that only 5 of 20 studies investigating the sleeper effect produced a pattern of findings consistent with the Traditional Model (Allen & Stiff, 1989).

The Forgetting Model

Because early research failed to replicate the Traditional Model, later researchers offered a revised version that has been labeled the Forgetting Model (Gillig & Greenwald, 1974). The Forgetting Model assumes that attitude change is a result of simple reinforcement and that source credibility is one form of reinforcement. Hence, messages from highly credible sources will produce more initial attitude change than those from less credible sources.

Thus, the Forgetting Model predicts that immediately following message exposure, the message attributed to the high-credibility source will produce more attitude change than the same message attributed to the low-credibility source. However, as the message source is forgotten, attitude change decays over time, regardless of the credibility of the source. Eventually, attitudes of people exposed to high- and low-credibility sources should converge, or become similar. Because initial attitude change produced by the highly credible source is greater, people exposed to this source will experience greater attitude decay once the source is forgotten. Thus, over time, there is a relative, but not absolute, increase in effectiveness of the low-credibility source.

Of the 20 experiments included in our review of this literature, only 10 were consistent with the predictions of the Forgetting Model. Though this model fared better in our review than the Traditional

Model, half of the findings from prior research are inconsistent with this model.

The Disassociation Model

This model assumes that persuasion is a function of both message and source factors (Cook, Gruder, Hennigan, & Flay, 1979). As does the Forgetting Model, the Disassociation Model argues that attitude change produced by the highly credible source decays over time. In this case, attitude decay occurs because the characteristics of the message source are disassociated from the message content. Message receivers remember message information that was persuasive, but they forget characteristics of the source. This process is evident in phrases such as, "I don't remember who told me this, but . . . . "

People exposed to a persuasive message from a low-credibility source experience little initial attitude change. For these message recipients, the persuasive effects of message content are offset by the negative characteristics of the message source. Over time, when the source is disassociated from the message, these message recipients are influenced by the persuasive content recalled in the message. Thus, the Disassociation Model predicts no initial change for recipients of messages from low-credibility sources, but increased attitude change once the source is disassociated from the message, assuming that the message content is persuasive.

This model is derived from an information processing view of persuasion in which credibility is not considered permanent information. Source credibility only operates in the short term to overstate or understate the evidential effects of the message. Over time, attitudes are a function of the information contained in the message, which is the same for recipients of messages from high- and low-credibility sources (Allen & Stiff, 1989, p. 417).

Gruder et al. (1978) argued that an effective test of this model requires a message that is sufficiently persuasive to offset the initial negative effects of a low-credibility source, but not persuasive so that it overcomes them. Gruder et al. argued that if a low-credibility source produces some initial attitude change, then the attitude decay that occurs when the source is disassociated from the message content will be obscured by the positive effects of message content. In such cases, it is impossible to determine if delayed attitude changes are due to simple disassociation or due to the positive effects of the evidence. Thus, a fair test of this model requires that the low-credibility group shows no initial attitude change.

Unfortunately, only 5 of 20 studies included in our review met this methodological requirement. However, four of these studies produced a pattern of immediate and delayed attitude change that was consistent with this model (Figure 5.2). Although there have been few tests of the Disassociation Model, relevant findings suggest it may be the best representation of the sleeper effect.

Implications of the Sleeper Effect

There are a number of theoretical and practical implications emerging from this literature. First, the persuasive effects of source expertise and trustworthiness are short-lived. Though only a few studies have investigated the short- and long-term effects of credibility, these investigations have demonstrated that initial persuasive effects of source expertise and trustworthiness decay over time.

Second, these findings suggest that long-term effects of single message presentations are a function of message content, not source characteristics. Once the source is disassociated from the message, the effects of source credibility diminish, and the effects of message content take over.

This literature has important implications for persuasion practitioners as well. Applied in natural persuasive settings, the Disassociation Model suggests that if short-term attitude change is desired, then the credibility of the message source is important. However, if persist-

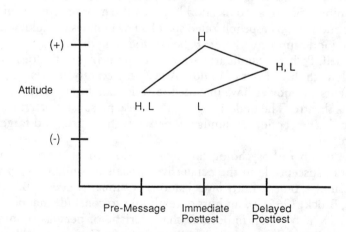

FIGURE 5.2. Attitudes predicted by the Disassociation Model. ("H" represents the highest average attitude of people receiving a message from a high-credibility source. "L" represents the average attitude of people receiving the same message from a low-credibility source.)

ing attitude change is the goal, then the credibility of the message source is less important. In such persuasive situations, evidence and message arguments are likely to be most influential. Of course, one caveat bears mentioning. Investigations of the sleeper effect have employed a single message presentation. Often, however, persuasive campaigns involve the use of repeated message presentations. Advertising, health promotion, and political campaigns all rely heavily on the use of source credibility factors. Though the influence of source characteristics may be temporary, repeated exposure to these factors during a persuasive campaign may create persisting attitude change. Unfortunately, research on the sleeper effect has not investigated the long-term effects of repeated exposure to highly credible message sources.

RELATED SOURCE CHARACTERISTICS

Although researchers have expended considerable effort to understand the persuasive effects of source expertise and trustworthiness, additional source characteristics have received somewhat less attention. Nevertheless, a sufficient number of investigations have examined the effects of source similarity and attractiveness to permit speculation about the influence of these factors in persuasive transactions.

Perceived Similarity

Practitioners have long believed that effective persuasion begins by establishing a personal connection between the message source and the target audience. Salespeople often spend a few minutes to build or maintain a good rapport with clients before focusing the discussion on the sale itself. Political candidates arrange for photo opportunities as they mingle with the masses of middle America. Recently, television advertisements for movies have included testimonials from viewers as they leave a theatre. The underlying goal of these persuasive activities is to create the perception of similarity between the source and target audience.

A number of psychological theories inform us that people should be more susceptible to the persuasive appeals of similar, as opposed to dissimilar, others. Early investigations of similarity effects (Berscheid, 1966; Brock, 1965) led authors of textbooks to conclude that perceived similarity may be an important characteristic of persuasive message sources (Bettinghaus & Cody, 1987; Petty & Cacioppo, 1981). In a thorough review of the literature, however, Simons, Berkowitz, and Moyer (1970) concluded that the persuasive effects of perceived similarity are less straightforward.

Simons and his colleagues identified two dimensions of a message source's similarity. They first distinguished between *membership similarity* and *attitudinal similarity*. Sources create membership similarity through references to demographic and social characteristics, personal experiences, and affiliations with groups and organizations that they share in common with the target audience. Politicians often emphasize their membership (or lack thereof) in national organizations to build a sense of rapport and trust with the target audience. In the 1988 Presidential campaign George Bush "accused" Michael Dukakis of being a member of the American Civil Liberties Union (ACLU). Aware of the negative attitude that many conservative Republicans held toward the ACLU, Bush strategically associated Dukakis with the values of the ACLU, while at the same time aligning himself with conservatives who were not members of the organization. Though less pronounced, college students often establish membership similarity during initial interactions. For example, sorority and fraternity members will often describe themselves in terms of membership in their particular organization.

Attitudinal similarity is established when speakers express opinions and values that are shared by members of the target audience. Television evangelists, for example, enhance their perceived trustworthiness by continuously expressing values and opinions that are deeply held by their target audience. The credibility enjoyed by those in the electronic ministry is persuasive when requests for financial contributions are made. Though indirect, the influence of attitude similarity on perceived trustworthiness can enhance the persuasiveness of message sources.

In addition to the distinction between membership and attitudinal similarity, Simons et al. (1970) described similarities in terms of their relevance to the persuasive context. Irrelevant similarities, they argued, are offered simply to build rapport and lack persuasive influence. Relevant similarities, on the other hand, may lead to greater perceptions of source trustworthiness or expertise and thus indirectly influence attitudes. After reviewing research on the persuasive effects of similarity, Simons et al. (1970) concluded that perceived similarity is not always a persuasive cue. In fact, Goethals and Nelson (1973) argued convincingly that agreement from dissimilar others was sometimes more compelling than agreement from similar others. They found that when the issue was a statement of fact, that is, a verifiable position, agreement from dissimilar others increased the confidence with which people held beliefs. Apparently, agreement from similar others leads people to question whether their assessment of the issue is subject to personal biases and the predispositions they share with a similar other. However, when agreement comes from another who does not share the same biases and predispositions, people are more confident about the position they hold. Although Goethals and Nelson (1973) focused on judgmental confidence, as opposed to attitudes, their finding is consistent with the following proposition about the persuasive influence of source similarity: "Attitude change toward the position advocated by the source depends on the extent to which interpersonal similarities or dissimilarities are perceived as having instrumental value for the receiver" (Simons et al., 1970, p. 12).

Applied to the Goethals and Nelson (1973) findings, this proposition suggests that agreement from similar others about a statement of fact had little informational value for people. However, agreement from a dissimilar other was more informative, because the other was not influenced by the same biases and predispositions. In much the same fashion, Simons et al. concluded that source similarity was not informative when it lacked relevance to the issue under consideration.

Relatively little has been learned about the effects of source similarity since the Simons et al. (1970) review. Presently, it is safe to advance two conclusions about its role in persuasive communication:

1. Source similarity does not always serve as a persuasive cue; in many situations it is unrelated to the persuasion process.
2. When similarity serves as a persuasive cue, it has a direct effect on source trustworthiness, and a smaller, indirect effect on attitudes.

Physical Attractiveness

Laboratory and field investigations of the persuasive effects of physical attractiveness produced findings similar to those found in studies of source similarity. In a review of this literature, Chaiken (1986) concluded that, like perceived similarity, source attractiveness is not always a persuasive cue. Instead, physical attractiveness seems to have its greatest influence in persuasive situations that are relatively unimportant. Unlike the effects of source similarity, however, the persuasive effects of source attractiveness are unrelated to evaluations of source expertise (Chaiken, 1979) and source trustworthiness (Norman, 1976). That is to say, the persuasive effects of source attractiveness are direct and not mediated by judgments of credibility.

Three different explanations have been advanced to account for the influence of source attractiveness (Chaiken, 1979, 1986). The *social reinforcement* explanation argues that the persuasive effects of physical attractiveness stem from the social rewards attractive people provide.

It is well established that we find attractive people to be socially rewarding, and when given a choice, we select attractive acquaintances over unattractive ones (Berscheid & Walster, 1974). Kelman (1961) argued that the process of *identification* increases susceptibility to influence from attractive sources. Thus, the social reinforcement explanation suggests that our desire to associate with attractive people leads us to accept influence from them.

A *cognitive processing* explanation has also been advanced to account for the persuasive effects of source attractiveness (Chaiken, 1980, 1987). Chaiken argues that people often rely on simple decision rules to make judgments about message recommendations. These decision rules are called "heuristics," and they substitute for careful thinking about the persuasive message. Chaiken argues that heuristics are cognitive shortcuts that eliminate the need for effortful thinking about the message (see discussion of the Heuristic Model of Persuasion, Chapter 9, this volume). For example, one heuristic, the "likeability–agreement heuristic," suggests that we tend to agree with people we like. Because physical attractiveness has been associated with likeability (Chaiken, 1986), the likeability–agreement heuristic may be the basis for agreement with attractive sources.

Finally, the *social skills* explanation suggests that physically attractive people are more persuasive because they have better social skills than less attractive people. For example, in a field study of physical attractiveness, Chaiken (1979) found a number of important differences between attractive and unattractive sources. Specifically, she found that attractive sources were significantly more fluent and slightly faster speakers than unattractive sources. Moreover, attractive sources reported higher SAT scores and more favorable self-impressions, and they were more confident of their persuasive skills than less attractive communicators. Although no specific test of the relationship between these communication factors and attitude change was made, it is likely that these factors contribute to the persuasive successes of attractive sources. Thus, the social skills explanation argues that attractive sources are more persuasive because they are more confident and skilled communicators than unattractive sources.

Regardless of the underlying explanations, the persuasive effects of physical attractiveness are clear. In situations where source characteristics are considered by message recipients, attractive sources enjoy a persuasive advantage over their less attractive counterparts. It bears mentioning that the three explanations for this effect are not mutually exclusive. More likely, some combination of the three explanations accounts for the persuasive effects of source attractiveness.

These explanations underscore the importance of understanding the influence of individual difference variables in persuasion research. The finding that attractive people have a persuasive advantage over unattractive sources has significant predictive utility for persuasion practioners, and it is equally important for persuasion theorists. Isolating the correct theoretical explanations for this effect will contribute to a broader understanding of how people process persuasive messages.

SUMMARY

This chapter examined several characteristics of message sources that affect the persuasion process. I began by discussing two dimensions of source credibility, source expertise and source trustworthiness, and argued that although they are often related, these are separate dimensions that people typically use to evaluate a source. Next I discussed the expectations people have about message sources and the positions the sources are likely to advocate. I argued that when these expectations are confirmed, people perceive the source to be biased and, hence, less convincing. However, when these expectations are disconfirmed, the source is perceived as less biased and more persuasive. I concluded the discussion of source credibility effects by reviewing research on the sleeper effect. Here, I argued that source credibility has its greatest persuasive influence in the short term and that, over time, people disassociate the source of a message from the message content. Thus, in the long term, message content features are much more persuasive than source characteristics.

Source similarity and physical attractiveness are two other factors that may affect the persuasion process. When characteristics of a message source that are relevant to the persuasive message are similar to characteristics of the audience, the trustworthiness of the source may be enhanced. In addition, research has shown that source attractiveness is only persuasive in some situations. Specifically, when the message is relatively unimportant to receivers, they are likely to be affected by the attractiveness of the source. Several possible explanations for these effects were discussed.

CHAPTER SIX

Persuasive Message Characteristics

LOOKING AHEAD . . .

This chapter examines features of messages that are influential in the persuasion process. I begin with a discussion of rational appeals and discuss how evidence is processed by message receivers and when it is likely to be most effective. Then I examine the effectiveness of one- and two-sided messages. The second part of the chapter examines the use of emotional appeals. In particular, I review the broad area of research on fear appeals.

The decade of the 1960s was witness to a proliferation of persuasion research that attempted to catalog the characteristics of persuasive messages. These investigations culminated in several avenues of research that are generally referred to as "message effects research," which helped to inform most of our classic and contemporary theories of persuasion. Unfortunately, a thorough review of each of these research programs is beyond the scope of this book. Instead this chapter examines the findings from four distinct avenues of message effects research. These four topics were selected because they made a significant contribution to the understanding of persuasive communication, and because they continue to motivate persuasion research 30 years after the genesis of the message effects research paradigm.

The chapter is divided into two major sections; the first examines the effectiveness of rational appeals and the second focuses on the use of emotional appeals. The discussion of rational appeals begins with a review of the research on the persuasive effects of evidence. Following this, several models of rational argumentation are examined, and the section concludes with a discussion of the effectiveness of one- and two-sided message presentations. The second major section of the chapter examines the role of emotional appeals in persuasion. In particular, I focus the discussion on the persuasive effects of fear appeals.

RATIONAL PERSUASIVE APPEALS

Persuasive messages that contain rational arguments are based on the assumption that people have an implicit understanding of formal rules of logic, and that they apply these rules when making judgments about a source's recommendations. Rational arguments derive their influence from sound reasoning and the quality of evidence that is offered in support of the conclusion. Though there are many types of rational appeals, the most basic form of an argument contains three components; a claim, data to support the claim, and a warrant that provides a logical connection between the data and the claim (Toulmin, 1964).

In Toulmin's terms, a *claim* is the conclusion of the argument, the position implied by reasoning and supporting information. Typically, the claim is the position a source is advocating in a message. *Data* are evidence that provide support for the claim. McCroskey defined evidence as "factual statements originating from a source other than the speaker, objects not created by the speaker, and opinions of persons other than the speaker that are offered in support of the speaker's claims" (1969, p. 170). Finally, a *warrant* is a propositional statement that connects the data to the claim. Its specific form may vary, but a warrant always provides the logical connection between the data and the claim. It is the justification for the claim, given the data provided.

For example, consider the following argument: "Recent tuition increases at most state universities make it increasingly difficult for people from lower- and middle-income families to obtain a college degree. Thus, we should cap tuition increases in order to make public education accessible to students from all economic backgrounds." In this argument, the claim is that we should cap tuition increases. Support for this claim comes from the first sentence, which states that tuition increases make it difficult for poorer students to attend college. However, this evidence is not relevant to the claim unless we also consider our longstanding commitment to make public education accessible to everyone. Hence, the warrant that connects the data to the claim is the statement that we must maintain our commitment to make public education accessible to everyone.

Toulmin's model of argument specifies an important role for evidence in the persuasion process and suggests two important questions for persuasion scholars. First, how persuasive is the evidence contained in rational appeals? Second, how do rational appeals influence the attitudes and beliefs of targets? The following sections of this chapter examine each of these questions. I begin with a discussion of the persuasive effects of evidence and then review studies that have modeled the effectiveness of rational appeals.

Persuasive Effects of Evidence

Investigations of persuasive communication after World War II sparked an interest in the use of evidence in persuasive appeals. Though Toulmin (1964) clearly specified the role of evidence in argumentation, persuasion scholars were curious about the importance of valid arguments in persuasive appeals. By the late 1960s, a plethora of variable-analytic studies had examined the persuasive effects of evidence (for reviews, see McCroskey, 1967, 1969; Reynolds & Burgoon, 1983). Unfortunately, these investigations often produced contradictory findings, and without a relevant theory to guide them, researchers had difficulty summarizing this literature.

In response to this state of affairs, Petty and Cacioppo (1981, 1986) developed the Elaboration Likelihood Model (ELM) of persuasion. A thorough discussion of this model and the controversy surrounding it appears in Chapter 9. For now, I will consider only the portion of the model pertaining to the effectiveness of evidence. In part, the ELM posits that the persuasiveness of supporting information is dependent on the *motivation* and *ability* of message recipients to process the evidence contained in the message. Each of these determining factors is discussed below.

Motivation to Scrutinize Message Content

Petty and Cacioppo hypothesized that one factor that affects people's willingness to scrutinize the content of a persuasive message is their involvement with the message topic. According to the ELM, when recipients are highly involved in a message topic, they are motivated to scrutinize the message content because they are concerned about the outcome of the persuasive attempt. Thus, when message receivers are highly involved with the message topic, message characteristics such as supporting evidence and argument quality should influence attitude change. Conversely, when targets are relatively uninvolved with the topic of the persuasive appeal, they will be less motivated to scrutinize message content. In these cases, evidence and argument quality will go relatively unnoticed by message recipients, and their persuasive effects will be minimal.

A meta-analytic review of the evidence literature provided support for this general hypothesis (Stiff, 1986). When the findings of 30 investigations were cumulated, I found an overall positive correlation between the use of evidence and attitude change ($r = .18$). However, as predicted by the ELM, there was an interaction between message recipient involvement and the effectiveness of evidence. That is, there was a direct linear relationship between the level of message recipient involvement and the persuasiveness of message evidence. Specifically, when the message topic was relatively uninvolving for recipients, evidence was least persuasive ($r = .12$). For moderately involving topics, the correlation between the amount or quality of evidence and attitude change was somewhat stronger ($r = .18$). Finally, the correlation was strongest when the topic was highly involving ($r = .30$). Although they are small in size, the differences among these effect sizes were statistically significant. Thus, the meta-analysis of the effects of supporting information on attitudes was consistent with the effects predicted by the ELM.

The investigations included in this meta-analytic review contained a variety of different evidence manipulations. Some studies manipulated the amount of evidence contained in the message, other studies varied the presence or absence of evidence in the message, and still others manipulated evidence by varying the quality of arguments contained in the message. Petty and his colleagues (Petty et al., 1987) criticized the decision to collapse these different types of evidence manipulations into a single evidence category. They argued that the different types of evidence manipulations would produce different persuasive effects. However, subsequent analysis of these studies produced the same pattern of effects for each type of evidence manipulation (Stiff & Boster, 1987).

Thus, the pattern of findings that emerged from my meta-analysis appears to be quite robust. Across many studies employing a variety of operational definitions, the persuasive effects of evidence seem dependent on the motivation of recipients to scrutinize message content. When they are motivated to consider its content, persuasive targets are likely to be influenced by the quality of supporting evidence in the message.

Ability to Scrutinize Message Content

In addition to motivation, the ELM also specifies that the effects of evidence are dependent on the ability of message recipients to scrutinize message content. Most studies tacitly assume that persuasive targets are capable of effectively judging the validity of message arguments. However, prior research has documented several errors in reasoning that people frequently commit.

In an early study, Janis and Frick (1943) hypothesized that people make two types of systematic errors when judging the logical validity of arguments. First, Janis and Frick hypothesized that when people agree with the conclusion of an argument, they are more likely to judge invalid arguments that support the conclusion as valid and judge valid arguments against the conclusion to be invalid. Conversely, Janis and Frick hypothesized that when people disagree with the conclusion of an argument, they are more likely to judge invalid arguments opposing the conclusion as valid and judge valid arguments favoring the conclusion as invalid. In short, Janis and Frick speculated that when asked to judge the logical validity of an argument, people are likely to let their preferences about the argument's claim affect their judgments.

To test these hypotheses, Janis and Frick presented college students with a series of arguments that were logically valid or logically invalid. A pretest revealed the arguments participants agreed with and those they opposed. Janis and Frick's analyses provided clear support for their hypotheses. When students made errors in reasoning, they tended to judge an invalid argument as valid if they agreed with the conclusion and a valid argument as invalid if they disagreed with its conclusion.

Bettinghaus and his colleagues extended this analysis, but argued that people are not equally likely to make errors in judging the logical validity of arguments (Bettinghaus, Miller, & Steinfatt, 1970). Instead, they argued that highly dogmatic people are more likely to let their preferences influence their judgments of argument validity. *Dogmatism* is a personality trait that reflects the extent to which a person is closed-minded. For example, a highly dogmatic person would most likely agree with statements such as, "Of all the different philosophies which exist in this world there is probably only one which is correct," and "There are two kinds of people in this world, those who are for truth and those who are against truth" (Trodahl & Powell, 1965). Bettinghaus et al. hypothesized that because of their rigid cognitive style, highly dogmatic people would be more likely to let their preference for an argument's conclusion influence their judgment of the argument's validity. Using the measure of dogmatism developed by Trodahl and Powell (1965), they replicated Janis and Frick's findings and also found support for their hypothesis. Specifically, they found that highly dogmatic people were more likely to judge an argument as valid if it came from a positive source than if it came from a negative source (Bettinghaus et al., 1973).

Together these studies suggest that people tend to make systematic errors when they judge the validity of arguments. Though the accuracy rates in studies like these are generally quite high, it bears mentioning that people can and do make errors in reasoning when processing persuasive messages.

Combined with the research on motivation, these findings challenge the tacit assumption that messages containing well-reasoned arguments with ample supporting information will be persuasive. In fact, it may be that in many instances people are unmotivated or unable to effectively scrutinize the content of persuasive messages. If message recipients are capable and sufficiently motivated, messages containing quality arguments and strong evidence are an effective means of persuasion.

Modeling the Effects of Rational Appeals

The preceding discussion of the limitations of rational appeals was not intended to create the impression that logical arguments and supporting information are ineffective for creating, changing, and reinforcing attitudes and behavior. Rather, it was intended to provide readers with a better understanding of the situations in which the influence of rational appeals is likely to be limited. Given that rational appeals are persuasive in a large majority of persuasive contexts, we should understand *how* they work to persuade targets.

Mathematical models of belief formation and change provide some insights into the effectiveness of rational persuasive appeals (Hample, 1977, 1978, 1979; McGuire, 1960; Wyer, 1970; Wyer & Goldberg, 1970). These models are derived from the logical syllogism as a form of rational argument, and they assume that humans are rational beings.

McGuire's Probabilistic Model

Belief in the conclusion of an argument is not always an all-or-nothing proposition. That is, people believe claims with a certain probability. Sometimes, people believe with a high degree of probability that a persuasive claim is true. Beliefs about abortion rights, for example, tend to be held with a high degree of certainty. Abortion rights advocates and their antiabortion adversaries often express all-or-nothing beliefs about abortion. The battle lines have been clearly drawn, and for many people on opposite sides of this continuing debate there is no gray area, no common ground.

On the other hand, most of our beliefs about issues are held with less certainty. For example, we may believe that Ross Perot would have been an effective president, or that the collapse of the Soviet Union has led to increased international conflict, but we may be less certain of these beliefs than we are about our beliefs surrounding the abortion issue. That is, we may hold these beliefs with a probability of less than 1.00.

To accommodate the variation in the extent to which people hold beliefs, McGuire (1960) developed a probabilistic model of beliefs. The foundation of this model is a form of argument known as a logical syllogism. Logical syllogisms have three components, a major premise, a minor premise, and a conclusion. If an argument is valid, its conclusion can be deduced from the major and the minor premises, providing they are true. Consider the following example:

Major Premise: If I attend class and study 3 hours a week, I will receive an "A" in my persuasion course.
Minor Premise: I will attend class and study 3 hours a week.
Conclusion: I will receive an "A" in my persuasion course.

In this example, if the major premise is true and the minor premise is true, then the conclusion is true by definition. Thus, if attending class and studying 3 hours a week is sufficient to receive an "A" in your persuasion course, then you should expect an "A" if you attend class and study 3 hours a week. However, McGuire (1960) argued you may be less than certain about the major or minor premise, yet still believe them. That is, you may believe with a high probability, say 90%, that the major premise is true, and believe with somewhat less probability, say 65% that the minor premise is true. According to McGuire's model, if either the major or minor premise is held with less than certain probability, then the conclusion will be held with less than certain probability.

Understanding this, the crux of McGuire's model is actually quite simple, and it can be easily represented in the following equation:

$$p(B) = p(B/A)\, p(A) \tag{6.1}$$

where $p(B)$ is the probability that the conclusion is true (read: the probability of B); $p(B/A)$ is the probability that the major premise is true (read: the probability of B given A); and $p(A)$ is the probability that the minor premise is true (read: the probability of A).

Thus, to estimate your belief in the conclusion of an argument you simply multiply the probability that you believe the major premise is true by the probability that you believe the minor premise is true. Applying this model to the earlier syllogism about receiving an "A" in your persuasion course is one way to examine the effects of probabilistic beliefs. If you assume that the probability of your belief in the major premise is .80 and the probability that you believe the minor premise is true is .70, then the probability that you believe the conclusion, that is, that you will receive an "A" in the course, should be .56. Conversely, the probability that you will receive something other than an "A" is .44 (1.00 − .56).

It bears mentioning that like any other model or theory of persuasion, McGuire's model is simply a hypothesis, one that describes how the components of logical syllogisms determine people's beliefs about an argument's conclusion. Tests of this hypothesis were relatively straightforward. People were asked to indicate the probability that a number of belief statements were true. Embedded in this list of belief statements were minor premises, major premises, and conclusions from syllogistic arguments. By multiplying a person's belief probability for the major premise of an argument by the belief probability of the minor premise, researchers could obtain a predicted value for the person's belief in the conclusion. The correlation between the predicted belief in the conclusion and the person's reported belief in the conclusion indicates the extent to which the model describes how people form beliefs about an argument's conclusion. That is, a strong positive correlation between the predicted and reported probabilities of belief in the conclusion provides support for the model's validity. Several tests of McGuire's model produced the anticipated positive correlations between predicted and observed belief probabilities, thus providing support for this model (McGuire, 1960).

Wyer's Extension of McGuire's Model

Although evidence existed to support McGuire's model, correlations between predicted and observed belief probabilities were far less than perfect. In an effort to improve its predictive value, Wyer (1970) and Wyer and Goldberg (1970) proposed an extension of McGuire's original model. They hypothesized that factors other than those included in an argument influenced the probability with which people believe the argument's conclusion. In fact, Wyer hypothesized that people could believe the conclusion of syllogism even if they did not believe the major and minor premises. For example, you may believe you will receive an "A" in your persuasion class even if you don't go to class and study. Instead, you may believe you will receive an "A" because you are brilliant, cheat well, or believe the class is remarkably easy. Wyer's extension can be represented in the following equation:

$$p(B) = p(B/A)\,p(A) + p(B/\overline{A})\,p(\overline{A}) \qquad (6.2)$$

where $p(B)$ is the probability that the conclusion is true (read: the probability of B); $p(B/A)$ is the probability that the major premise is true (read: the probability of B given A); $p(A)$ is the probability that the minor premise is true (read: the probability of A); $p(B/\overline{A})$ is the probability that the conclusion is true even if the minor premise is false (read: the probability of B given *not A); and* $p(\overline{A})$ is the probability that the minor premise is false (read: the probability of *not A*. By definition, this value is $1 - p[A]$).

Thus, Wyer's model suggests that a person's belief in the conclusion is determined by belief in the major and minor premises plus the effects of factors not included in the syllogism. Extending our syllogism about the grade you believe you will receive, recall that your belief in the major premise is .80, your belief in the minor premise is .70, and the product of these two belief probabilities is .56. Wyer's model requires that you also consider your belief that you will receive an "A" even if you do not attend class and study 3 hours a week, $p(B/\overline{A})$, multiplied by the probability that you will not attend class and study 3 hours a week, $p(\overline{A})$. Assume that you believe the probability that you will receive an "A" even if you do not attend class and study 3 hours a week is .40. Because $p(\overline{A})$ equals $1 - (A)$, you believe the probability that you will not attend class and study 3 hours a week is .30. Multiplying these latter two values produces a belief in the conclusion of .12 that is due to factors other than those contained in the argument. Combined with the probability that the conclusion is true because the major and minor premises are true (.56), the overall belief probability in the conclusion is .68.

Thus, in this example, Wyer's model predicts that you believe there is a .68 probability of getting an "A" in your persuasion class compared to the .56 probability predicted by the McGuire model. As does the previous model, Wyer's probabilistic model represents a hypothesis about the structure of people's beliefs. Tests of this hypothesis, however, produced disappointing results. In comparative tests of the two models, Hample (1979) found that the McGuire model predicted beliefs much better than the Wyer model.

Hample's Refinement of Wyer's Model

Hample (1979) found that when added together, the two components in the Wyer model tended to offset one another. Because the $p(A)$ is inversely related to $p(\overline{A})$—recall that $p(\overline{A}) = 1 - p(A)$—the values for the first multiplicative term in Wyer's equation were negatively correlated with the values of the second multiplicative term in the equation. The result was a model with less predictive validity than the original model offered by McGuire.

To alleviate this concern, Hample suggested applying a weight to each of the multiplicative components in the Wyer model. Using regression analyses, Hample (1979) demonstrated that applying weights to both parts of the Wyer model allowed each to work independently to predict people's belief in the conclusion of an argument (p. 144). That is, the weights consider separate contributions of the two components in Wyer's model without having the contributions of each component offset one another. In short, Hample applied a statistical solution to the problems associated with Wyer's model. Hample further demonstrated that his weighted version of Wyer's model produced uniformly strong correlations between people's predicted and reported beliefs in the conclusions of various arguments. Hample's revision of the Wyer model provided a better explanation of people's beliefs in a conclusion than either the Wyer (1970) or McGuire (1960) models.

Why These Models Are Important

Students often question the value of these models for persuasion practitioners. I frequently field inquiries about the relevance of probabilistic models for everyday interaction, or even the development of persuasive campaigns. Although their value may not be intuitively obvious, these models provide considerable insight into the role that evidence plays in persuasion.

Recall the earlier discussion of Toulmin's (1964) model of argument. A valid argument contains a claim, data to support the claim, and a warrant that connects the data to the claim. Hample argued that whatever verbal form an argument may ultimately take, its warrant must serve the logical function of asserting "if D then C, where D represents the data and C represents the claim" (1978, p. 220). In a logical syllogism, the argument's warrant is the major premise of the syllogism. The data are represented in the minor premise, and the argument's claim is represented in the conclusion. Thus, the probabilistic models describe the effect of an argument's evidence and warrant on adherence to its claim. Hample's (1979) revision of Wyer's (1970) model accurately predicted people's acceptance of an argument's conclusion and thus provides insights into the operation of evidence in the persuasion process.

Hample's model underscores the importance of evidence in the success of a logical appeal. Furthermore, the model implies that belief in the argument's warrant is as important as the acceptance of supporting evidence. Given the importance of the warrant to the overall acceptance of the argument, sources may gain a persuasive advantage by explicitly stating the connection between the data and the claim and avoiding the use of implicit warrants. Because they are unstated, implicit warrants allow targets to provide their own connection between the data and the claim, or to leave the evidence logically unconnected. Indeed, Burgoon cautioned against the use of implicit conclusions for the same reason. He argued that "persuaders must be cautious in assuming that the audience will draw the *correct* conclusion from the data" (1989, p. 144). Arguments with explicit warrants also require less cognitive participation from targets who may be content to adopt the logic, and hence the conclusion, of a source's argument.

One- and Two-Sided Rational Appeals

One characteristic of rational persuasion is that two or more opposing positions can be advocated for any persuasive topic. Because there are at least two sides to every persuasive story, persuaders must decide how much recognition they should direct toward opposing viewpoints. Messages can be crafted to focus exclusively on arguments in favor of a source's position, or they can be expanded to acknowledge the existence of opposing arguments. Messages that contain only supporting arguments are labeled *one-sided messages;* those that also address opposing viewpoints are *two-sided messages.*

Hovland and his colleagues were the first to investigate the relative persuasiveness of one- and two-sided messages. Like most variable analytic researchers of their day, Hovland et al. (1949) were motivated by a practical concern; they wanted to determine which type of message structure would enjoy the greatest persuasive success.

Initial investigations of this issue found that premessage agreement with the position advocated in the message and the education level of message recipients influence the relative persuasiveness of one- and two-sided messages. Participants who already agreed with the position advocated in a message were persuaded more by one-sided messages, whereas two-sided messages were more effective for targets who initially disagreed with the source's position (Lumsdaine & Janis, 1953). Moreover, two-sided messages proved more successful for targets with some high school education whereas one-sided messages were more successful for less educated targets (Hovland et al., 1949).

These early research efforts sparked a considerable amount of interest in the structure of persuasive messages. At issue in this literature was the extent to which one- and two-sided messages influenced credibility assessments of the speaker. Presumably, well-informed audiences and audiences that disagree with the speaker's position are cognizant of opposing viewpoints and expect the source to address both sides of the issue. One-sided message presentations to these types of audiences were hypothesized to produce lower judgments of source expertise and trustworthiness and to limit the effectiveness of the message.

Unfortunately, subsequent investigations of message sidedness produced an array of conflicting findings. Some studies found two-sided messages to be more persuasive, some found one-sided messages more persuasive, and some revealed no effects for message sidedness. Moreover, the pattern of findings in these investigations did not support the anticipated effects of audience characteristics (for a review, see Allen, 1991).

Extending their review of this literature, Allen and his colleagues (Allen et al., 1990; Jackson & Allen, 1987) noted widespread differences in the message sidedness manipulations of prior research. Although the definition of a one-sided message is relatively straightforward, defining a two-sided message is conceptually more difficult. For example, some investigations constructed two-sided messages that acknowledged, but did not refute, opposing arguments. Allen and his colleagues labeled these as "two-sided, nonrefutational messages." Other researchers developed two-sided messages that not only recognized opposing viewpoints, but also refuted them. These were labeled as "two-sided, refutational messages."

Allen and his colleagues hypothesized that the apparently conflicting findings in this literature may have resulted from a failure to recognize the operational differences of two-sided messages in prior research. They hypothesized that sources who recognize the existence of opposing viewpoints, but do not refute them, are likely to be viewed as having less expertise than sources who recognize and refute opposing viewpoints. In fact, they speculated that two-sided, nonrefutational messages would be less persuasive than one-sided messages.

To test their hypothesis, they conducted three studies involving 17 topics, 51 messages, and over 1,000 research participants. For each of the 17 topics, they developed, or had students develop, 3 persuasive messages—a one-sided message; a two-sided, refutational message; and a two-sided, nonrefutational message. These messages were presented to research participants and measures of their attitudes following the message were obtained. A consistent pattern of findings emerged from their analyses. Two-sided, refutational messages were more persuasive than one-sided messages, and one-sided messages were more persuasive than two-sided, nonrefutational messages. The pattern for source credibility assessments was consistent with the attitude data. Targets who read the two-sided, refutational messages provided the most favorable assessments of source credibility, followed by targets who read the one-sided messages and two-sided, nonrefutational messages, respectively (Allen et al., 1990).

A subsequent meta-analytic review of the literature confirmed the importance of the distinction drawn by Allen and his colleagues. Allen (1991) divided prior investigations into two categories, those that employed two-sided, refutational messages and those that employed two-sided nonrefutational messages. His analyses revealed that two-sided, refutational messages were more persuasive than one-sided messages, and that two-sided, nonrefutational messages were less persuasive than their one-sided counterparts. Although the size of these persuasive effects were not large, Allen noted that the two-sided, refutational messages were significantly more persuasive than two-sided, nonrefutational messages. Moreover, the effect sizes he observed indicated that two-sided, refutational messages were about *20% more effective* than one-sided messages, whereas two-sided, nonrefutational messages were about *20% less effective* than one-sided messages (1991, p. 400). It also bears mentioning that early predictions of the relative effectiveness of one-sided messages for favorable audiences and two-sided messages for unfavorable audiences were not confirmed in Allen's review. He found that audience favorability toward the topic was unrelated to message effectiveness.

Hale, Mongeau, and Thomas (1991) employed cognitive response processes to explain the enhanced persuasiveness of two-sided, refutational messages. They found that two-sided, messages produced more favorable thoughts about the message recommendation, which led to more favorable evaluation of the message and greater attitude change. Although this same causal process was found for both types of two-sided messages, the effect of the refutational message on positive cognitions ($B = .18$) was almost twice as strong as the effect of nonrefutational message ($B = .10$). Thus, one explanation for the effectiveness of two-sided, refutational messages is that they engender more favorable thoughts about the message recommendation. In combination, the findings of Allen's (1991) meta-analysis and the Hale et al. (1991) study suggest that two-sided, refutational messages are more persuasive because they produce more favorable thoughts about the message recommendation and more favorable evaluations of the source's credibility.

EMOTIONAL PERSUASIVE APPEALS

When people use rational persuasive appeals their success rests on the assumption that persuasive targets behave as rational human beings. However, in many persuasive contexts, message recipients are unable or unmotivated to effectively process rational appeals. In these circumstances, persuaders often turn to emotional persuasive appeals. Although there are many types of emotional appeals, ranging from humor to sympathy, fear appeals have received the most attention from persuasion scholars and practitioners.

Fear appeals are frequently employed in prevention and safety campaigns directed at adolescents. "Don't drink and drive" campaigns, for example, routinely rely on the use of fear-arousing messages to attract the attention of teenagers and motivate them to change their attitudes and driving behavior. Sponsors of these campaigns believe that fear-arousing messages are persuasive, but a review of prior research (Boster & Mongeau, 1984) suggests that the effectiveness of fear appeals *may* be restricted to older audiences. These findings lead to questions about the utility of fear appeals. Are these types of messages persuasive? The answer to this question is a qualified yes: Given certain message and audience characteristics, fear-appeal messages can be persuasive. In this section of the chapter I examine the fear-appeal literature. I begin by defining a fear appeal and identifying models that describe how fear appeals work. Following this, I summarize some of the important findings from previous studies of this genre of persuasive messages.

Defining Fear Appeals

Over the years, a number of definitions have been used to separate fear appeals from other types of persuasive messages. For the most part, these definitions focus on message content and/or audience reactions to a message (O'Keefe, 1990). For example, a definition emphasizing message content would describe a fear appeal as a message that contains "gruesome content" (Leventhal, 1970). The gory films of crash victims we all watched during high school driver education classes reflect this type of definition. A second approach defines a fear appeal as a message that invokes considerable fear in message recipients. Studies adopting this definitional approach use manipulation checks to assess the amount of fear people report after exposure to a message. Messages that produce significant levels of self-reported fear in message recipients are defined as fear-arousing messages. Though some studies adopt one of these two approaches, many investigations incorporate features of both definitions. That is, many studies have defined a fear appeal in terms of message content, but have also employed manipulation checks to assess audience perceptions of fear. For our purposes, a fear appeal can be defined as a persuasive message that arouses fear by depicting a personally relevant and significant threat, followed by a description of feasible recommendations for deterring the threat (Witte, 1992a).

Embedded in this definition are three concepts, —*fear, threat,* and *perceived efficacy,*—that have guided thinking about fear appeals for over 40 years. Fear is a negatively valenced emotion that is usually accompanied by heightened physiological arousal. Threat is an external stimulus that creates a perception in message receivers that they are susceptible to some negative situation or outcome. For example, a message that links cigarette smoking to lung cancer is likely to be perceived as threatening by many smokers because it links their behavior with some negative outcome. Finally, perceived efficacy is similar to the concept of perceived behavioral control that I discussed in Chapter 3 (see also Chapter 11, this volume). As applied in the fear-appeal literature, perceived efficacy is a person's belief that message recommendations can be implemented and will effectively reduce the threat depicted in the message (Rogers, 1975, 1983; Witte, 1992a).

The conceptual importance of these concepts is reflected in the three families of models,—*drive theories, parallel response models,* and *subjective expected utility models,*—that have been proposed to explain the persuasive effects of fear appeals (Dillard, in press; Witte, 1992a). Each of these models is described below.

Modeling the Effects of Fear Appeals

Humble Beginnings

One of the first investigations of the effects of fear-arousing persuasive messages speculated about the possibility of a curvilinear (inverted-U) relationship between the amount of fear-arousing content and acceptance of message recommendations. Janis and Feshbach hypothesized that "when emotional tension is aroused, the audience will become more highly motivated to accept the reassuring beliefs or recommendations advocated by the communicator" (1953, p. 78). However, they cautioned that the arousal of extreme emotional tension can activate defensive mechanisms that may thwart the persuasive effects of the message. Under conditions of high fear, for example, they speculated that persuasive targets may be inattentive to the message content in hopes of alleviating their anxiety.

To test their speculation, they exposed 200 college freshmen to messages advocating better dental hygiene. The strong fear message contained several references to the painful consequences of tooth decay and gum disease that result from poor dental hygiene. The moderate fear message contained the same information, but was less graphic in its depiction of the effects of poor dental hygiene. Finally, the minimal fear message contained the same hygiene information, but rarely described the negative effects of poor hygiene. Both 1 week before and 1 week after exposure to the persuasive messages, participants in the study completed a questionnaire describing their dental hygiene practices.

Janis and Feshbach's findings disconfirmed their expectations; they found no support for the curvilinear relationship they had hypothesized. Instead, they found that the minimal fear message induced the most compliance with the message recommendations and the strong fear message produced the least amount of compliance. In other words, they hypothesized a curvilinear (inverted-U) relationship between fear and attitude change, but they found a negative linear relationship.

Although their study found no evidence for the effectiveness of fear-arousing messages, Janis and Feshbach (1953) ignited considerable research and theorizing about the persuasive effects of fear appeals. Specifically, this early research laid the conceptual groundwork for the family of fear-appeal models known as drive models.

Drive Models

The first theoretical explanation for the effects of fear-arousing messages conceptualized fear as acquired drive (Janis, 1967; Janis & Feshbach, 1953; McGuire, 1968; Miller, 1963). *Drive* is a psychological term that reflects an unpleasant state that people strive to reduce or eliminate. These bodily states initiate activity and are frequently experienced as feelings of tension or restlessness (Newcomb, Turner, & Converse, 1965, p. 23).

Applied to the study of fear appeals, fear is a drive state that is usually initiated by a graphic description of negative consequences that message receivers are likely to experience if they do not adopt the message recommendations. Consider again the gory films that are part of many high school driver education courses. These films depict the consequences of drinking and driving and are designed to create a drive state. To effectively reduce this fear, these films also contain recommendations for safe driving. "When a response reduces fear, it is reinforced and becomes part of one's permanent response repertory" (Leventhal, 1970, p. 123).

Thus, the drive model suggests a sequence in which a fear appeal arouses fear in message receivers. Acceptance of message recommendations reduces this fear and leads to attitude or behavior change. However, message receivers might also reduce fear by denying that the negative consequences of drinking and driving are likely to occur. This is particularly relevant for adolescents, who sometimes feel invulnerable. The mechanism that reduces this fear, whether adaptive (e.g., behavioral change) or maladaptive (e.g., denial), is reinforced and becomes the preferred response to the threat (Janis, 1967; Witte, 1992b). This process is depicted in Figure 6.1 and implies that "a fear appeal should have two components: a part of the message that instills fear and another that assuages it" (Dillard, in press).

Drive models posit a curvilinear (inverted-U) relationship between the level of fear aroused by a message and message acceptance (Janis, 1967; McGuire, 1968). According to these models, messages that arouse very little fear are ineffective because people are relatively unaffected by mild warnings (Janis, 1967). That is, low levels of fear do not produce the drive necessary to motivate acceptance of message recommendations. Moderate levels of fear produce the drive that causes people to accept the message recommendations. Finally, messages that arouse high levels of fear may cause a defensive avoidance process in which people ignore or deny the threat contained in the message (Miller, 1963). Thus, the drive models predict that messages that arouse moderate levels of fear will be more effective than those that arouse very low or extremely high levels of fear (Figure 6.2).

Little evidence has been garnered to support drive models of fear appeals. Beginning with the Janis and Feshbach (1953) experiment, researchers have consistently failed to observe the curvilinear relationship between fear and message acceptance. A recent meta-analytic review of this literature produced no evidence of a curvilinear relationship (Boster & Mongeau, 1984). Instead, they found a positive linear relationship between manipulated fear and attitude change ($r = .21$). Indeed, by 1970, the lack of empirical support and growing concerns about the specification of variables that moderate the relationship between fear and message acceptance led Leventhal (1970) to propose an alternative model, the parallel response model, to explain the persuasive effects of fear appeals.

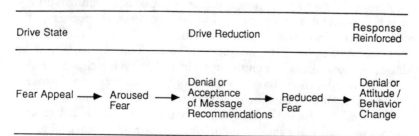

FIGURE 6.1. A drive model of fear appeals.

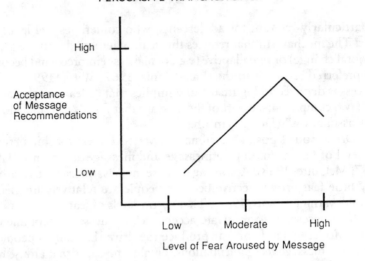

High ─┤

Acceptance
of Message
Recommendations

Low ─┤

           Low   Moderate   High

Level of Fear Aroused by Message

FIGURE 6.2. The relationship between aroused fear and message acceptance predicted by the drive model.

Parallel Response Model

Leventhal's (1970) solution to the mixed findings in the fear-appeal literature was to propose two separate, but parallel, responses in message recipients. *Fear control* is one response people have to fear-arousing messages. This process involves the "initiation of responses in an attempt to reduce the unpleasant feeling of fear, and is guided by internal cues" (Sutton, 1982, p. 324). As such, this response is consistent with the process depicted by the drive models, and it functions to reduce the fear. A second, parallel, response to fear appeals is *danger control*. Danger control involves the evaluation and selection of responses that will avert the danger.

Perhaps the clearest distinction between these two responses stems from their focus on emotion and cognition. Fear control is basically an emotional response, whereas danger control is a cognitive process that is dependent on information available to message receivers. Outcomes of the fear control process include avoidance of the situation and denial of the threat contained in the message. Outcomes of the danger control process include attitude and behavior change (Figure 6.3). Thus, adaptive behavior results from the danger control process, while maladaptive behavior is attributed to the fear control process.

Leventhal's (1970) distinction between fear control and danger control was a significant shift in theorizing about fear appeals. "The importance of the parallel response model lies largely in its movement

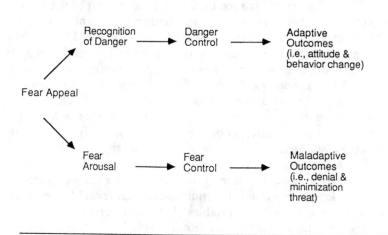

FIGURE 6.3. The parallel response model of fear appeals.

away from the notion of fear as the central explanatory concept . . . " (Sutton, 1982, p. 324). Dillard (in press) put it differently when he noted:

> During the heyday of the drive theories, fear was at the center of the theoretical stage. With the coming of the parallel response model, it was forced to share the limelight with the cognitive machinations of the danger control process.

Since its introduction, research has failed to support the predictions of the parallel response model. Failure to find empirical support stems largely from a lack of precision. That is, the model is not sufficiently precise to permit specific predictions to be made about the factors that mediate the relationship between fear appeals and message acceptance (Beck & Frankel, 1981; Rogers, 1975; Sutton, 1982). Although it lacked empirical support, the model drew an important distinction between emotional and cognitive reactions to fear appeals, and it provided the conceptual framework for a third family of fear appeal models — subjective expected utility models.

Subjective Expected Utility Models

Subjective expected utility models have been developed to explain a variety of human behavior. For example, in Chapter 3 I discussed two models, Fishbein and Ajzen's (1975) Theory of Reasoned Action and

Ajzen's (1985) Theory of Planned Behavior, that are part of the family of subjective expected utility models. In Chapter 11, I examine another member of this family, the Health Belief Model (Becker, 1974). This family of models adopts a rational view of humans and posits that people choose behaviors that maximize rewards and minimize punishments (Edwards, 1961; Lewin, 1935). According to these models, a person faced with two or more alternative courses of action will choose the one with the greatest *subjective expected utility* (SEU). The SEU for a course of action is a function of the *subjective value* (or utility) of the outcome associated with a course of action and the *subjective probability* that the course of action will produce the outcome (Sutton, 1982, p. 325). Thus, the basic structure of these models is a simple equation in which the dependent variable is a multiplicative function (the product) of two or more independent variables (Dillard, in press).

Protection Motivation Theory (Rogers, 1975, 1983) is an application of a SEU model to the study of fear appeals. Rogers argued that the effectiveness of a fear appeal was dependent on its ability to create three perceptions in message receivers; the perceived severity or noxiousness of the threat contained in the message, the perception of susceptibility to the threat contained in the message, and the perception that the recommended response will effectively reduce or eliminate the threat.

The original formulation of this model (Rogers, 1975) proposed that all three components were necessary ingredients in an effective fear appeal. That is, the model proposed that a person's intention to adopt a recommended behavior was a multiplicative function of *perceived noxiousness, perceived susceptibility,* and *perceived efficacy of the response* (Figure 6.4).

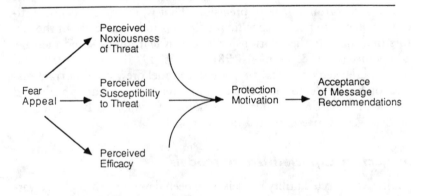

FIGURE 6.4. The protection motivation model of fear appeals.

By the 1980s, several studies failed to find evidence of the multiplicative relationship (i.e., the predicted three-way interaction) among these three variables and raised doubts about the validity of Rogers' model. In response, alternative SEU models were introduced (Sutton & Eiser, 1984), and modifications of the original model were suggested. For example, Beck and Frankel (1981) distinguished the concepts of *response efficacy* (i.e., the perception that a recommended response will effectively reduce the threat) and *self-efficacy* (i.e., the perception that one can personally execute the response), and they suggested that both dimensions of efficacy were important features of fear appeals. By 1983, Rogers revised his Protection Motivation Theory by incorporating the concept of self-efficacy and altering the predictions concerning the separate and combined effects of the four predictor variables.[1]

Tests of these models produced mixed findings regarding the specific effects of perceived noxiousness of the threat, of perceived susceptibility to the threat, and of the efficacy of the recommended responses on the intentions to adopt the action recommended in the fear appeal. Nevertheless, two important implications emerged from investigations of these models. First, these perceptual variables are "important sources of information for individuals attempting to determine what response to make to a potential threat" (Dillard, in press). Second, the emergence of this family of fear-appeal models virtually excluded the concept of fear from the study of fear appeals (Dillard, in press). Instead of describing emotional reactions to a fear-arousing message, the SEU models emphasize cognitive, or rational, reactions to these messages. Indeed, over a 30-year period, beginning with Janis and Feshbach's (1953) seminal study, theorizing about fear appeals has evolved to the point where fear is no longer an essential construct.

Summarizing the Research Findings

One conclusion that is widely accepted among fear-appeal researchers is that the findings from past research paint a confusing picture of the effects of fear appeals (for reviews, see Boster & Mongeau, 1984; Dillard, in press; Rogers, 1975; Sutton, 1982). Nevertheless, two relatively clear conclusions can be drawn from this literature. The first involves the combined effects of fear and age on message acceptance, and the second involves the combined effects of threat and perceived efficacy on attitudes.

---

[1]Dillard (in press) provides a more complete discussion of these models and modifications.

Fear by Age Interaction

In their meta-analytic review of the literature, Boster and Mongeau (1984) found evidence of a fear by age interaction. Specifically, fear appeals were much more effective for older message receivers than they were for adolescents and children. To observe this effect, they correlated the estimated age of participants in previous studies with the effect that the fear appeal had on message recipient attitudes. They found a strong positive correlation ($r = .52$) between message receiver age and the effectiveness of the fear appeal. This finding is ironic, and a bit unsettling, given the extensive use of fear appeals in persuasive campaigns targeted at children and adolescents.

Threat by Efficacy Interaction

A second conclusion about this literature concerns the importance of response efficacy and self-efficacy in the fear-appeal process. Several studies provide evidence to suggest that when efficacy is high, threatening information contained in a fear appeal is positively related to message acceptance (for a review, see Witte, 1992a). In other words, messages that create high levels of perceived threat and efficacy are maximally effective. Conversely, when perceived efficacy is low, perceived threat is negatively related to message acceptance. This finding suggests that effective fear appeals must include information that poses a threat to message receivers and then prescribe effective action for alleviating the threat. Fear appeals that fail to accomplish *both* objectives are unlikely to be persuasive. Thus, fear appeals that warn teenagers about their susceptibility to the AIDS virus without also providing workable recommendations for prevention are unlikely to be persuasive.

Directions for Future Research

There appears to be a rekindled interest in the study of fear appeals. This interest may be due in part to the conflicting findings that permeate this literature and in part to the continued application of fear appeals in everyday persuasive campaigns. Regardless of its source, recent conceptual developments have revived an interest in studying the "fear" component of fear-arousing messages. In a thoughtful review of the fear-appeal literature, Dillard (in press) chronicles the decreasing emphasis on fear in fear-appeal models and suggests that a reinstatement of the fear construct, and a renewed interest in emotional reactions to fear appeals, may be essential to our better understanding of their effects.

Witte (1992a) echoed this concern and introduced a new model, the Extended Parallel Process Model (EPPM), to explain the effects of fear appeals. The EPPM extends Leventhal's (1970) distinction between fear control and danger control processes by specifying a series of propositions that predict when each process is likely to dominate a person's reaction to a fear appeal. Essentially, the EPPM posits that when a message creates a perceived threat, but perceived efficacy remains low, fear control processes are enacted. When a message creates high perceived threat *and* perceived efficacy, danger control processes are enacted.

When danger control processes are dominant, people respond to the danger and not to their fear, and they are likely to accept the message recommendation. However, when fear control processes are dominant, people respond to their fear and adopt maladaptive responses like rejecting the message recommendation (Witte, 1992a). The EPPM articulates both emotional and cognitive reactions to fear appeals, and it specifies the conditions that are likely to produce these reactions. Although an initial test of this model produced promising findings (Witte, 1992b), additional research is needed before we can confidently endorse this model of the fear-appeal process.

THE CHOICE BETWEEN RATIONAL AND EMOTIONAL APPEALS

Prior research has documented the effectiveness of both rational and emotional persuasive appeals. Although we seem to understand the process of rational argument more clearly than we do emotional appeals, research supports the persuasive value of both types of appeals. Given this, one might speculate about the merits of integrating rational and emotional appeals.

Though no research bears directly on this issue, investigations of heightened arousal on cognitive processing suggest that rational appeals may lose their effectiveness when combined with fear-arousing content. For example, investigations of short-term memory (Bacon, 1974; Mandler, 1984) suggest that heightened arousal may interfere with information processing. In fact, these investigations indicate that a variety of stressors can contribute to memory impairment. However, a recent investigation of college women found that arousal was unrelated to their learning and recall of contraceptive information (Goldfarb, Gerrard, Gibbons, & Plante, 1988). Thus, the relationship between arousal and cognitive processing appears unsettled. In addition, there may be some conceptual slippage between the arousal of fear and the physiological arousal induced in these studies. Nevertheless, these investigations provide little reason to expect that the arousal of fear or anxiety will facilitate the persuasive influence of rational appeals.

Because emotional and rational appeals appear to be incompatible persuasive companions, persuaders often rely on one or the other. A recent investigation provided information that may assist persuaders in choosing between these alternatives. M. B. Millar and K. U. Millar (1990) hypothesized that attitudes that are cognitively based, that is, formed through careful consideration of rational arguments, are more susceptible to affective appeals and that attitudes that are affectively based are more susceptible to rational appeals. M. B. Millar and K. U. Millar argued that when attitudes and arguments against them are based on the same class of information (rational/cognitive or emotional/affective), the argument threatens the way in which the person has thought about the object (1990, p. 217). Because receivers often react defensively to threatening messages, such arguments may be ineffective. In the three investigations that provided support for their general hypothesis, when attitudes were formed through cognitive processes, affective appeals were more persuasive. Conversely, when attitudes were affectively based, rational appeals were more persuasive (M. G. Millar & K. U. Millar, 1990). Although the affective appeals in these studies were not fear appeals, these findings provide some recommendations for the use of rational and emotional persuasive appeals. Knowledge about the affective or cognitive basis of a target's attitude may be instructive in determining whether to construct a rational or emotional appeal to alter that attitude.[2]

SUMMARY

This chapter examined the use of rational and emotional appeals in persuasive messages. I began by examining the structure of rational ap-

[2]Edwards (1990) argued that affect-based attitudes are most susceptible to affective appeals and that cognition-based attitudes are most susceptible to rational appeals. Three studies provide support for these predictions and appear to contradict the M. G. Millar and K. U. Millar (1990) findings. However, important differences exist between these investigations. For example, the manipulations employed in the Edwards (1990) studies appear to create a positive or negative mood state in participants. The stimuli used to create these mood states are unrelated to the attitude objects investigated in these studies. By comparison, the M. G. Millar and K. U. Millar (1990) studies assess the affective and cognitive dimensions of *existing* attitudes. Moreover, these dimensions were directly related to the attitude objects investigated in M. G. Millar and K. U. Millar's (1990) studies. Although the Edwards (1990) studies have important implications for the role of affect in persuasion, the M. G. Millar and K. U. Millar (1990) investigations are more relevant to the notion of affective-based and cognitive-based attitudes.

peals and how they functioned to influence attitudes and behavior. I concluded that when people are motivated and able to process the content of a persuasive message, rational appeals are an effective persuasive technique, and the quality of supporting information in these appeals determines the persuasiveness of the message. Although we are often accurate judges of the logical validity of a rational appeal, when we make errors, they tend to be systematic and reflect our agreement or disagreement with the argument's conclusion. I also considered the relative merits of one- and two-sided rational appeals and concluded that two-sided, refutational messages were more effective than both one-sided messages and two-sided, nonrefutational messages.

The review of emotional appeals focused primarily on the fear-appeal literature. The development of this literature, from the drive models to parallel response and SEU models, coincided with the reduced emphasis on the role of fear in these appeals. I concluded that all three families of models are instructive, but that none provides a satisfying description of the effects of fear appeals. Nevertheless, recent summaries of this literature provide a number of empirical conclusions that can safely be drawn about the effects of fear appeals. Recent theoretical developments provide important recommendations for future research. The chapter concluded with a discussion of the effectiveness of emotional and rational appeals for changing affectively based and cognitively based attitudes.

CHAPTER SEVEN

Receiver Characteristics

L OOKING AHEAD . . .

A receiver-oriented approach to persuasion focuses attention on characteristics of message receivers that affect the persuasion process. In this chapter I review the research on these
characteristics and discuss how they influence persuasion. I begin with a discussion of gender and answer the question, "Are
women more easily persuaded than men?" Then I look at the
message discrepancy literature and describe how the difference
between a receiver's opinion and the position advocated in the
message affects the persuasiveness of the message. Finally, I look
at the effects of receiver involvement with the message topic.
Three types of receiver involvement will be identified, and for
each type, I describe its effect on the persuasion process.

In the previous two chapters I focused on the characteristics of persuasive messages and persuasive message sources. Although carefully crafted
messages from highly trustworthy sources can promote response formation, reinforcement, and change processes, persuasion scholars have
long recognized the importance of message receivers in the persuasion
process. The persuasive effects of target characteristics were initially
investigated by Hovland and his colleagues (Hovland et al., 1953) and
gained prominence in the development of cognitive response theories
of the late 1960s and 1970s (Greenwald, Brock, & Ostrom, 1968; Petty, Ostrom, & Brock, 1981).

This chapter examines the role of receiver characteristics in the
persuasion process. Historically, persuasion scholars have paid considerable attention to three characteristics of persuasive targets; gender, message discrepancy, and involvement. In fact, these three characteristics

continue to motivate contemporary programs of research on persuasive communication. The chapter begins with a discussion of the effects of gender in persuasive communication, focusing on the question of gender differences in persuasibility. Following this is a discussion of message discrepancy research, which examines the persuasive effects of the discrepancy between the position advocated in a message and the position held by a message recipient. The chapter concludes with a discussion of the influence of receiver involvement on the processing and effectiveness of persuasive appeals. Researchers have traditionally employed a variety of conceptual definitions for the term "involvement," and as a result, investigations of the effects of involvement have produced apparently contradictory findings. Each of these definitional approaches, along with their related research findings, is examined in this chapter.

GENDER EFFECTS AND PERSUASIBILITY

One colloquial truism about persuasive communication is that women are more easily persuaded than men. Indeed, for years social scientists have argued that clear and convincing evidence exists to support such a proposition. Even today, I suspect that if you ask most communication scholars if gender influences persuasibility, many would indicate that women are easier persuasive targets. However, close scrutiny of research on this topic reveals that there is insufficient evidence to sustain this belief. This examination of research on gender differences in social influence studies will conclude that the small gender effects that have been found are largely attributable to artifacts of the investigations rather than differences between men and women.

Eagly and her colleagues have been largely responsible for summarizing the research on gender effects into a cohesive set of defensible conclusions. Thus, the following discussion will draw heavily upon the findings of their reviews. Before beginning, a brief comment about the variable, *gender,* is in order. Most frequently, biological definitions of gender (i.e., male and female) are employed in persuasion research. However, persuasion researchers are rarely interested in biological differences between men and women. Instead, biological gender (sex) is used as a marker for socialization and cultural differences between men and women. Although cultural and social differences are invoked to explain persuasive differences between men and women, they are rarely measured in persuasion research. The biological definition of gender that is frequently used in persuasion research is an imprecise way to measure social and cultural differences that exist among people, as a biological definition of gender inevitably miscategorizes people who have not experienced traditional sex-role socialization and do not identify with the social or cultural characteristics of their biological group. Nevertheless, because of its prevalent use in prior research, the following review of gender effects will employ this imprecise categorization of socialization differences between male and female message recipients.

A Narrative Review

Eagly (1978) conducted a narrative review of research on gender differences in social influence. She noted several prior reviews of the persuasion and conformity literature that concluded there were strong gender effects in prior research. She then examined two categories of prior investigations; traditional persuasion studies in which message receivers were individually exposed to a persuasive message, and conformity studies in which participants formed a small group and attempted to achieve consensus on an issue. Three types of findings were recorded for these studies; either women were more easily persuaded or conformed more than men, men were more easily persuaded or conformed more then women, or there were no differences in persuasibility and conformity between men and women. Of the 62 persuasion studies included in her review, Eagly (1978) found that 51 (82%) revealed no gender difference in persuasibility. Ten studies (16%) found that women were more easily persuaded than men, and one study (2%) found that men were more easily persuaded. The conformity studies yielded larger differences. Of the 61 group conformity studies, 38 (62%) found no gender differences, 21 (34%) found that women conformed more than men, and 2 studies (3%) found that men conformed more frequently than women. These findings clearly dampen the claims of strong gender effects that had been advanced in prior literature reviews.

Eagly speculated that the studies in her review that found significant gender differences may have been affected by cultural and experimental factors. She found that many of the studies finding significant gender effects were conducted prior to 1970 and the onset of the women's movement. In addition, she argued that many of these studies employed gender-biased persuasion topics. That is, studies finding that women conformed more readily, or were more easily persuaded, than men may have used male-oriented topics. At the risk of appearing sexist, examples of traditional female topics might include nutrition and child development. That is, women in traditional sex roles may have more knowledge and experience with these issues than men. Conversely, examples of traditional males topics might include auto mechanics and football. Eagly argued that the use of gender-biased topics prior to the women's movement may have made women more susceptible to influence in some studies. In fact, prior research has found that people, regardless of gender, are more susceptible to influence when they lack knowledge of (McGuire & Papageorgis, 1961) or are uninterested in the persuasive topic (Miller, 1965). If these factors combined to influence susceptibility to persuasion in prior studies, then it is even less likely that gender is an important receiver characteristic in persuasive transactions.

A Meta-Analytic Review

Eagly's (1978) review was limited by the use of a "counting procedure" for summarizing the findings of prior research. Because this review . predated the development of more sophisticated meta-analytic procedures (see Chapter 2, this volume), a subsequent review of this literature was conducted to obtain more precise estimates of the effects of cultural and experimental factors in studies reporting gender effects (Eagly & Carli, 1981).

The primary advantage of the meta-analytic review is a precise estimate of the *size* of a gender effect in each study. Averaging these effect sizes across studies provides a much more precise estimate of gender effects in persuasion. Although the meta-analysis found that, for both persuasion and group conformity studies, women were more susceptible to influence than men, the size of this effect was small. In fact, less than 1% of the variance in influenceability was attributed to subject gender. Eagly and Carli (1981) concluded that "a sex difference as small as this may have few implications for social interaction" (p. 11).

In addition, their review failed to find evidence of gender bias in the topics employed in prior research. To examine this issue, they presented students with a list of topics from these studies and asked them to rate their interest and knowledge about the topics. Some topics were found to be biased in favor of men, (e.g., football, soccer, the military, and automobiles), some were found to be biased in favor of women (e.g., cancer checkups and social work), and others were not biased toward either sex. Although many of the topics were gender biased, there was no support for the position that male-oriented topics were overrepresented in prior studies. That is, the average sex difference on the interest and knowledge ratings for topics used in these studies was not significantly different from zero (Eagly & Carli, 1981). It should be emphasized that these interest and knowledge ratings were made by students in 1981, not by the original participants in these studies. Given that the majority of the studies included in this review were conducted prior to 1970, and before the onset of the women's movement, it is possible that participants in many of these original studies may have had different knowledge and interest levels than the students who made the ratings for this review. Thus, these findings should be interpreted cautiously (Eagly & Carli, 1981).

Summary of Gender Effects Research

Together, these reviews provide little evidence to suggest that the gender of persuasive targets is an important feature of persuasive transactions. Although this belief has been widespread among the scholarly and lay community, the findings of these two reviews have laid this issue to rest. No doubt, there are some persuasive situations in which women and men find themselves more susceptible to influence than members of the opposite sex, but these situations are not sufficiently frequent to maintain the belief that important gender differences exist in persuasibility.

MESSAGE DISCREPANCY AND PERSUASION

The goal of many persuasive transactions is attitude or belief change in a target person or audience. When persuaders attempt to alter attitudes or behaviors, the position advocated in the persuasive message is likely to differ from the position held by message recipients. This difference is generally referred to as *message discrepancy*, that is, the extent to which a persuader's message recommendation is discrepant from the position held by the target person or audience.

As discussed in Chapter 6 of this volume, evaluation of persuasive issues is rarely an all-or-nothing proposition. Instead, a continuum can be constructed to represent the differing positions people hold for most attitude objects. At the risk of confounding legal and financial issues and appearing overly simplistic, let's consider the variety of positions people hold on the controversy over abortion rights. Some people oppose abortion under any circumstances, and their position is represented on the right end of the continuum in Figure 7.1. However, there are a variety of positions that globally oppose abortion, but find it acceptable under extenuating circumstances. For example, some would advocate abortion only when the life of the mother is at risk, and in cases of rape or incest. These positions are represented to the right of center on this continuum. At the other end of the continuum are people who support the right of every woman to have an abortion, even if it requires government assistance for women who are unable to afford the procedure. This position is represented at the extreme left end of the continuum. Less extreme, but still to the left of center on this con-

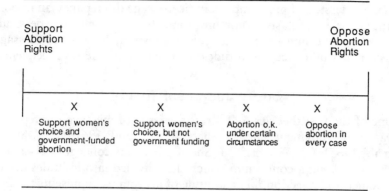

FIGURE 7.1. Hypothetical attitude continuum.

tinuum, are people who favor a woman's right to have an abortion, but oppose government funding of this procedure.

The diversity of viewpoints on the abortion issue is apparent in this example. As with many persuasive topics, people may hold similar global views about abortion, yet differ when more precise statements of their positions are outlined. As a result, persuaders who blindly assume that an audience's views on a topic are homogeneous may overlook subtle but important variations in the positions held. In other words, it is important to recognize that even when people generally agree on an issue, they are likely to differ somewhat in the specific positions they hold. Indeed, this may be one reason why politicians become "fuzzy" on some issues. In their attempt to appeal to a wide spectrum of voters, politicians often attempt to minimize the perceived discrepancy between their position and the positions held by their constituents.

Most persuasive messages advocate acceptance of a particular position. Combined with the fact that audience members are likely to hold a variety of positions on an issue, message discrepancy is likely to differ among message recipients. Extending the abortion rights example a bit further, it should be apparent that a persuasive message advocating a ban on all abortions will be mildly discrepant for some people (e.g., those who favor abortion only under extenuating circumstances) and highly discrepant for others (e.g., those who believe that every woman should have the right to an abortion regardless of the circumstances). To the extent that message discrepancy affects attitude or behavior change, the persuasive effects of any message are likely to differ among message recipients.

The concept of message discrepancy raises two questions for persuaders. First, and most important, is message discrepancy an important factor in persuasive communication? If so, then effective persuaders should be interested in a second question; How does message discrepancy influence the attitudes and behaviors of message recipients?

Social Judgment Theory

One of the first theories to address the issue of message discrepancy was Social Judgment Theory (Sherif & Hovland, 1961; C. W. Sherif et al., 1965). C. W. Sherif, M. Sherif, and their colleagues classified attitudes along a continuum which they divided into latitudes of acceptance and rejection.[1] The latitude of acceptance represents the positions on the attitude continuum that a person finds acceptable. By definition, a person's ideal or preferred position is centered within this latitude. Positions that are unacceptable to a message recipient constitute the latitude of rejection. People holding a moderate position on an issue may have a latitude of rejection on either side of their latitude of acceptance (Figure 7.2). However, when a person's attitude is extreme, then a single latitude of acceptance will be located on one end of the latitude continuum, and a latitude of rejection will be located on the other end (Figure 7.3).

Predicting Attitude Change

Underpinning the attitude change process are a series of perceptual judgments people make about message content and message sources. When people perceive that a message recommendation falls within their latitude of acceptance, *assimilation* is hypothesized to occur. That is, receivers judge the message recommendation as being closer to their own position than it actually is. However, when a message recommendation is perceived to fall within the latitude of rejection, *contrast effects* are hypothesized. A contrast effect causes receivers to judge the message as more discrepant from their own position than it actually is. Although assimilation and contrast effects were a central feature of early descriptions of the theory (C. W. Sherif et al., 1965), they are not central to predictions of attitude change. Instead, attitude change can be predicted succinctly from knowledge about the latitudes of acceptance and rejection (Figure 7.4). "Attitude change increases with [message] discrepancy as long as the message falls within the latitude of

---

[1]Some variations of the theory also include a latitude of noncommitment that represents a range of positions that are neither acceptable nor unacceptable. Unfortunately, few testable hypotheses were ever offered about attitudes falling within this latitude.

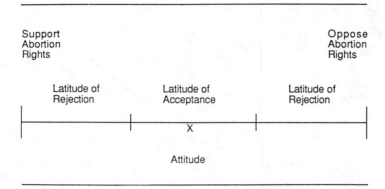

FIGURE 7.2. Latitudes of acceptance and rejection for a moderate attitude.

acceptance, but then it decreases if the discrepancy is so large that the message falls in the latitude of rejection" (Hunter, Danes, & Cohen, 1984, p. 57).

Predicting Changes in Source Credibility

Social Judgment Theory did not offer specific predictions about the effects of message discrepancy on perceived source credibility. However, descriptions of the theory provide a clear set of expectations regarding this relationship. For example, M. Sherif and C. Sherif (1967) argued that source credibility was related to latitudes of acceptance and rejection and, hence, to attitude change. Moreover, they identified source derogation as one outcome of extreme message discrepancy. They con-

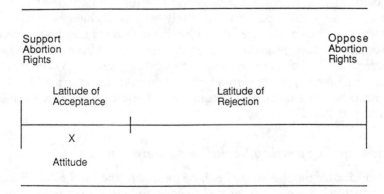

FIGURE 7.3. Latitudes of acceptance and rejection for an extreme attitude.

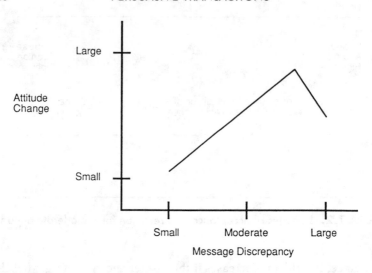

FIGURE 7.4. Curvilinear relationship between message discrepancy and attitude change as predicted by Social Judgment Theory.

cluded that "when a communication is discrepant from a source's position on an issue, the source is dubbed as unreasonable, propagandistic, false, and even obnoxious. Conversely, when messages fall within the latitude of acceptance, the source is viewed as more truthful, factual, and less biased (C. W. Sherif et al., 1965, p. 227).

This discussion of source derogation led Hunter et al. (1984) to argue that *if* predictions regarding message discrepancy and source credibility had been posited by social judgment theorists, the hypothesized relationship would mirror the message discrepancy–attitude change prediction. That is, when a message falls within the latitude of acceptance, message discrepancy is positively related to changes in source credibility. When a message falls within the latitude of rejection, source derogation occurs, producing a negative relationship between message discrepancy and changes in source credibility (Figure 7.5). In short, Social Judgment Theory would predict a curvilinear (inverted-U) relationship between message discrepancy and source credibility change (Hunter et al., 1984).

Evidence Supporting Social Judgment Theory

A considerable number of studies have found evidence of the curvilinear relationship between message discrepancy and attitude change (Aronson, Turner, & Carlsmith, 1963; Bochner & Insko, 1966; C. W. Sherif

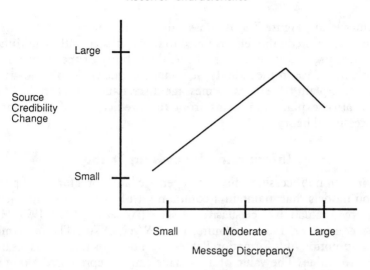

FIGURE 7.5. Curvilinear relationship between message discrepancy and changes in perceived source credibility as predicted by Social Judgment Theory.

et al., 1965; Whittaker, 1967). These studies provided evidence of a "discrepancy curve" reflecting a positive relationship between message discrepancy and attitude change up to a point, beyond which further increases in discrepancy decreased the amount of observed attitude change. These findings are consistent with the pattern of attitude change predicted by Social Judgment Theory.

Unfortunately, evidence for the predicted change in source credibility is less encouraging. In an extensive investigation of message discrepancy effects, Hunter et al. (1984) failed to find evidence of a curvilinear relationship between message discrepancy and source credibility change. Instead, they found that changes in source credibility were a positive linear function of message discrepancy. Moreover, prior message discrepancy studies that measured changes in source credibility (Bochner & Insko, 1966; Rhine & Severance, 1970; Tannenbaum, 1953) found the same positive linear relationship between message discrepancy and changes in source credibility.

In summary, the attitude change data suggest that discrepancy is positively related to attitude change until the message becomes sufficiently discrepant to fall within a receiver's latitude of rejection. In this regard, there is support for the theory. However, predictions concerning source credibility pose problems for the theory. Although source credibility predictions were not specifically offered by C. W. Sherif, M. Sherif, and their colleagues, the curvilinear hypothesis advanced by

Hunter et al. (Figure 7.5) is consistent with the theory. Studies measuring source credibility effects failed to find evidence of this curvilinear relationship, and thus they challenge the validity of the theory. If we lack confidence in the validity of Social Judgment Theory, how then can we explain the effects of message discrepancy on attitudes? One alternative explanation stems from the predictions of Information Processing Theory.

Information Processing Theory

Information Processing Theory is a generic label for a family of persuasion models that maintain a common set of assumptions about the cognitive evaluation of persuasive messages (Anderson, 1959, 1971; Hovland & Pritzker, 1957; McGuire, 1968; Wyer, 1970). The fundamental assumption of Information Processing Theory is that messages have affective value. The value of a message can be represented along the same continuum that was developed to represent a person's attitude on a topic. The position of a message along the continuum is determined by the value of the attitude reflected in the message (Hunter et al., 1984). For example, the value of a message advocating a total ban on abortions would be represented on the right end of the continuum in Figure 7.1. Conversely, the value of a pro-choice message could be represented near the left end of this continuum.

According to the theory, message processing involves an internal comparison of one's own position to the position advocated in the message. The difference between these two positions is defined as message discrepancy, and it stimulates attitude change. Several theorists propose a "distance-proportional" model in which attitude change is proportional to message discrepancy and is always in the direction advocated by the message (Anderson, 1959; Anderson & Hovland, 1957; Hunter et al., 1984, p. 36).

Linear Discrepancy Model

Hunter et al. (1984) demonstrate that the attitude change predictions of Information Processing Theory are formally equivalent to a simple Linear Discrepancy Model in which the amount of attitude change produced by a persuasive message will be a linear function of message discrepancy:

$$\Delta a = \alpha(m - a) \qquad (7.1)$$

where Δa represents attitude change; m is the value of the message; and a is the receiver's premessage attitude. α is the coefficient that represents the strength of the relationship between message discrepancy $(m - a)$ and attitude change.

There are two important differences between the predictions of Information Processing Theory and Social Judgment Theory. First, Social Judgment Theory predicts a curvilinear (inverted-U) relationship between message discrepancy and attitude change, whereas Information Processing Theory predicts a positive linear relationship between message discrepancy and attitude change (Figure 7.6). Second, Social Judgment Theory suggests that source derogation will occur when message discrepancy is large, producing a curvilinear relationship between message discrepancy and changes in perceived source credibility. Information Processing Theory, on the other hand, predicts that changes in perceived source credibility are a linear function of message value and premessage evaluations of source credibility (Figure 7.7).

Evidence Supporting Information Processing Theory

Several experiments provide support for the predictions of Information Processing Theory. First, there is considerable evidence of a linear relationship between message discrepancy and attitude change. Tests of Anderson's Information Integration Model (Anderson, 1971, 1981) and the Linear Discrepancy Model (Hunter et al., 1984) provide evidence of a positive linear relationship between message discrepancy and atti-

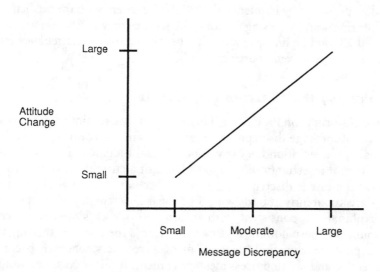

FIGURE 7.6. Linear relationship between message discrepancy and attitude change as predicted by Information Processing Theory.

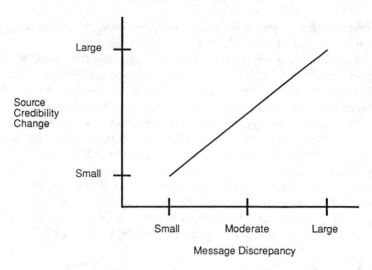

FIGURE 7.7. Linear relationship between message discrepancy and changes in perceived source credibility as predicted by Information Processing Theory.

tude change. That is, greater persuasive effects are associated with increased, not decreased, message discrepancy.

Perhaps the most compelling evidence for the information processing explanation of discrepancy effects stems from the source credibility data presented by Hunter et al. (1984). Consistent with the predictions of Information Processing Theory, the studies they reviewed and conducted all found a linear relationship between message discrepancy and changes in perceived source credibility.

Explaining the ''Discrepancy Curves''

Before Information Processing Theory can fully explain the persuasive effects of message discrepancy, however, it must account for the "discrepancy curves" found in early tests of Social Judgment Theory. Recall that several investigations found evidence of a curvilinear relationship between message discrepancy and attitude change. Though these findings are apparently at odds with the Linear Discrepancy Model, several explanations consistent with Information Processing Theory can account for these nonlinear curves. First, it is the possible that highly discrepant messages will "turn off" message receivers, who may become inattentive and fail to process message content. If this occurs, one would expect highly discrepant messages to lose their effectiveness.

A second explanation follows from cognitive response models of persuasion. Brock (1967) found that highly discrepant messages resulted in more counterarguing from message recipients than less discrepant messages. In his study, participants were told they would be the target of a persuasive appeal and were given time to generate arguments against the message. Receivers exposed to highly discrepant messages listed significantly more reasons to oppose the message recommendation than receivers exposed to less discrepant messages. Brock argued that these thoughts were evidence of subvocal arguing on the part of message receivers. It bears mentioning that counterarguing is consistent with the general position of Information Processing Theory. That is, to the extent that message processing includes counterarguing of highly discrepant appeals, the decrease in persuasiveness of highly discrepant messages is consistent with Information Processing Theory (Hunter et al., 1984, p. 176).

A third explanation for the discrepancy curves stems from investigations that have examined the effects of *positional* and *psychological* discrepancy (Fink, Kaplowitz, & Bauer, 1983). Positional discrepancy refers to the absolute difference between a receiver's attitude and the position advocated in the message. Psychological discrepancy refers to the difference a receiver perceives between his or her attitude and the position advocated by a message. Fink et al. (1983) argued that situational characteristics can cause receivers to perceive a message recommendation to be more or less discrepant than it objectively is. For example, they argued that a message advocating a moderately discrepant position would be perceived as less psychologically discrepant if it was preceded by a message advocating an extremely discrepant position than if it was presented alone. In addition, they argued that a message without supporting arguments, or with weak arguments, may produce a higher level of psychological discrepancy than a message with strong supporting arguments (Fink et al., 1983, p. 418).

To test the importance of psychological discrepancy, Fink et al. constructed a mathematical model that assumed that, all other things being equal, positional discrepancy facilitates attitude change, and psychological discrepancy inhibits change (1983, p. 420). When they tested a basic linear model without psychological discrepancy, they found that positional discrepancy was associated with greater attitude change. However, when the effects of psychological discrepancy were considered, they found that greater psychological discrepancy inhibited attitude change. Moreover, they found that psychological discrepancy of a message was indeed influenced by surrounding messages.

Applied to Information Processing Theory, these findings suggest that messages with extreme positional discrepancy may also serve to heighten the psychological discrepancy of message recipients. If these two types of discrepancy are confounded, one would expect the non-linear discrepancy curve observed in prior tests of Social Judgment Theory.

Summarizing Message Discrepancy Research

In summary, the body of existing evidence is more supportive of an information processing explanation than a social judgment explanation. Information Processing Theory can explain both the linear and nonlinear relationships between message discrepancy and attitude change found in prior studies. Moreover, the linear source credibility effects found in several studies can only be explained through Information Processing Theory.

It bears mentioning that social judgment theorists may claim that the source credibility prediction is a nonessential feature of the theory and discount the importance of the source credibility findings. Even if one discounts the theoretical importance of the source credibility data, Social Judgment Theory cannot explain the linear effects of message discrepancy on attitudes found in many investigations.

Of course, one could argue that studies finding a linear relationship between message discrepancy and attitude change failed to use the extremely discrepant messages that are necessary to produce the nonlinear relationship predicted by Social Judgment Theory. This argument is untenable, however, because the highly discrepant messages in many of the tests of Information Processing Theory fell within message recipients' latitudes of rejection. For example, participants in one study read a high-discrepancy message that recommended a 50% increase in tuition! Because student participants had already experienced significant increases, they rated this message as extremely discrepant. Nevertheless, there was a positive linear relationship between the level of message discrepancy and the size of a tuition increase advocated by students after hearing the persuasive message (Fink et al., 1983, p. 424). Thus, it is unlikely that the linear discrepancy effects found in prior research are an artifactual limitation of these studies. It is more likely that these findings are incompatible with Social Judgment Theory.

Regardless of the correct theoretical interpretation for these effects, the practical implications of message discrepancy research are clear. The discrepancy between the position held by a target audience and the one advocated in a message appears to enhance message persuasiveness. In many situations, highly discrepant messages will produce greater attitude change than less discrepant messages. However, there is probably a practical limit to the effects of message discrepancy. Extremely discrepant messages (those falling within a receiver's latitude of rejection) may cause receivers to discount the message, counterargue against it, or perceive it to be more psychologically discrepant than it objectively is. Any of these outcomes could limit the persuasiveness of the message. The most confident practical recommendation is one of moderation: Message discrepancy enhances attitude change, but don't overdo it. In the end, this recommendation is one that both information processing and social judgment theorists can endorse.

RECEIVER INVOLVEMENT AND PERSUASION

A third characteristic of message receivers that has captured the attention of persuasion researchers is *involvement*. Over the years, receiver involvement has assumed a variety different theoretical roles in the development of persuasion theories. Beginning with the social judgment theorists in the early 1960s, involvement referred to the activation of ego-defensive mechanisms in message receivers that motivated them to reject persuasive appeals (C. W. Sherif et al., 1965). By the late 1960s social-cognitive theories of persuasion began to dominate persuasion research (Greenwald et al., 1968; Petty et al., 1981). This theoretical shift led to the development of several social-cognitive theories in which involvement was hypothesized to stimulate thinking in message receivers (Chaiken, 1987; Petty & Cacioppo, 1981, 1986). In yet a third conceptual approach, Cialdini and his colleagues argued that receiver involvement can stimulate impression management behaviors and influence the persuasibility of message receivers (Cialdini, Levy, Herman, & Evenbeck, 1973; Cialdini, Levy, Herman, Kozlowski, & Petty, 1976).

The use of widely divergent definitions for the term "involvement" has produced a body of persuasion studies that appear contradictory. In their recent review of this literature Johnson and Eagly (1989) identified the different conceptual meanings underlying the use of this term and clarified the various roles of involvement in the persuasion process. They defined involvement as "the motivational state induced by an association between an activated attitude and some aspect of the self-concept" (Johnson & Eagly, 1989, p. 293).

Three research traditions of involvement—*value-relevant, outcome-relevant,* and *impression-relevant*—summarized in Johnson and Eagly's review, reflect the different functions that involvement may serve in the persuasion process. Although Johnson and Eagly (1989) did not endorse a functional perspective for defining involvement, such a framework provides an excellent conceptual backdrop for understanding the essential characteristics of these research traditions. Three of Katz's

(1960) psychological functions of attitudes;—*ego-defensive, instrumental,* and *value-expressive*—highlight differences among the three traditions of involvement research. These traditions and their psychological functions are reviewed in the following sections of this chapter.

Value-Relevant Involvement

This tradition of research on the persuasive effects of involvement evolved from investigations of Social Judgment Theory (C. W. Sherif et al., 1965; M. Sherif & Hovland, 1961; M. Sherif & C. W. Sherif, 1967). Earlier in this chapter I examined the latitudes of acceptance and rejection that define an attitude's evaluative continuum. I discussed the predicted effectiveness of messages falling within each of these latitudes, but did not indicate how these latitudes were formed. As it turns out, value-relevant involvement determines the width of these latitudes. Social Judgment Theory posits that when message receivers are highly involved in a message topic, their latitudes of rejection become wider, increasing the number of positions along the attitude evaluation continuum that are unacceptable. Conversely, when receivers are uninvolved, their latitudes of rejection become more narrow, increasing the number of positions that receive an acceptable evaluation.

Social Judgment theorists used the term *ego-involvement* to reflect a set of core values or beliefs that constitute a person's self-concept. Thus, ego-involving attitudes define a person's system of values. For example, gun control legislation is a highly involving topic for many National Rifle Association members because their attitudes on this topic define their core social and political values. Abortion rights is a highly involving topic because, for many people, this issue has come to symbolize fundamental characteristics of their religious and political self-concepts.

Johnson and Eagly (1989) labeled this type of involvement *value-relevant involvement* because it reflects a concern about values that define a person's self-concept. Regardless of the label, this type of involvement serves an ego-defensive function. People become highly concerned about particular topics because their involvement in these issues is an essential defense of the values that make up their self-concepts.

Given this function, the predicted relationship between this type of involvement and attitude change should be obvious. Value-relevant involvement should increase the number of unacceptable positions along the attitude-evaluation continuum and inhibit attitude change. Johnson and Eagly's (1989) meta-analytic review found a moderately strong negative correlation between value-relevant involvement and attitude change. In short, this type of involvement appears to inhibit attitude change.

Outcome-Relevant Involvement

A second category of involvement identified by Johnson and Eagly was labeled *outcome-relevant involvement*. This tradition of involvement research began with the social-cognitive approaches to persuasion. During the 1980s two related, yet distinct, models of persuasion identified an important role for outcome-relevant involvement. Both the Heuristic Model of Persuasion (Chaiken, 1987) and the Elaboration Likelihood Model (ELM) (Petty & Cacioppo, 1986) posited that outcome-relevant involvement is one factor that motivates receivers to carefully scrutinize the content of persuasive messages (see Chapter 9, this volume).

In this research tradition, involvement serves an *instrumental function* similar to the one described by Katz (1960). This type of involvement reflects a concern about achieving particular outcomes. Typical investigations of the ELM, for example, manipulate outcome-relevant involvement by presenting college students with messages that warn of comprehensive exams for undergraduates or higher tuition rates. Both of these topics are central to the educational goals of the student participants in these studies. Though only a handful of topics have been used in these investigations, people are likely to exhibit outcome-relevant involvement with a wide variety of persuasive topics. For example, a young couple preparing to purchase their first home may become highly interested in the Federal Reserve Board's policy decisions that ultimately influence home mortgage interest rates. However, after purchasing a home, this couple will likely become less concerned with the policy decisions that determine interest rates, especially if their mortgage has a fixed interest rate.

Outcome-relevant involvement with an issue is likely to rise as people work toward achieving an issue-related goal and decline once the goal has been achieved and the instrumental function of involvement declines. This characteristic distinguishes outcome-relevant involvement from value-relevant involvement. Value-relevant involvement is likely to be much more stable because of its connection to a person's core values.

The persuasive effects of outcome-relevant involvement are somewhat complicated. Social-cognitive models of persuasion (Chapter 9, this volume) posit that highly involved message recipients will scrutinize the content of persuasive messages more than less involved recipients. Thus, the persuasive effects of this type of involvement are dependent on the quality of arguments and supporting material in the persuasive message. Consistent with this general prediction, Johnson and Eagly (1989) found that involvement enhanced the persuasive effects of strong persuasive messages and inhibited the effectiveness of weak persuasive messages.[2] Thus, when outcome-relevant involvement of message receivers is high, the quality of arguments and evidence in the persuasive message will determine the extent of attitude change.

Impression-Relevant Involvement

The third tradition of involvement research emphasizes *impression-relevant involvement*. Investigations by Cialdini and his colleagues (Cialdini et al., 1973, 1976; Cialdini & Petty, 1981) evolved from Zimbardo's (1960) concept of response involvement. Research on this type of involvement has consistently found that when people are concerned about the impressions they make on others, they may be reluctant to endorse positions that are incompatible with those of message sources. Cialdini's research found that when people are under public scrutiny, they tend to advocate more flexible and moderate attitudes than when their position is unlikely to be publicly evaluated.

Because concerns about impression management influence the attitudes people endorse, Johnson and Eagly prefer the label impression-relevant involvement to Zimbardo's response involvement. In this regard, impression-relevant involvement serves a value-expressive function (Katz, 1960). Values of groups, organizations, and cultures are formed and regulated through social interaction. Impression management reflects the extent to which people are motivated to endorse socially accepted values of a particular group, organization, or culture. For example, this concern is evident in the behavior of many job applicants who are cautious not to endorse an extreme value unless they are certain their potential employer endorses the same value.

Given its social function, it should come as no surprise that impression-relevant involvement inhibits attitude change (Johnson & Eagly, 1989). Although the size of this effect was small, highly involved receivers were less likely to change their attitude or endorse an extreme position than receivers who were less concerned with impression management.

---

[2]This finding was not consistent across all studies. Johnson and Eagly (1989) found that researchers associated with Ohio State University (Petty, Cacioppo, and their colleagues) consistently found this pattern of effects, but that scholars with different research backgrounds were unable to replicate them. Johnson and Eagly were at a loss to explain these differences and suggested caution when interpreting them. Although this effect was not consistent across researchers, the overall pattern of findings suggests that the persuasive effects of outcome-relevant involvement differ from those of value-relevant involvement.

Summarizing the Effects of Involvement

Johnson and Eagly (1989) offer convincing evidence of the theoretical and empirical distinctions among these three research traditions of involvement research.[3] Although the pattern of effects for value-relevant and impression-relevant involvement are similar, the theoretical foundations for these traditions are clearly distinct. Whereas value-relevant involvement reflects concern about a set of core values, impression-relevant involvement stems from more superficial concerns about self-presentation. Although outcome-relevant involvement may be transient, the hypothesized effects of this type of involvement on the cognitive processes of message receivers distinguishes it from the other two types of involvement.

For scholars of persuasion, differences among the research traditions highlighted by Johnson and Eagly may help resolve many of the apparent inconsistencies among prior investigations of the persuasive effects of involvement. For persuasion practitioners, this analysis suggests considerable caution in the development and presentation of persuasive appeals. Because the specific type of receiver involvement is likely to influence the effectiveness of persuasive messages, persuaders are cautioned to carefully consider the values and goals that message receivers bring to each persuasive transaction.

SUMMARY

This chapter examined three characteristics of persuasive targets that have received considerable attention from persuasion scholars. I concluded that although some weak effects were found in prior research, the gender of message receivers is not an important feature in the effectiveness of persuasive messages. That is, there is scant evidence to suggest that women are more easily persuaded than men.

The discussion of message discrepancy effects was considerably more complicated. Social Judgment Theory and Information Processing Theory offered competing predictions about the persuasive effects of message discrepancy. Although some evidence supported both in-

---

[3]It bears mentioning that not everyone endorsed the conceptual distinctions drawn by Johnson and Eagly (1989). Petty and Cacioppo (1990) criticized the distinction between value-relevant and outcome-relevant involvement, opting instead for a broader concept they labeled "personal involvement." They also criticized the merits of the meta-analytic review that supported Johnson and Eagly's distinction. Interested readers are encouraged to carefully examine these arguments along with a comprehensive response provided by Johnson and Eagly (1990).

terpretations, Information Processing Theory can more fully explain the findings of prior investigations. Regardless of the underlying theoretical mechanism, however, I concluded that moderation was the best policy. Message discrepancy appears to enhance attitude change up to a point, but messages that advocate extremely discrepant positions may lose their effectiveness.

Involvement is an important characteristic of message receivers. I described three types of receiver involvement along with functions they serve. The ego-defensive function served by value-relevant involvement has a moderately strong inhibiting effect on attitude change. Outcome-relevant involvement interacts with message quality to influence the effectiveness of message appeals, although there was some inconsistency among these research findings. Finally, impression-relevant involvement appears to have an inhibiting effect on attitude change, but this effect is much weaker than the one found for value-relevant involvement.

CHAPTER EIGHT

Characteristics of Persuasive Settings

L OOKING AHEAD . . .

This chapter examines three situational characteristics that influence the persuasion process. The chapter begins with a discussion of the relative effectiveness of various modes of presenting persuasive appeals. After this, I examine the influence of distracting stimuli on the persuasiveness of a message. The chapter concludes with a discussion of group influences in the persuasion process.

In the preceding three chapters, I discussed the effects of source, message, and receiver characteristics in persuasive transactions. The present chapter concludes the discussion of the persuasive effects literature by examining characteristics of persuasive situations. I begin with a discussion of modality research and review the relative effectiveness of video, audio, and written modes of presenting persuasive messages. Following this, I review the distraction literature, which examines the influence of distracting stimuli on the comprehension and effectiveness of persuasive messages. The final section of this chapter is devoted to a discussion of the influence of others in the persuasion process. Though few persuasion textbooks consider the persuasive effects of small groups, a considerable portion of our persuasive activities occur in group settings. Although a comprehensive review of group influences is beyond the scope of this book, I review two avenues of research that reflect important social and informational influences of groups on the attitudes and behaviors of individuals.

MODE OF MESSAGE PRESENTATION

Perhaps the most fundamental decision facing would-be persuaders is a decision about how best to present their persuasive appeals. With a larger variety of technological alternatives available to persuaders, this choice has become somewhat more difficult in recent years. Advertisers, politicians, business organizations, and relational partners routinely choose among several methods of message presentation. Sometimes, these choices are based on research, but often they reflect personal preferences based on prior persuasive success. Since the mid-1970s, for example, television has been the media staple of politicians seeking to present their positions and cultivate their images. This trend was marked by the election of Ronald Reagan in 1980, a former actor with a strong television persona. Advertisers employ a wide spectrum of media alternatives to establish and maintain brand loyalty, while relational partners frequently choose among face-to-face, telephone, and written forms of communication when attempting to influence one another.

Although these choices often become routine, one might question their effectiveness. Is television the most effective method for outlining the political positions of a candidate? When are various forms of media effective for achieving the particular goals of advertisers? Are face-to-face interactions the most effective method for making persuasive appeals to relational partners? Most likely, these questions require complex answers that depend on a variety of source, receiver, and message characteristics. Nevertheless, a growing body of research provides some preliminary insights about the persuasive merits of various modes of message presentation.

Research on the effects of message modality has found no simple effects for any mode of message presentation. That is, no overall persuasive advantage exists for live, video, audio, or written messages. Instead, message modality serves to influence other factors, including the salience of the source and message comprehension, which in turn determine the effectiveness of a persuasive message.

Message Modality and Source Salience

With respect to receiver involvement, two studies found that live and video messages were more likely to heighten the involvement of message receivers than audio or written messages (Andreoli & Worchel, 1978; Worchel, Andreoli, & Eason, 1975). Involvement was conceptualized in these studies as attentiveness to the message and the message source. Live and video message presentations more effectively focused receiver attention on the characteristics of the message and its source than written messages. When the source was perceived as trustworthy, this attention enhanced the persuasiveness of the message presentation. However, when the source was perceived as untrustworthy, this heightened attention decreased the persuasiveness of the message.

Chaiken and Eagly (1983) also investigated this issue and found similar effects. They argued that video presentations would make communicator-based cues more salient to message receivers than audio or written messages. Consistent with this hypothesis, they found that a video presentation presented by a likeable source was more effective than the same message presented in audio or written format. Conversely, for unlikeable sources, audio and written message presentations were more persuasive than video message presentations.

Taken together, these investigations provide a consistent pattern of effects. Live and video presentations focus attention on the source of the message more than audio and written presentations do. If the source's attributes are persuasive, this attention should enhance the effectiveness of the message. However, if the source lacks trustworthiness, or is for some reason unlikeable, then the use of a live or video presentation may inhibit the persuasiveness of the message. These findings provide a relatively straightforward set of recommendations for persuaders; live or video presentations should be most effective for favorable message sources, whereas written and audio presentations should be most effective for sources who are viewed less favorably.

Modality and Message Comprehension

Message modality has also been related to message comprehension. Once again, however, the persuasive effects of this relationship are not straightforward. Chaiken and Eagly (1976) argued that the relative persuasiveness of video, audio, and written messages depends on the difficulty of message content. In one study they manipulated message difficulty by creating one message that contained complicated language but was equivalent in all other respects to a more easily understood second message. They presented these difficult and simple messages in a video, audio, and written format.

Chaiken and Eagly (1976) found that *comprehension* of the simple message did not vary across video, audio, and written message presentations. However, the difficult message was best comprehended when it was presented in a written format, as compared to the audio or video format. This finding should come as no surprise when one considers that messages presented in written format afford receivers the opportunity to reread portions of the message that are not initially understood. This opportunity is typically unavailable to receivers exposed to audio and video message presentations.

Chaiken and Eagly (1976) also found that simple messages were most persuasive when presented in a video presentation, and that difficult messages were more persuasive when presented in written format. Given the positive relationship between message comprehension and message acceptance, these findings regarding the difficult message are easy to interpret; the difficult message was more persuasive when presented in a written format because message comprehension was highest in that format. The finding that the video presentation was most effective for the simple message may reflect an increased salience of favorable source characteristics, or increased attentiveness to the message when it was presented in a video format.

Summary of Modality Effects

In combination, research on source salience and message comprehension provides a clear description of the persuasive effects of message modality. When a source's attributes are favorable and likely to engender attitude change, video and live message presentations are an effective way to emphasize these characteristics. If a source's characteristics are unfavorable and likely to inhibit persuasion, written and audio message formats appear most effective because they do not accentuate these characteristics.

A similar interaction effect was found for message comprehension. Written messages aid comprehension, and consequently persuasion, when the message content is difficult to understand. However, when message content is simple and comprehension is less of a concern, live and video presentations appear to be more persuasive. Another feature of some persuasive situations is the presence of distracting stimuli. The next section describes two types of distracting stimuli and examines this influence on persuasive outcomes.

PERSUASIVE EFFECTS OF DISTRACTING STIMULI

Several years ago, I went shopping for a waterbed and experienced first-hand the use of distraction as a persuasive strategy. I entered a waterbed store and was immediately approached by a slick salesperson who was eager to describe the line of waterbeds the store had to offer. After listening to his sales pitch for several minutes, I had formed several questions about the reliability of the mattress and heating element. Just as he stopped to ask if I had any questions about the beds, another salesperson came over and told us a joke that was in poor taste. After the second salesperson left, the first salesperson asked, "Well, are there any more questions I can answer before you make a decision?" When I reminded him that his partner's rude interruption prevented me from asking any questions, he looked somewhat disappointed. Luckily, I was able to recall the questions I formulated prior to the interruption. I was somewhat skeptical about whether the interruption was a planned distraction, but after talking with several friends who were former salespeople, I became convinced that the distraction was indeed intentional. Most of these former salespeople indicated that planned interruptions were part of their sales pitches, and most believed these distractions facilitated their sales performance.

Fortunately, a large body of scientific research provides some insights about the practical application of distraction techniques. Following a seminal investigation by Festinger and Maccoby (1964), many persuasion scholars have examined the effects of a variety of distracting stimuli on the attitudes and behaviors of persuasive targets.

A cursory review of these investigations reveals two relatively distinct categories of distraction research. One research tradition has conceptualized distractors as stimuli that are external to the message presentation. Many different *external distractors* have been manipulated in these studies, including using flashing lights (Osterhouse & Brock, 1970), playing audio feedback (Zimbardo & Ebbesen, 1970), and having receivers eat while they read a persuasive message (Janis, Kaye, & Kirschner, 1965). These distractors are hypothesized to divert attention away from the message presentation and toward the source of the distraction.

The second category of studies has conceptualized distractors as communicator-relevant behaviors. *Communicator-relevant distractors* are defined as behaviors that are intentionally manipulated by the speaker that cause receivers to shift attention away from the content of the message and toward characteristics of the speaker (Buller, 1986, p. 109). Manipulations of this type of distractor include varying the synchrony of a source's nonverbal behaviors (Woodall & Burgoon, 1981), violations of interpersonal distancing expectations (Burgoon, Stacks, & Burch, 1982), and the use of intense language (Burgoon, Cohen, Miller, & Montgomery, 1978). Studies employing external and communicator-based distractors reflect fundamentally distinct conceptualizations about persuasive communication.

Studies of external distractors are primarily concerned with the effect of distraction on message processing and subsequent attitude change. Conversely, studies of communicator-relevant distractors are primarily concerned with the effect of the distracting aspects of a source's communicative behavior on perceptions of source credibility and subsequent attitude change.

Examining the Effects of External Distraction

To explain the persuasive effects of external distractors, researchers frequently rely on *cognitive response* and *information processing* theories of persuasion. Cognitive response explanations were initially invoked to explain the findings of Festinger and Maccoby's (1964) seminal investigation. Shortly thereafter, McGuire (1966, 1969) applied an information processing explanation to explain distraction effects. He argued that distraction would limit message learning and recall and thus inhibit acceptance of the message recommendation. The competing predictions offered by these two theoretical perspectives are considered in the following sections.

Cognitive Response Explanations

Cognitive response approaches to persuasion reflect a theoretical perspective that the cognitive responses (a fancy term for thoughts) generated by message receivers contribute significantly to the effectiveness of a persuasive appeal. These theorists argue that when receivers process a message, they generate favorable or unfavorable thoughts about the merits of the message recommendation. These self-generated thoughts combine with message content to influence the postmessage attitudes and behaviors of receivers (see Chapter 9, this volume).

According to a cognitive response explanation, distracting stimuli interfere with the production of cognitive responses. That is, when the message recommendation is counterattitudinal, distraction is hypothesized to inhibit the production of counterarguments (Osterhouse & Brock, 1970; Zimbardo & Ebbesen, 1970). When the message recommendation is proattitudinal, distractors are hypothesized to limit a receiver's favorable thoughts about the message (Harkins & Petty, 1981; Insko, Turnbull, & Yandell, 1974; Petty, Wells, & Brock, 1976).

Information Processing Explanations

A second genre of explanations stems from Information Processing Theory. Information processing explanations suggest that in order for a message to be persuasive, the arguments and evidence contained in it must be understood by message recipients. Failure to learn the arguments favoring a recommendation should reduce the effectiveness of the persuasive appeal (McGuire, 1969).

According to information processing explanations, external distractors interfere with message comprehension and hence reduce the persuasiveness of the message. Because distractors divert attention away from the message, receivers have a more difficult time understanding the arguments and evidence supporting the message recommendations (Haaland & Venkatesen, 1968; Vohs & Garrett, 1968).

Specific Predictions and Supporting Evidence

In short, both the cognitive response and information processing explanations posit that distractors divert attention away from message processing and toward the distracting stimulus, but the hypothesized effects of this distraction differ. Cognitive response theorists argue that when the message is counterattitudinal, distraction inhibits counterargument generation, enhancing acceptance of the message recommendations. However, distraction interferes with the generation of favorable thoughts when the message recommendation is congruent with receiver attitudes, and thus inhibits the persuasive effects of the message.

Several investigations provide support for the first half of this prediction. For example, Osterhouse and Brock (1970) found that external distractors reduced the number of counterarguments generated by receivers and increased attitude change. However, evidence for the second half of the prediction has been limited. Petty, Wells, and Brock (1976) did find that distraction enhanced attitude change when the message presentation was counterattitudinal, and that it inhibited message acceptance when the message was proattitudinal. However, in this investigation, distraction was unrelated to the production of favorable thoughts and counterarguments, limiting confidence in the cognitive response explanation examined by the study.

Although investigations provided mixed support for the cognitive response explanation, other tests of distraction effects produced findings that are consistent with Information Processing Theory, which predicts that distraction interferes with message learning and reduces the effectiveness of persuasive messages. Studies supporting this explanation found that distraction reduced message recall (an indication of learning) and led to less acceptance of message recommendations (Haaland & Venkatesen, 1968; Vohs & Garrett, 1968).

Although the findings from these studies are contradictory, a recent meta-analytic review revealed stronger support for the information processing hypothesis than for the cognitive response hypothesis (Buller, 1986). Across studies using a variety of different manipulations of external distraction, Buller consistently found a stronger negative relationship between distraction and message comprehension than between distraction and the generation of favorable and unfavorable thoughts. This finding provides stronger support for the information processing explanation than for the cognitive response explanation. A second finding from Buller's (1986) analysis, that distraction was negatively related to attitude change, provides additional support for the information processing explanation.

Thus, although some individual studies provide evidence for each of these explanations, a cumulative summary of these studies suggests that persuasive effects of an external distraction are mediated by the distraction's negative effect on message comprehension. "Contrary to the conclusion of many other researchers, communication irrelevant distraction generally reduces the effectiveness of a persuasive message" (Buller, 1986, p. 109). Several researchers have noted, however, that a significant distraction is needed to create the reduction in message comprehension necessary to reduce message effectiveness. That is, rather small distractors are unlikely to produce the significant reduction in comprehension necessary to reduce acceptance of message recommendations.

Examining the Effects
of Communicator-Relevant Distraction

A second category of distraction studies has produced much more consistent findings. Investigations of communicator-relevant distraction hypothesize that the distraction diverts attention away from the content of the message presentation and toward the characteristics of the communicator. Information processing and cognitive responses are not central to this explanation. Instead, the persuasive effects of communicator-relevant distraction are dependent on features of the source that affect persuasion.

Studies of this type of distraction were analyzed separately in Buller's (1986) review. These analyses revealed that communicator-relevant distraction enhanced attitude change when the source was highly credible and decreased attitude change when the message source lacked credibility. The estimates for these effects were consistent across studies, though small in size. Nevertheless, the difference between the persuasive effect of communicator-relevant distraction among high-credibility ($r = +.15$) and low-credibility ($r = -.10$) sources provides compelling support for the importance of this explanation. In addition, Buller (1986) found that communicator-relevant distraction was unrelated to counterarguing ($r = .00$) and message comprehension ($r = -.02$), providing further evidence of the distinction between source-based and external distractors.

Summary of Distraction Effects

Differences in the persuasive effects of external and communicator-based distraction underscore the importance of manipulations created by researchers in prior studies. More important, they provide a fuller understanding of situational features that affect the persuasion process. When a distraction that is external to the source occurs during a message presentation, it apparently shifts the attention of message receivers away from processing message content and toward the irrelevant distractor. The effect of this distraction appears to be a reduction in message comprehension and message effectiveness.

However, when distraction stems from the source of the message, the distractor shifts attention away from processing message content and toward the characteristics of the message source. The effectiveness of this type of distraction is dependent on the favorability of source characteristics. In this regard, the effects of communicator-relevant distractors mirror the modality effects discussed earlier in this chapter. In both cases, the effect is to increase the salience of source characteristics, which may enhance or restrict acceptance of the message recommendation.

PERSUASIVE INFLUENCES OF COLLECTIVITIES

Another important situational factor that influences persuasion is the presence of others. Every day, we spend a considerable amount of time working and socializing with other people. Whether we communicate in large organizations or small groups, we are rarely immune from the social influences of collectives. Although communication scholars and social psychologists have sought to understand the persuasive effects of social and work collectives, these social effects are routinely neglected in persuasion textbooks. Though a complete discussion of these effects is beyond the scope of this book, the remainder of this chapter examines two types of influence that collectives have on their individual members. This section begins with a discussion of conformity effects and concludes with an examination of the persuasive effects of group discussion.

Conformity Effects

Most of the communicative messages that are exchanged in small groups and organizations are expressions of the values, beliefs, and goals of people in those small groups and organizations. Over time, these individual expressions are codified into a collective set of values, beliefs, and goals that establish a norm of acceptable behavior for individual group members. Once these norms have been established, social pressure is exerted on individual members to adopt them. Pressures toward attitudinal and behavioral uniformity in collectives have been well documented (for a review, see Forsyth, 1983). *Conformity* is the general label for this genre of social influence processes and is commonly defined as "a change in attitude, belief, or behavior as a function of real or perceived group pressure" (Aronson, 1984, p. 17). People often conform because they perceive that the collective, or its individual members, exerts pressure on them to behave in a particular manner. However, overt pressure is not necessary to produce conforming behavior; all that is required is a *perception* of group pressure.

The Asch experiments provide a compelling example of the influence that collectives can have on their members. Asch (1955, 1956) was interested in the effect of apparent group consensus on the judgments of individuals. His experiment involved several confederates, who played the role of research participants, and an actual research participant who was naive about the purpose of the study. Asch presented the confederates and research participant with a series of card pairs. There were 18 pairs of cards in the series. For each pair, the first card contained three lines of different length. On the second card was a single line which was the same length as one of the lines on the first card. The task was to determine which line on the first card was the same length as the line on the second card.

When participants completed this task alone, they were correct 99% of the time. However, when they were placed in a group setting, their decisions were influenced by the choices of the confederates. Asch identified 12 of the 18 trials as critical trials. On the critical trials, confederates were instructed to choose the same wrong response. On the noncritical trials confederates were instructed to choose the correct response. The experimenter asked each of the confederates for their judgment before asking the naive research participant who was seated at the end of the row.

On each trial, the judgments of the confederates established a group norm. On the critical trials, this norm was obviously in error. Recall that participants who made these decisions alone were correct 99% of the time, indicating that the correct response was obvious. Asch (1956) was interested in knowing how often research participants would choose the wrong response in order to conform with the group norm. The findings were remarkable. Asch found that more that 75% of the participants conformed to the group norm on at least one of the 12 critical trials. In fact, over 35% of the total judgments made on critical trials were in error! Although a very small percentage of people conformed on all

12 critical trials, participants frequently conformed to the norm established by the group.

It bears mentioning that the confederates and participant in this study did not form a group in the everyday usage of the term. There was no group history, no leader, and no anticipation of future interaction. It also bears mentioning that the confederates exerted no overt pressure on the naive research participant, they simply established a norm by choosing the wrong response. However, despite the fact that the participants in Asch's study had little commitment to the group and there was no overt pressure on them to conform, they were influenced by the pressures of an established group norm. Subsequent research has demonstrated that group norms can be quickly established, and that once established, members tend to maintain these norms even when group members are no longer present (M. Sherif & C. Sherif, 1956). These studies indicate the pervasive effect of conformity influences on individual behavior.

Conformity occurs in a variety of ways. Conformity occurs when an employee agrees to work late into the evening in order to complete an important project. Conformity also occurs when advertisers successfully employ sports personalities and movie stars to promote their products. Kelman (1958) provided a conceptual framework for categorizing conformity behavior by identifying *compliance, identification,* and *internalization* as three distinct types of conformity processes.

Compliance

When compliance occurs, people accept influence from a group or organization in hopes of attaining some reward or avoiding punishment. Festinger (1953) defined this type of influence as "public conformity without private acceptance." That is, compliance does not require an actual change in attitude, only a change in observable behavior. People routinely engage in conforming behavior without changing their corresponding attitude or belief. For example, many drivers routinely exceed posted speed limits so long as they perceive they will not be caught. The sight of a highway patrol officer, however, triggers an immediate change in most people's driving behavior. The presence of the highway patrol officer increases the likelihood of sanctions for noncompliance and causes drivers to obey the speed limit or only exceed it by an acceptable margin. The fact that many drivers routinely disobey posted speed limits suggests that they do not privately believe the limits are reasonable. In this case, surveillance and the threat of a monetary fine are required to produce compliance with the law.

Compliance processes are not always motivated by a desire to avoid punishment. People often comply in order to gain rewards. A young professional may work overtime in hopes of impressing a supervisor and gaining consideration for an upcoming promotion. Hospital volunteers follow rules and procedures necessary to enjoy rewarding work with patients. College students may agree to participate in a persuasion experiment in order to gain extra credit. Behaviors like these are motivated by the rewards they offer and not the threat of reprisal.

Regardless of the motivation, however, the fundamental characteristic of compliance processes is that they are motivated by a desire to *avoid punishment* or *gain a reward*. As a result, compliance is only effective so long as the controlling agent is likely to offer rewards for compliance or apply sanctions for noncompliance. Although I have focused on the ways that collectives affect this type of conformity, compliance processes are also prominent in interpersonal interaction. In fact, Chapter 10 of this volume examines the large body of research that has investigated compliance processes in interpersonal settings.

Identification

A second type of conformity identified by Kelman is *identification*. When identification occurs, people accept influence from a controlling agent in order to "develop and maintain a favorable self-defining relationship with the controlling agent" (Kelman, 1958, p. 35). These self-defining relationships allow people to construct favorable self-images. Identification processes are often sufficiently subtle that they are unrecognized by sources and targets of influence. For example, college fraternity and sorority members often wear "Greek clothing" that identifies the organization to which they belong. Although the decision to purchase and wear clothing bearing an organization's label is clearly an identification process, few people would argue that this form of influence is a conscious effort to promote conformity among organization members. Nevertheless, these identification processes represent a type of conformity that facilitates the adoption of collective norms and values.

Though frequently subtle, identification processes can also be explicit. The recent "Be Like Mike" advertising campaign to promote a sports drink product is a prime example of an explicit identification appeal. The ad campaign, featuring basketball superstar Michael Jordan, encouraged people to be like Mike and drink the product. Though often less explicit, most ad campaigns that involve an endorsement by a sports figure derive their effectiveness from identification processes.

Kelman (1958) noted that the success of identification appeals is dependent on the maintenance of a favorable social relationship between the source of the influence and the target audience. As people grow, their attraction to reference groups changes, altering the effectiveness of persuasion agents who rely on identification processes. Because the social attractiveness of an individual, group, or organization is subject to rapid change, influence stemming from identification processes may not persist for extended periods of time.

Internalization

Kelman's third type of conformity was labeled *internalization*. Internalization processes are similar to traditional conceptions of attitude change. When people internalize a behavior, they do so after careful consideration of the reasons offered to adopt a particular behavior. This type of conformity is akin to Festinger's (1953) concept of public conformity with private acceptance. In this regard, internalization reflects the use of rational message appeals (see Chapter 6, this volume) that are the cornerstone of Information Processing Theory (see Chapter 7, this volume).

Internalization is the type of conformity that is the most stable of Kelman's three types of conformity. Internalized behaviors stem from a person's beliefs and values and thus are likely to persist in the absence of a controlling agent.

Summary of Conformity Effects

Regardless of their specific characteristics, conformity processes are a prominent form of social influence in collectives. Normative expectations emerge from interaction with other people, and once formed they exert pressure on people to conform with them. Although compliance, identification, and internalization are qualitatively distinct forms of conformity, they all stem from the desire of individuals in collectives to behave in a uniform fashion. Pressure toward uniformity is most apparent in group discussions that require a single decision. In the next section I extend the discussion of group influence by examining the effects of group discussion on the attitudes of individual members.

Polarization of Group Decisions

Another important influence of group interaction on the attitudes and behaviors of individual members is apparent from investigations of group decision-making processes. Beginning in the 1960s, social psychologists examined what was initially labeled the *risky shift phenomenon,* the tendency for groups to make more risky decisions than individuals. These investigations relied primarily on the methodology of a choice-dilemma item (Kogan & Wallach, 1967). This methodology presents research participants with a problem and two potential solutions. One solution is almost certain to resolve the dilemma and has a moderately rewarding outcome. The probability of success for the second alternative is uncertain, but if successful it will provide a much more rewarding outcome. Perhaps the adage, "A bird in the hand is worth two in the bush," represents the dilemma created by items like these. Respondents must choose between a certain, but less rewarding, alternative, and an uncertain, but potentially more rewarding, alternative. For example, financial planning often involves choosing between a safe investment that almost certainly will produce moderate profits and a risky investment that if successful will produce much greater returns, but if unsuccessful will lose money.

Researchers investigating this phenomenon typically ask research participants to read a choice-dilemma scenario and make an individual choice prior to participating in a group discussion of the dilemma. A risky shift is said to occur when the group decision, or average post-discussion choices of individual group members, is more risky than the average prediscussion decision of individual group members.

Using this methodology, several investigations found that small group discussions produced more risky choices than those made by individuals (Dion, Baron, & Miller, 1970; Kogan & Wallach, 1967). Subsequent research, however, found evidence that groups may also make more cautious decisions than individuals (Baron, Baron, & Roper, 1974; Stoner, 1968), leading researchers to relabel the risky shift phenomenon as the *polarity shift phenomenon*. That is, groups tend to make more extreme decisions (either more risky or more cautious) than individuals.

Since these initial investigations, several studies have provided evidence of a polarity shift phenomenon in group discussions (for reviews, see Boster, 1990; Lamm & Myers, 1978). How can these opinion shifts be explained? The most likely explanation stems from the influence of group interaction on the attitudes and judgments of individual group members. Two theoretical explanations that emphasize group communication have received most of the attention from researchers. Consistent with Deutsch and Gerard's (1955) distinction between normative and informational social influence, researchers have examined the merits of *social comparison* and *persuasive arguments* explanations of the polarity shift phenomenon.

Social Comparison Explanations

Social normative explanations of the polarity shift phenomenon evolved from Festinger's (1954) description of Social Comparison Theory and

Deutsch and Gerard's (1955) concept of normative social influence. Social Comparison Theory posits that people are concerned about the correctness or appropriateness of positions they hold, and this concern motivates them to validate their positions through interaction with others. In highly ambiguous situations, people are less certain about the validity of their positions, so social comparison processes become more likely. Consistent with the earlier discussion of conformity effects, discussion about a particular issue creates a social norm. Once a norm has been established, social influence is exerted on group members to conform to the normative position.

Social comparison processes occur in daily interaction. For example, college students often engage in social comparison processes after an exam when they gather just outside the classroom to discuss their impressions about the test's difficulty, fairness, and so forth. Students engage in this comparison process to reduce their uncertainty about the exam. Social pressure to conform to a normative position about the perceived difficulty of the exam may be limited, but a normative position is likely to emerge during discussions like these. That is, students participating in these discussions may collectively conclude that the exam was difficult, or that a particular question was unfair.

In much the same fashion, group discussions are social comparison processes that produce normative positions about the issue under consideration. The fundamental assumption of Social Comparison Theory is that people view themselves as "better embodiments of socially desired abilities, traits, and attitudes than are most members of their groups" (Lamm & Myers, 1978, p. 176). Lamm and Myers (1978) provide a variety of evidence to support this assumption, including the fact that most businesspeople view themselves as more ethical than the average businessperson (Baumhart, 1968) and research indicating that most people perceive they are less prejudiced than the average person (Lenihan, 1965). But, as Lamm and Myers point out, people's perceptions that they are superior to the average person are distorted because "the average person is not better than the average person" (1978, p. 176).

Applied to the polarity shift phenomenon, a social comparison (or normative influence) explanation posits that our desire to view ourselves more favorably than we view the average person affects the extremeness of positions we advocate. That is, social comparison processes in group discussions disconfirm the average group member's belief that his or her position is more favorable than the group norm. If discussion reveals that a cautious position is favored by the group, then members striving to maintain the perception that they are more favorable than the average group member will advocate a position that is more cautious than the group norm. On the other hand, if group discussion reveals a risky norm, then members will endorse a position that is more risky than the group norm. The result of social comparison processes is to cause individuals to endorse a more extreme position, either risky or cautious, than the group norm. The result of these individual position shifts is a postdiscussion position that is more extreme than the prediscussion position of the group.

Persuasive Arguments Explanations

An alternative explanation of the polarity shift phenomenon is more straightforward. The persuasive arguments explanation posits that group discussions expose members to novel arguments that are persuasive. Consistent with Information Processing Theory, this explanation holds that if the group norm favors a cautious position, then the distribution of these novel arguments is likely to be skewed in the cautious direction. That is, novel arguments are more likely to favor a cautious position than risky one. On the other hand, if group members favor a risky position, then novel arguments are more likely to be risky than cautious.

The informational influence of these novel arguments is hypothesized to produce the shifts in group discussions. Group discussions produce more reasons for advocating the normative group position than individual members could develop on their own. Armed with these additional new arguments, individual members become more confident in their judgments and advocate a more extreme position following group discussion. Thus, when the group norm favors caution, group discussion should produce a more cautious decision than the average prediscussion decision of individual group members. However, if the normative position is risky, group discussion should produce a decision that is more risky than the average prediscussion position of individual group members.

Testing Competing Explanations

Examining the validity of these two explanations is a difficult task. Social comparison explanations posit all that is required to produce a group shift is knowledge of the positions held by group members. Persuasive arguments explanations argue that information content, and not the normative positions of individual members, is responsible for the polarity shift phenomenon.

Unfortunately, these two forms of information are confounded in naturally occurring group discussions. As Boster (1990) aptly noted, an argument offered during group discussion contains both types of information; it provides an indication of another member's position on the issue as well as reasons for advocating that position. Thus, if the argument is persuasive, social comparison theorists might conclude that it was due to the statement of opinion contained in the argument and not the argument itself. However, persuasive arguments theorists would contend that the argument itself was persuasive. Conversely, if a person offered an opinion statement with no explicit argument to support it, social comparison theorists would argue that any persuasive effects were caused by the normative information in the opinion statement. However, persuasive arguments theorists might conclude that opinion statements include implicit arguments, and that these arguments, rather than group pressure, are responsible for the persuasive effects of the message (Boster, 1990, p. 305).

To examine each of these explanations, researchers have employed a variety of experimental procedures that systematically control group composition and the number of risky and cautious arguments that emerge during group discussion. For example, one study created groups with either a risky or cautious majority by selecting members on the basis of their prediscussion responses to a choice-dilemma item. These groups then discussed an issue that tended to produce either a risky or cautious shift (Boster, Fryrear, Mongeau, & Hunter, 1982). These researchers argued that a group's composition and the type of choice-dilemma item they discussed would combine to influence the number of risky and cautious arguments that emerged in group discussion. Boster and Mayer (1984) employed a more direct manipulation of persuasive arguments and normative influences by having research participants observe videotaped discussions that varied both the number of arguments favoring a risky and cautious position *and* the majority of group members with risky and cautious positions. Although this procedure did not involve research subjects in a group discussion, it more precisely controlled the social normative information and persuasive arguments to which they were exposed.

Investigations like these have examined the relative merits of the social comparison and persuasive arguments explanations (for reviews, see Lamm & Myers, 1978; Mayer, 1986). Support for the social comparison explanation has been found in studies where participants altered their positions after being exposed to only the positions of others. Evidence of this *mere exposure effect* was found in a recent meta-analysis of group polarization experiments. Isenberg (1986) reported that the average effect of social comparison processes in these studies was substantial ($r = .44$).

Considerable support has also been found for the persuasive arguments explanation. In fact, Isenberg's review found the average effect of persuasive arguments processes was quite strong ($r = .75$). Indeed, further support for the persuasive arguments explanation has emerged from studies employing the linear discrepancy model (see Chapter 7, this volume) to explain group polarization effects (Boster et al., 1982; Boster, Mayer, Hunter, & Hale, 1980). Although efforts to understand the interactive processes that create persuasive arguments effects in group discussions have only recently begun (Meyers, 1989; Meyers & Seibold, 1990), informational influences of group discussion on polarization of attitudes are well established.

Evidence supporting both explanations might cause one to question whether social comparison or persuasive arguments influences are responsible for the group polarization effects. Most likely, both informational and social normative influences affect polarity shifts in group discussions (Boster, 1990). One recent study that was designed to examine the relative importance of both processes found evidence supporting both explanations, although the persuasive arguments explanation accounted for more variance in polarity shifts than the social comparison explanation did (Mayer, 1986). This finding is consistent with Isenberg's (1986) meta-analytic review, which found a much stronger persuasive arguments effect, though the influence of social comparison processes was also large. Furthermore, a strong correlation between the persuasive arguments and social comparison effects led Isenberg to conclude that "at this point in time there is very good evidence that there are two conceptually independent processes even though outside of the laboratory they almost always co-occur" (1986, p. 1149). Regardless of the relative contributions of these theoretical processes, investigations of the polarity shift phenomenon provide compelling evidence for the influence groups have on their individual members.

SUMMARY

The present chapter examined characteristics of persuasive situations that influence the attitudes and behaviors of persuasive targets. Persuasive effects of the mode of message presentation appear to be moderated by characteristics of the message and message source. Live and video presentations focus attention on message sources and enhance the persuasiveness of highly attractive and credible sources. Written presentations were found to be more effective for complex messages that are difficult to understand.

Distracting stimuli are a second category of situational factors that affect the persuasiveness of messages. Distractions that are external to the message source seem to interfere with message learning and restrict the persuasiveness of the message. However, the effect of communicator-based distractions is to direct attention toward the message source, enhancing the persuasiveness of highly credible sources and restricting the effectiveness of less credible sources.

Finally, investigations of conformity effects and the polarization of individual attitudes provided clear evidence of the influence that collectives have on their individual members. Conformity research suggests that social norms are developed in the presence of others. Once these norms are established, groups and organizations exert influence on their members to adopt them. Investigations of the polarity shift phenomenon reflect a different type of influence that groups have on individual members. These investigations found that group discussion causes individuals to advocate more extreme positions (either risky or cautious) than they did prior to group discussion. Social comparison effects and the influence of novel persuasive arguments are two prominent explanations that account for these effects.

PART III

PERSUASION MODELS

This last section of the book describes persuasion models that incorporate the essential features of persuasive transactions discussed in Part II. This section of the book is divided into three chapters. Chapter 9 reviews several models of persuasion that emphasize the cognitive processes of message recipients and their influence on the persuasion process. Chapter 10 reviews three research traditions on interpersonal influence. And finally, Chapter 11 examines models of persuasive communication that are frequently employed in media campaigns.

CHAPTER NINE

Cognitive Models
of Persuasion

LOOKING AHEAD . . .

In this chapter I discuss cognitive models of persuasion.
These models incorporate the essential elements of persuasive
activity that I discussed in previous chapters into a set of cohesive predictions about persuasive communication. After discussing how people cognitively process messages, I describe and
evaluate two models, the Elaboration Likelihood Model (ELM)
and the Heuristic Model of Persuasion (HMP), which explain how
people's cognitive responses influence the effectiveness of persuasive messages.

Early persuasion research largely examined the influence of source and
message factors on the psychological processes that affect message
recipients' attitudes and behaviors. By the early 1960s, however, persuasion scholars began to consider the importance of message receivers
in the attitude change process. For example, Inoculation Theory
(McGuire, 1964) described a technique for increasing people's resistance
to persuasive attempts by providing them with counterarguments. Armed
with such arguments, people are somewhat more effective at counterarguing a subsequent persuasive appeal. This focus on individual
responses to persuasive appeals became more pronounced by the late
1960s and has since evolved into present-day cognitive theories of persuasion.

Though it has only recently assumed theoretical prominence, the
concept of cognitive processing during message reception is not new.
The seeds of this contemporary approach to persuasion were sown by

early persuasion scholars. Indeed, one of the earliest programs of persuasion research suggested that an audience can protect itself against
persuasion by going over its own arguments against the persuasion while
hearing a presentation (Hovland et al., 1949).

The primary assumption of many cognitive theories of persuasion
is that message receivers may play an active role in the formation, reinforcement, and change of their own attitudes and behaviors. According to this approach, when people are exposed to a persuasive message
presentation, they attempt to integrate the message appeal with their
existing attitudes and knowledge about the topic. In the course of this
integration process, message recipients may generate additional arguments and information to support or oppose the message recommendation. These self-generated thoughts and arguments contribute to the
overall persuasiveness of the message. To the extent that the communication evokes favorable thoughts in message recipients, receiver-generated
cognitions should enhance the effectiveness of the persuasive appeal.
If, however, the communication evokes counterarguing by message
recipients, receivers' cognitive responses are likely to inhibit the persuasiveness of the appeal.

Two empirical issues are fundamental to the utility of this theoretical perspective. First, research must document that people generate
favorable and unfavorable thoughts as they process persuasive messages
and that these self-generated thoughts influence their attitudes about
the message recommendation. Second, research must identify characteristics of persuasive situations that affect the production and valence
of these cognitive responses.

This first issue was the focus of a program of research by Abra-
ham Tesser and his colleagues (Sadler & Tesser, 1973; Tesser, 1978;
Tesser & Conlee, 1975), who established a link between cognitive
processes and attitudes. More recently, two models, the Elaboration
Likelihood Model (ELM) (Petty & Cacioppo, 1981, 1986) and the
Heuristic Model of Persuasion (HMP) (Chaiken 1987), have sought
to address the second issue by identifying factors that motivate and guide
the generation of these cognitive responses. Details of these research
programs are presented in the following sections of the chapter.

THE PERSUASIVE EFFECTS OF "MERE THOUGHT"

A basic assumption of cognitive models of persuasion is that people
are capable of recalling and evaluating previously held information about
a particular issue as they process persuasive messages. These self-
generated cognitions (thoughts) combine with message content and the

persuasive characteristics of the communicator to affect a receiver's evaluation of the message recommendation. To demonstrate the influence of these self-generated thoughts on subsequent evaluation of a stimulus object, Tesser and his colleagues conducted a series of investigations of the effects of "mere thought" on attitudes (Sadler & Tesser, 1973; Tesser, 1978; Tesser & Conlee, 1975).

In the first study, research participants were told they were participating in a study of "first impressions." Participants were told they were being matched with another person in an adjoining cubicle and asked to briefly introduce themselves. After their self-descriptions, participants listened to a simulated self-description of their partner via a recorded message. Half of the participants heard a description of a likeable person and half heard a less favorable description. Following these introductions, half of the participants were asked to think about the person who had just been described and half were asked to complete an irrelevant task. The irrelevant task was designed to distract participants from thinking about the description they had just heard. Following the relevant or irrelevant thinking task, participants evaluated their partner.

As expected, participants evaluated the likeable partner more positively than the unlikeable partner. More important, these differences were most pronounced among the participants who were given time to think about their partner before offering their impressions. That is, when offered a chance to think about their partner, people's reactions became more extreme, in either a positive or negative direction, depending on the valence of the initial introduction (Sadler & Tesser, 1973).

A second study examined the effects of the amount of time spent thinking about an issue on evaluation of the issue. In two experiments, Tesser and Conlee (1975) found a direct positive relationship between the amount of time participants spent thinking about an issue and the polarization of their attitudes about the issue. It is likely, however, that this positive linear relationship does not extend indefinitely. For example, Tesser found that the positive relationship between self-reported thought and attitude polarization diminished after a period of several minutes. As Tesser noted, "Thoughtful people simply don't walk around with more and more extreme attitudes" (Tesser, 1978, p. 301). Indeed, there seem to be practical limits to the persuasive effects of the "mere thought" phenomenon.

Nevertheless, these studies document the influence of self-generated thoughts on the evaluation of stimulus objects. Whether the object under consideration is a political issue or another person, the opportunity to think about the stimulus object is likely to make favorable evaluations more favorable, and unfavorable evaluations more unfavorable. This attitude polarization process is similar to the group polarization effects discussed in Chapter 8 of this volume. In the present case, however, *biased processing* (i.e., recalling either favorable or unfavorable thoughts) is the result of individual cognitive processes rather than group interaction.

Tesser (1978) argued that the persuasive effects of "mere thought" were guided by individuals' cognitive structures. Cognitive schemas assist information processing by directing attention toward certain stimuli and away from others and by providing rules for making inferences about the stimuli under evaluation. In the case of the Sadler and Tesser (1973) study, the likeable (unlikeable) introduction served to activate favorable (unfavorable) cognitive structures that guided the generation of thoughts about the stimulus object. These cognitive structures result in biased processing by affecting the favorableness (unfavorableness) of self-generated thoughts and information recall. Thus, when given time to think about an issue, people who favorably evaluate the issue are likely to generate mostly favorable thoughts about the issue, while people with unfavorable evaluations are likely to generate mostly unfavorable thoughts. Combined with research on cognitive schema, Tesser's investigations of the "mere thought" phenomenon establish an important link between individual cognitive responses toward a stimulus object and evaluations of that object.

Applied in persuasive transactions, this body of research suggests that message recipients' thought processes play a significant role in determining the effectiveness of a persuasive message. Investigations of several different persuasive phenomena have established that people are capable of generating their own arguments to support a message recommendation (Vinokur & Burnstein, 1974), or oppose it (Burgoon, Cohen, Miller, & Montgomery, 1978; McGuire, 1961a; Miller & Burgoon, 1978). Given the potential persuasive influence of self-generated arguments, researchers have recently focused attention on the processes that guide the generation of these cognitive responses and determine their persuasive effects.

During the 1980s, two contemporaneous programs of research attempted to model factors that affect the production of cognitive responses to persuasive messages and explain the influence of these self-generated thoughts on individual attitudes. The Elaboration Likelihood Model (ELM) of persuasion (Petty & Cacioppo, 1981, 1986) has received the most attention from persuasion scholars and is most closely associated with traditional cognitive response approaches to persuasion (see Petty et al., 1981). A second model, the Heuristic Model of Persuasion (HMP) (Chaiken, 1987), is more firmly rooted in theories of social cognition. Though the two models are similar in many respects, important differences exist between them. Because their differences are more subtle than their obvious similarities, students of persuasion often discuss these models as though their conceptual components are interchangeable. However, the theoretical differences between these two programs of research necessitate a separate discussion of the respective models.

THE ELABORATION LIKELIHOOD MODEL OF PERSUASION

The ELM evolved from a dissatisfaction with the contradictory findings of various theoretical approaches to studying persuasive communication. Based on their review of prior persuasion research, Petty and Cacioppo argued that many of these approaches reflect one of two distinct routes to persuasion. The *central route* to persuasion is marked by a careful scrutiny of message content and posits that attitude change is a function of message content and elaboration. A second general approach, the *peripheral route,* reflects an attitude change process that is marked by the association of message recommendations with positive or negative cues in the message environment (Petty & Cacioppo, 1981).

The ELM posits that when message receivers engage in central processing, characteristics of persuasive messages (e.g., argument quality, supporting information, and logical consistency) determine the extent and direction of attitude change. When people engage in peripheral processing, persuasive cues that are peripheral to the message itself (e.g., source expertise, source trustworthiness, and source attractiveness) determine the extent and direction of attitude change.

Distinguishing Central and Peripheral Processing

Given the distinction between central and peripheral routes to persuasion, the utility of the ELM stems from its ability to predict a priori the conditions under which message receivers engage in central and peripheral processing. The ELM's first two postulates were derived to assist in this prediction process. The primary postulate of this model is that people are motivated to hold "correct" attitudes. Referring to Festinger's (1954) Social Comparison Theory, Petty and Cacioppo argued as follows: "Incorrect or improper attitudes are generally maladaptive and can have deleterious behavioral, affective, and cognitive consequences" (1986, p. 6). As a result, people are often motivated to actively process persuasive messages in an effort to adopt an appropriate or correct attitude about message recommendations. However, the ELM's second postulate recognizes that although people are often motivated to actively process persuasive messages, the amount of cognitive effort people are willing or able to engage in to process persuasive appeals varies widely across people and situations (Petty & Cacioppo, 1986, p. 6).

To represent the range of processing activity available to message receivers, Petty and Cacioppo introduced the concept of an *elaboration likelihood continuum*. One end of this continuum represents highly active cognitive processing, in which message receivers scrutinize message content and generate their own cognitive responses to it. According to the ELM, when conditions are ripe for this type of message processing, elaboration likelihood is high and the central route to persuasion is most probable. Issue-relevant thoughts generated by receivers during message elaboration affect attitude change and contribute to the overall effectiveness of the message. If these thoughts are favorable toward the message recommendation, acceptance of the message recommendation is more likely. Conversely, thoughts opposing the message recommendation are likely to decrease acceptance.

The other end of the continuum represents message processing that requires very little cognitive effort. Instead of careful attention to message content, receivers rely on persuasive cues in the message environment to make decisions about message recommendations. When conditions are ripe for this type of processing, elaboration likelihood is low and the peripheral route to persuasion is most probable. When receivers use a peripheral route to persuasion, positive persuasion cues in the message environment (e.g., a highly attractive source) increase message acceptance, whereas negative persuasion cues decrease message acceptance.

Predicting Message Elaboration

The ELM's second postulate suggests that cognitive elaboration of persuasive messages varies across people and situations. Thus, the crux of this model is specifying the conditions under which message elaboration is likely to occur. Though a variety of situational and personal characteristics may affect elaboration likelihood, three factors—*motivation, ability,* and *need for cognition*—have received the most attention from ELM researchers.

Motivation

Message receivers must be motivated to hold a socially appropriate or correct attitude on a particular issue before they will engage in effortful cognitive elaboration of a persuasive message on that issue. One factor that reflects the motivation of message recipients is the personal relevance of the issue. Accordingly, receivers who perceive a high degree of outcome-relevant involvement (see Chapter 7, this volume) should be motivated to carefully scrutinize message content in hopes of making the correct decision about the message recommendation. Though other factors, such as need for social approval and self-monitoring, may also influence a person's motivation to scrutinize a message, outcome-relevant involvement has been used most often to manipulate receiver motivation in prior ELM research (see Petty & Cacioppo, 1986).

Ability

A second factor that affects message elaboration is cognitive ability. According to the ELM, recipients must be both willing *and* able to cognitively elaborate message content. This factor has been largely ignored by ELM researchers, although investigations of message comprehension underscore the importance of this variable. For example, distracting stimuli (Buller, 1986), message distortion (Eagly, 1974; Eagly & Warren, 1976), and message difficulty (Chaiken & Eagly, 1976) have all been found to reduce message learning and comprehension, affecting cognitive evaluation of message content. Though many persuasive situations involve message recipients who have the cognitive ability to elaborate message content, message presentations that are cognitively challenging are less likely to result in cognitive elaboration.

Need for Cognition

One individual characteristic that affects a person's motivation, and perhaps ability, to elaborate message content is *need for cognition* (Cohen, Stotland, & Wolfe, 1955). This personality characteristic was developed to reflect differences among individuals in their "need to engage in and enjoy effortful cognitive endeavors" (Petty & Cacioppo, 1986, p. 48). Questionnaire measures of this construct were refined (Cacioppo & Petty, 1982, 1984), and have been employed to represent another motivational factor that influences elaboration likelihood. Although this factor has been used mainly to reflect a person's motivation to scrutinize persuasive messages, it may also reflect a person's ability to do so. If you have a high need for cognition and routinely scrutinize persuasive message content, you are likely to develop cognitive skills necessary to effectively scrutinize messages. Thus, people with a strong need for cognition are probably better able to scrutinize message content than people with relatively little need for cognition.

In summary, the ELM posits that receivers must be willing and able to cognitively elaborate messages in order to travel the central route to persuasion. Outcome-relevant involvement is one factor that reflects motivation, message comprehensibility is one factor that affects ability, and need for cognition is an individual factor that probably affects both motivation and ability to scrutinize message content.

Message Elaboration and Attitude Change

The ELM's predictions regarding message processing are straightforward: "As motivation and/or ability to process arguments is decreased, peripheral cues become relatively more important determinants of persuasion. Conversely, as argument scrutiny is increased, peripheral cues become relatively less important determinants of persuasion" (Petty & Cacioppo, 1986, p. 5). That is, when central processing occurs, message content will influence attitudes more than peripheral cues in the persuasive situation. However, when peripheral processing is predominant, message content becomes relatively unimportant and persuasion cues external to the message itself affect attitude change. Thus, when people centrally process a message, its persuasiveness depends mostly on the quality of arguments and supporting evidence. When people engage in peripheral processing, the persuasive appeal's effectiveness depends mostly on the valence of persuasive cues, including source credibility and source attractiveness.

An impressive number of experiments have examined the validity of the ELM, though for the most part, these investigations have employed the same experimental procedure. This general procedure evolved from original tests of the model (Petty, Cacioppo, & Goldman, 1981) and involves creating two persuasive messages that advocate the same position (typically a tuition increase or comprehensive exams for undergraduate students). One message contains strong arguments supporting the message recommendation and the other contains weak arguments. These messages are attributed to a highly or less expert source as they are presented to research participants (usually college students).

To control the motivation factor, experimenters usually tell half of the message recipients that the message is personally relevant to them, while telling the remaining participants that the message has little relevance for them. For example, when messages advocate a tuition increase or comprehensive exams, half of the student participants are told that the advocated action will begin the following year, while the remaining participants are told that the recommended action is not scheduled to occur for several years. When the recommended action is proposed for the following year, outcome-relevant involvement is high for students who are not in the final year of their degree program. When the recommended action is proposed for several years in the future, the message has low outcome-relevant involvement for message recipients.

The three variables manipulated with this procedure reflect three important components of the ELM. Receiver motivation to scrutinize message content is manipulated by varying levels of outcome-relevant involvement.[1] Argument quality represents a central cue that may or may not be scrutinized by message recipients, and source expertise represents a peripheral cue that is external to the message content.[2] Consistent with ELM predictions, Petty and his colleagues have repeatedly found that under conditions of high outcome-relevant involvement, argument quality has a stronger effect on attitudes than source expertise. When receiver involvement is low the source expertise manipulation routinely has a much stronger effect on attitudes than the argument quality manipulation (see Petty & Cacioppo, 1986). In statistical terms, two two-way interactions provide support for the ELM. In the first interaction, outcome-relevant involvement and argument quality combine to affect attitudes (Figure 9.1). The second interaction reflects the combined effects of outcome-relevant involvement and source expertise on attitudes (Figure 9.2).

Evaluating the Utility of the ELM

Although Petty and Cacioppo, and their colleagues, have marshalled considerable evidence in support of the ELM, several recent investigations have raised a number of concerns about the logical validity and practical utility of this model. These concerns stem from the theoretical specificity of the model and the quality of empirical support for the model.

Theoretical Limitations of the ELM

In the first published critique of the ELM, I questioned the extent to which it accurately reflected human information processing capacities (Stiff, 1986) and argued that the ELM depicted humans as single-channel

---

[1] It bears mentioning that a number of other factors, including need for cognition, can motivate cognitive elaboration of messages.

[2] Although early tests of the ELM uniformly associated the persuasive effects of argument quality with central processing and the persuasive effects of source expertise with peripheral processing, Petty and Cacioppo (1986) later specify that these variables can serve multiple roles. As is revealed later in the chapter, this conceptual flexibility raises serious concerns about whether the model can be falsified.

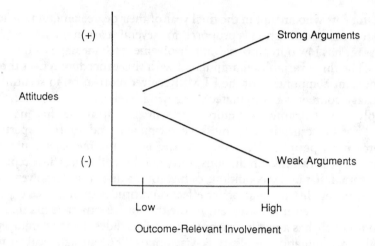

FIGURE 9.1. Combined effect of outcome-relevant involvement and argument quality on attitudes.

information processors, even though current theories of information processing argue that humans are capable of parallel information processing (see Kahneman, 1973; Stiff, 1986). At issue is whether people are able to engage in both central and peripheral processing of persuasive messages simultaneously. If central message content and peripheral cues can be processed in parallel, then both types of information may

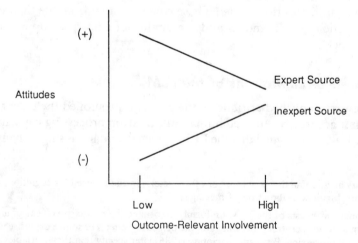

FIGURE 9.2. Combined effect of outcome-relevant involvement and source expertise on attitudes.

affect attitudes. However, as articulated by Petty and Cacioppo, the ELM postulates "a trade-off between argument elaboration and the operation of peripheral cues" (Petty & Cacioppo, 1986, p. 21). This postulate led to an interpretation of the ELM as a single-channel processing model (Stiff, 1986).

Rejecting this conceptualization of the ELM as a single-channel processing model, Petty and his colleagues argued that their description of the ELM "does not mean that people are incapable of processing *both* arguments and cues" (Petty et al., 1987, p. 238). Nevertheless, the schematic diagram of the ELM (Petty and Cacioppo, 1981, 1986) does not reflect the parallel processing capacities of message receivers. Indeed, it is difficult to imagine how their diagram of the ELM can be used to explain parallel processing. "At each decision point along the flow chart individuals are depicted as channeling their efforts toward *either* central *or* peripheral processing, but not both" (Stiff & Boster, 1987, p. 250).

The practical implication of this debate centers around the persuasive effects of cues that are processed centrally and peripherally. That is, in many persuasive situations, message content is processed centrally and source characteristics are processed peripherally. In these situations, single-channel processing models would predict that either message content or source characteristics are processed and subsequently influence attitudes. Conversely, parallel processing models predict the simultaneous evaluation of both message and source characteristics and specify that both types of processing may contribute to attitude change. Specifically, parallel processing models allow for equal contributions from both types of processing, a clear departure from the processing trade-off described by Petty and Cacioppo (1986, p. 21).

To reflect the persuasive effects of parallel processing, I (Stiff, 1986) proposed an alternative model derived from Kahneman's (1973) Elastic Capacity Model (ECM) of human information processing. Applied in persuasive settings, the ECM posits that message receivers are capable of parallel processing and specifies the conditions under which they engage in central and peripheral processing. Under conditions of low outcome-relevant involvement, receivers are unmotivated to engage in central or peripheral processing. At moderate levels of involvement, receivers are motivated to engage in central and peripheral processing. At high levels of involvement, although parallel processing is possible, the ECM specifies that receivers will focus attention on a single processing task. Given the importance of holding an appropriate position on the issue, I (Stiff, 1986) hypothesized that central processing would receive primary attention of highly involved receivers.

The predictive differences between the ELM and my application of the ECM are apparent. The ELM predicts a negative relationship between a person's level of involvement and the influence of peripheral processing on attitudes and a positive relationship between involvement and the influence of central processing on attitudes (Figure 9.3). Conversely, applied in persuasive settings, the ECM predicts a curvilinear (inverted-U) relationship between receiver involvement and the influence of peripheral processing on attitudes. Similar to the ELM, however, the ECM predicts a positive linear relationship between receiver involvement and the influence of central processing on attitudes (Figure 9.4).

A meta-analytic review of the persuasion literature tested the predictions of the ELM and ECM (Stiff, 1986). The positive linear relationship between outcome-relevant involvement and the effects of supporting information on attitudes was consistent with both the ELM and ECM. However, the review also found a curvilinear relationship between receiver involvement and the effects of source credibility on attitudes. Assuming that source credibility effects reflected peripheral processing, this latter finding is consistent with the ECM and incompatible with the ELM (Stiff, 1986).

Although the merits of this alternative model and the evidence supporting it have been debated (see Petty et al., 1987; Stiff & Boster, 1987), this debate in no way diminishes the fact that the ELM has failed to explicitly consider the implications of parallel information processing in persuasive transactions. "In no instance do they predict that both central and peripheral information influence attitudes" (Stiff & Boster,

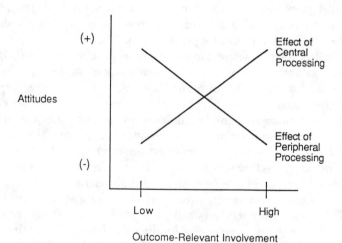

FIGURE 9.3. Effects of central and peripheral processing on attitudes across levels of outcome-relevant involvement as predicted by the ELM.

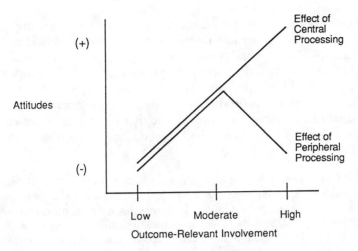

FIGURE 9.4. Effects of central and peripheral processing on attitudes across levels of outcome-relevant involvement as predicted by the ELM.

1987, p. 251). Before the ELM can fully explain the persuasive effects of cognitive responses, it must carefully consider the implications of parallel information processing on the production of cognitive responses.

A second theoretical limitation of the theory is its inability to specify a priori the conditions under which particular cues will be processed centrally and peripherally. Original investigations of this model uniformly associated message content cues such as argument quality with central processing and persuasion cues such as source expertise and attractiveness with peripheral processing (Petty, Cacioppo, & Goldman, 1981). That is, under conditions of high receiver involvement, the positive relationship between argument quality and attitudes was interpreted as evidence of central processing. Under conditions of low receiver involvement, the positive relationship between source expertise and attitudes was interpreted as evidence of peripheral processing (Petty, Cacioppo, & Goldman, 1981). However, by 1986, Petty and Cacioppo had specified that the same variable can serve multiple persuasive roles. They postulated that "Variables can affect the amount and direction of attitude change by (a) serving as persuasive arguments, (b) serving as peripheral cues, and/or (c) affecting the extent or direction of issue and argument elaboration" (1986, p. 5). For example, the beautiful hair of a female model may provide a peripheral cue in an automobile advertisement, whereas the same stimulus may be processed centrally in a commercial promoting hair shampoo.

The problem with this conceptual flexibility is that it "allows the

ELM to explain all possible outcomes of an experimental study" making it practically impossible to falsify (Stiff & Boster, 1987, p. 251). For example, under conditions of high involvement, if the quality of a model's hair is positively related to attitudes, then ELM proponents can argue that this stimulus must have been processed centrally. However, if the same conditions produce a nonsignificant effect for this stimulus, then ELM proponents could argue that this stimulus served as a peripheral cue. As Burgoon (1989) noted, classification of these cues is often

> . . . derived from inferring antecedents from consequents, or a teleological method of explanation. Thus, *if* specific outcomes occur (e.g., attitude change), then certain kinds of intrapsychic message processing had to have occurred. Such an explanatory mechanism is relatively unproductive for people interested in the social effects of strategy choices. The more appropriate approach is to specify a priori how message variables affect the persuasive process. (p. 157)

Thus, until the ELM specifies a priori the conditions under which important stimulus variables reflect central processing, a peripheral cue, or both, it will remain impossible to falsify, and consequently have little theoretical or practical value (Stiff & Boster, 1987. p. 251).

A third theoretical limitation of the ELM stems from its failure to describe and examine the specific intervening processes that mediate the influence of source and message cues on attitudes (Mongeau & Stiff, 1993). As a cognitive response theory, the ELM hypothesizes that characteristics of persuasive message presentations, such as argument quality and source expertise, produce cognitive responses in message receivers. In turn, these cognitive responses are hypothesized to affect attitudes. Thus, the ELM specifies a causal string, in which the message presentation (Factor A) causes cognitive responses (Factor B), which in turn affect attitudes (Factor C). However, prior studies have tested only a portion of the model, the A–B and A–C relationships. That is, most ELM studies assess the effects of a message presentation (A) on cognitive responses (B) and the effect of a message presentation (A) on attitudes (C). Although prior tests examined the A–B and A–C relationships, few studies have tested the hypothesized relationship between cognitive responses (B) and attitudes and behaviors (C). Nor have they attempted to simultaneously test the entire causal model (A causes B causes C) (Mongeau & Stiff, 1993).

Most likely, this error has resulted from reliance on analysis of variance techniques, which permit researchers to assume that if exogenous variables produce their predicted effects on outcome variables, then the hypothesized intervening processes that produced these effects must have occurred. As long as the predicted outcomes are observed, this reasoning permits researchers to misspecify causal processes without consequence. For example, three different sets of intervening cognitive processes are consistent with the general predictions of the ELM (Mongeau & Stiff, 1993). Although these alternative intervening processes may produce similar outcomes, each paints a distinctly different picture of the cognitive processes that determine the effectiveness of persuasive messages. Clearly, more precise specification and examination of these intervening cognitive processes are necessary before we can have confidence in the explanatory utility of the ELM.

Empirical Limitations of the ELM

In addition to the theoretical shortcomings of the ELM, recent reviews of the persuasion literature have challenged the validity of empirical support for the model. Perhaps the most important revelation emerged from a meta-analysis of the involvement literature (Johnson & Eagly, 1989). When cumulating the effects of outcome-relevant involvement on attitudes, Johnson and Eagly found evidence of an involvement by argument quality interaction. However, there was considerable variance in the overall estimate of this interaction. That is, there were significant differences among the findings of individual studies that contributed to this overall estimate. Specifically, studies authored by Petty, Cacioppo, and their colleagues obtained the predicted interaction between argument quality and involvement, whereas studies authored by other researchers found weak or no evidence of this same interaction (Johnson & Eagly, 1989, p. 304). That is, studies conducted by Petty, Cacioppo, and their colleagues consistently found a significant positive relationship between involvement and attitudes when receivers heard strong arguments and a significant negative relationship between involvement and attitudes when they heard messages containing weak arguments. However these effects were small and not significantly different from zero when similar studies were conducted by other researchers.[3]

One possible explanation for the difference in the findings of studies conducted by Petty, Cacioppo, and associates and studies conducted by other researchers stems from Petty and Cacioppo's operational definition of strong and weak arguments. Although this definition was not

---

[3]Petty and Cacioppo (1990) contested the conceptual and methodological decisions made by Johnson and Eagly (1989). However, the quality of Johnson and Eagly's (1990) response to this critique reaffirms the serious challenge their findings pose for proponents of the ELM.

revealed until their 1986 review of this literature, Petty and Cacioppo arbitrarily defined a strong argument as information that, when scrutinized, causes message receivers to generate 65% favorable or supportive cognitions and 35% unfavorable cognitions. They defined a weak argument as information that, when scrutinized by message receivers, produces only 35% favorable cognitions (1986, pp. 54–55).

Given this definition and the conceptual and empirical relationship between cognitions and attitudes (see Chapter 1, this volume), the predicted effects of central processing on attitudes are tautological. That is, if one operationally defines a strong argument as information that when processed centrally produces favorable cognitions, the finding that central processing of strong arguments leads to message acceptance is of little theoretical importance (Mongeau & Stiff, 1993). D. J. O'Keefe (1990) put this concern in perspective when he argued that the observed argument quality by involvement interaction:

> . . . is not a discovery; it is not an empirical result or finding, it is not something that research "shows" to be true, it is not something that could have been otherwise. . . . The described relationship is true by definition, given the definition of argument strength used by ELM research. (p. 110)

Indeed, if central processing of strong arguments failed to produce favorable attitudes under these conditions, the argument quality manipulation would be called into question (Mongeau & Stiff, 1993, D. J. O'Keefe, 1990).

Although somewhat obscure, the operational definitions adopted by Petty and Cacioppo may be responsible for their ability to consistently produce the argument quality by involvement interaction that has eluded many other researchers. If studies conducted by people other than Petty, Cacioppo, and colleagues employed more traditional definitions of argument quality—for example, definitions based on the structure or logical validity of arguments (cf., Reinard, 1988; Toulmin, 1964) and not the pattern of cognitions they produce—then their failure to replicate the argument quality by involvement interaction may stem from the use of a different operational definition of argument quality. Thus, speculative, careful examination of these methodological issues may resolve the conflicting findings of experiments conducted by Petty, Cacioppo, and their associates and those conducted by other researchers.

A second empirical limitation of many investigations of the ELM stems from the repeated use of a relatively small sample of message and source manipulations. Indeed, a large majority of investigations of the ELM have employed one of two topics; one advocating tuition increases and the other recommending comprehensive exams for under-graduates. D. J. O'Keefe (1990) succinctly summarized this concern when he wrote,

> What is worrisome about this, of course, is that the ELM purports to be a theory of persuasion generally, not a theory of persuasion about com-prehensive exams and tuition charges. One would naturally have reser-vations about a theory of persuasion resting on evidence from just a few human respondents, and one should similarly have reservations about a theory that rests on evidence from just a few message topics. (p. 109)

Of course, concerns about the importance of message diversity in persuasion research are not new (see Jackson & Jacobs, 1983). Although methods for message generalization have been vigorously debated (Jackson, D. J. O'Keefe, & Jacobs, 1988; Morely, 1988a, 1988b; D. J. O'Keefe, Jackson, & Jacobs, 1988), persuasion scholars generally agree about the importance of message diversity in establishing the breadth of theories.

Summary of ELM Limitations

For the better part of a decade, the ELM dominated thinking about the effects of cognitive responses in persuasion. Although the model has provoked significant research and considerable speculation about the persuasion process, several theoretical shortcomings call into ques-tion the theoretical validity and practical utility of the model. Specifi-cally, researchers have questioned whether the ELM is compatible with the parallel information processing capacities of message receivers; whether it can in principle be falsified; and whether it is sufficiently articulated to explain the precise cognitive processes that mediate the effectiveness of persuasive messages. Combined with these theoretical limitations, contradictory findings of prior studies limit the confidence some researchers have about the validity of the model.

Although questions remain about some aspects of the model, the ELM has provided strong evidence of two types of message processing and established an important relationship between receiver motivation, message scrutiny, and cognitive responses. In addition, the ELM has spawned a considerable amount of research and renewed interest in the study of persuasive message processing. A second cognitive model of persuasion, the HMP (Chaiken, 1987) coincided with the develop-ment of the ELM. Although the two models share a number of con-ceptual similarities, they differ in several important respects.

THE HEURISTIC MODEL OF PERSUASION

Although Chaiken's (1987) HMP has received considerably less attention from persuasion scholars than the ELM, the HMP provides an
attractive alternative to persuasion researchers seeking a cognitive model
of persuasion. Like the ELM, the HMP posits that two distinct cognitive processes guide the evaluation of persuasive messages. One process,
labeled *systematic processing,* involves the careful scrutiny of message
content and is similar to Petty and Cacioppo's concept of central processing. A second type of processing, labeled *heuristic processing,* involves
very little cognitive effort by message receivers.

Although Chaiken's (1987) systematic processing is similar to Petty and Cacioppo's (1986) central processing, the concepts of peripheral and heuristic processing are distinct. Petty and Cacioppo's peripheral
processing reflects a theoretical association with reactance theory
(Brehm, 1966), identification processes (Kelman, 1961), and models
of classical conditioning (Staats & Staats, 1957). Chaiken argues that
these theoretical perspectives "feature motivational orientations *other*
than assessing the validity of persuasive messages" (1987, p. 7, italics
added). Conversely, heuristic processing reflects a single theoretical orientation about the evaluation of persuasive messages in which receivers
employ cognitive heuristics to assess the validity of a persuasive message. *Heuristics* are simple decision rules that allow people to evaluate
message recommendations without effortful scrutiny of message content. For example, the heuristic that "experts are usually correct," permits receivers to make a decision about a message recommendation
based on a quick assessment of the source's expertise. Thus, peripheral processing reflects a variety of psychological motivations emphasizing the association of a speaker's position with rewarding or unrewarding
persuasive cues. Conversely, heuristic processing reflects a single motivation, that is, evaluation of the message recommendation with minimal
cognitive effort.

The centerpiece of the HMP is the explicit recognition that people are often "minimalist information processors" who are unwilling
to engage in highly active, conscious processing of persuasive message
content. Applying prior investigations of cognitive heuristics (Kahneman & Tversky, 1973; Tversky & Kahneman, 1974, 1982), Chaiken
argued that many distal persuasion cues are processed by means of simple schemas or decision rules that have been learned on the basis of
past experiences and observations (1987, p. 4). For example, many people hold a cognitive schema that "taxes are bad," which leads to a simple decision rule that messages advocating tax increases should be
rejected. Indeed, the political effectiveness of George Bush's 1988 cam-

paign promise, "Read my lips, no new taxes," was derived from the assumption that voters would enact this simple heuristic and vote for him.

Other, more general, heuristics may guide the processing of a variety of different persuasive messages. For example, the heuristic that "expert sources are probably correct" is a decision rule that evolves over time as sources with expertise demonstrate a propensity for advocating correct positions on issues. Once established, this heuristic is available to people for use in evaluating the statements of expert and inexpert sources. Applied in a persuasive situation, this heuristic may lead message receivers to accept the recommendations of an expert source without the need for careful examination of the reasons offered in support of such recommendations. In much the same fashion, the heuristic "more is better" may produce greater message acceptance of messages containing four supporting arguments than those messages containing a single supporting argument.

Unlike the careful scrutiny of message content, the use of cognitive heuristics requires little cognitive effort. In general, all that is required is the application of a situation to the heuristic. If characteristics of the persuasive appeal under consideration are representative of a general, prototypical example of the heuristic, then the heuristic is likely to guide the evaluation of the persuasive appeal. Thus, the heuristic "experts are likely to be correct" may guide the evaluation of a speaker's recommendation once the level of the speaker's expertise has been established.

Once formed, these heuristics are available in message receiver's cognitive structures. The operation (accessibility) of these heuristics depends not only on their existence (availability), but also on the frequency and recency of their use (Fiske & Taylor, 1991; Higgins & King, 1981; Wyer & Srull, 1981). For example, Higgins, King, and Mavin (1982) concluded that the cognitive constructs that people frequently use to evaluate others are likely to become chronically accessible. Bargh and Pratto argued that the "frequency of use of a cognitive process results in its becoming more efficient, and eventually in its automation" (1986, p. 295–296). Thus, cognitive heuristics allow many persuasive cues to be processed automatically, requiring minimal cognitive effort from message receivers.

Predicting Systematic and Heuristic Processing

Although the HMP is a cognitive model of persuasion, it does not emphasize message receiver's cognitive responses. Instead, Chaiken (1987) describes how cognitive processes permit message receivers to evaluate persuasive messages without much conscious control or cognitive activity. As "cognitive misers" (Fiske & Taylor, 1991) people generally seek to minimize their cognitive activity, preferring less effortful methods of information processing. Thus, although systematic processing is one method of message evaluation, it is employed less often than cognitive heuristics.

The central predictions of the HMP describe the conditions that determine when message receivers will rely on cognitive heuristics and when they will engage in systematic processing to evaluate persuasive messages. A critical assumption of the HMP is that "heuristic and systematic processing of persuasion cues represent parallel, rather than mutually exclusive, modes of message processing" (Chaiken, 1987, p. 11). Thus, whereas the ELM posits "a trade-off between argument elaboration and the operation of peripheral cues" (Petty & Cacioppo, 1986, p. 21), the HMP clearly views systematic and heuristic processing as complementary forms of information processing. Given the minimal requirements of cognitive load necessary for heuristic processing, it is likely that most persuasive messages can be processed in this manner. Thus, people with minimal motivation to scrutinize a message can nevertheless process the appeal with cognitive heuristics. However, the systematic evaluation of persuasive messages is predicated on the ability of receivers to comprehend the message and their motivation to exert the cognitive effort required for systematic processing (Chaiken, 1987). Thus, although they are derived from separate theoretical perspectives, the HMP and ELM hypothesize similar roles for motivation and ability in determining the extent of systematic (central) processing. As a result, the situational and individual difference factors that affect receiver ability and motivation are equally relevant to the HMP as to the ELM.

Comparison of the HMP and the ELM

Because it reflected a bold attempt to integrate the conflicting predictions and findings from a variety of different persuasion theories, the ELM has received considerably more attention from persuasion scholars than the HMP. However, the HMP offers an attractive alternative to researchers and practitioners who have concerns about the theoretical and empirical limitations of the ELM.

Perhaps the single greatest asset of the HMP is that it was derived from a single theoretical perspective, a cognitive approach to information processing. Because the ELM is clearly aligned with cognitive response approaches to persuasion, it also represents a conglomeration of motivational and learning theory perspectives. Indeed, the theoretical breadth of the ELM is reflected in the claim that "many theories of attitude change could be roughly placed along an elaboration likelihood continuum" (Petty & Cacioppo, 1986, p. 8). For example, the ELM has been applied in fields as diverse as clinical psychology and marketing. However, the theoretical breadth of the ELM may be related to the lack of depth in its specification of the precise cognitive processes that mediate the effects of messages on attitudes.

The most important distinction between these two models stems from the HMP's explicit recognition of the parallel processing capacities of message receivers. Not only is this recognition consistent with current theories of human information processing (Stiff, 1986), it alleviates the source of several limitations of the ELM. Because it posits a tradeoff between central and peripheral processing, the ELM cannot explain findings that both types of processes contribute equally to a message's persuasiveness (cf. Stiff, 1986). Because the HMP posits that systematic and heuristic processing can occur in parallel, evidence of the effects of parallel processing is not a problem for this model.

Their shortcomings aside, these two models have made significant contributions to an understanding of speaker, message, and receiver factors that affect attitude change. Specific tests of these models produced an overwhelming volume of persuasion research during the past decade. Though far from complete, these research programs reflect the dramatic shift from the source-centered approaches to persuasion that were prevalent in the 1960s and early 1970s to a receiver-centered focus, which is apparent in much of today's theorizing about persuasive communication.

SUMMARY

This chapter examined two recently developed cognitive models of persuasion. After reviewing research by Tesser and his colleagues that documented the effects of "mere thought" on the extremity of people's attitudes, the ELM was introduced as one model of persuasion that posits an important role for message receivers' cognitive responses. The ELM specified conditions that cause people to carefully consider the substance of persuasive messages and argued that when such conditions were met, message characteristics such as argument quality and supporting evidence would influence attitudes. According to the model, when people are unwilling or unable to carefully scrutinize message content, they base their message evaluation on persuasion cues that are peripheral to the message itself. Several concerns were raised about the theoretical validity and empirical support of the ELM. These theoretical and empirical limitations of the ELM call into question the validity of the model. The HMP was introduced as one alternative that is free of several of these limitations. Although they have many similarities, the HMP and the ELM represent distinct conceptualizations about the persuasion process. For example, the HMP reflects a single theoretical approach, rather than an attempt to integrate many different theoretical perspectives. In addition, the HMP explicitly accommodates the ability of message receivers to simultaneously conduct systematic and heuristic processing.

In summary, these models reflect a recent movement among persuasion scholars to a more careful consideration of the contributions of message receivers to the persuasion process. Recent theorizing about this issue has stimulated scholarly inquiry and debate and promises to provide a more comprehensive understanding of persuasive communication.

Models of Interpersonal Compliance

L OOKING AHEAD . . .

This chapter reviews three traditions of research on interpersonal influence. I begin the review with a discussion of studies that examine factors that affect the evaluation and selection of strategies for gaining compliance in interpersonal contexts. Following this, I review investigations of sequential request strategies, that is, compliance strategies that require multiple persuasive messages. Finally, I conclude with a review of an emerging tradition of research that examines factors that affect the generation of interpersonal influence messages.

In Chapter 9 of this volume I reviewed two models of persuasion that examined the cognitive responses people generate as they process persuasive messages. The focus of that chapter was on the contributions of message recipients to the overall effectiveness of a persuasive appeal. In the present chapter, I shift attention to examining characteristics of message sources in interpersonal persuasive transactions. Three avenues of research reflect the efforts of persuasion scholars to understand the production, evaluation, and use of messages designed to gain compliance in interpersonal settings.

The first avenue, labeled *compliance-gaining message selection* research, has been advanced primarily by communication scholars, though its genesis is in the field of sociology. In 1967, sociologists Marwell and Schmitt identified a typology of persuasive strategies that individuals might use to gain compliance from one another. This typology was subsequently adopted by communication scholars who examined situational factors that affect the evaluation of these strategies (Miller, Boster, Roloff, & Seibold, 1977). Together, these early investigations provided a research paradigm for examining compliance-gaining messages (for a review, see Seibold, Cantrill, & Meyers, 1985). Though these investigations were typically labeled as compliance-gaining "message selection" or "message use" studies, very few of these studies examined actual communicative behavior. Instead, researchers were content to rely on research participants' evaluations of the likelihood that they would use various strategies to gain compliance in a particular situation. This failure to investigate actual communicative behavior produced questions about the predictive utility of these evaluations and the generalizability of this research paradigm (Dillard, 1988; Seibold et al., 1985).

Concurrent with the efforts of communication scholars, a second avenue of research was instigated by social psychologists who studied the effectiveness of several sequential request strategies. Unlike compliance-gaining research in communication, many of these investigations observed actual communicative behavior and focused attention on persuasive outcomes, rather than the generation of interpersonal persuasive messages (for a review, see Cialdini, 1987).

Finally, as interest in the message selection paradigm waned, researchers began the search for alternative approaches to investigating interpersonal persuasion. A third avenue of research on interpersonal persuasion emerged from this search and focused attention on how people think about and produce interpersonal influence messages. Recently, several models have been proposed to explain factors that affect the production of persuasive messages (Dillard, 1990; B. J. O'Keefe, 1988; Wilson, 1990). Although these models hold promise for scholars of interpersonal persuasion, evidence regarding their utility is still being gathered, and few of these investigations have examined persuasive behavior in actual communicative transactions.

This chapter examines each of these three traditions of interpersonal persuasion research. I examine the theoretical foundations of each tradition and empirical findings of representative investigations within each tradition. Along the way, I identify the shortcomings of each approach and attempt to integrate the findings across these research traditions.

It bears mentioning that researchers have examined other aspects of interpersonal compliance interactions. For example, a number of studies have investigated the influence of nonverbal behavior on interpersonal social influence (Buller & Burgoon, 1986; Kleinke, 1980; Willis & Hamm, 1980; Woodall & Burgoon, 1981), while others have explored the use of compliance resisting strategies (McLaughlin, Cody, & Robey, 1980; McQuillen & Higginbotham, 1986). These programs of research, and others like them, are no doubt consistent with the focus of this chapter. However, a review of the entire literature on interpersonal social influence is beyond the scope and mission of this book. Hence, I restrict discussion to the three research traditions described above, as they are representative of the larger body of research on interpersonal compliance.

COMPLIANCE-GAINING MESSAGE SELECTION

The most visible tradition of research investigating interpersonal persuasion has been labeled message selection research. Indeed, well over 40 published articles and convention papers have emerged since 1977 when Miller and his colleagues first applied Marwell and Schmitt's (1967) typology of compliance-gaining strategies to the study of interpersonal communication.

Relying primarily on French and Raven's (1960) review of power and influence literature, Marwell and Schmitt developed a list of 16 compliance-gaining strategies. To examine how people would evaluate each of these strategies, Marwell and Schmitt (1967) created hypothetical scenarios that described a source attempting to gain compliance from a target. For example, in one scenario a father was attempting to persuade his son Dick, to improve his study habits. Marwell and Schmitt developed 16 messages, specific to the hypothetical situation, to reflect each of the 16 compliance-gaining strategies. Research participants read the scenario and rated how likely they would be to use each of the 16 messages to gain compliance from the son described in the hypothetical situation (Table 10.1). Factor analysis of these likelihood-of-use ratings produced five factors. That is, five clusters of messages emerged, which were interpreted as reflecting French and Raven's (1960) five bases of social power. These factors were labeled: Rewarding Activity, Punishing Activity, Expertise, Activation of Interpersonal Commitments, and Activation of Personal Commitments.

A decade later, Miller and his colleagues (1977) adopted this approach and examined the influence of two situational factors on the evaluation of compliance-gaining messages. They created scenarios that varied the type of relationship (interpersonal vs. noninterpersonal) between the source and target of the compliance request and the nature of the consequences (short-term vs. long-term) associated with compliance. For example, a high intimacy, long-term scenario might involve a college senior, considering a new job across the country,

TABLE 10.1. A List of Marwell and Schmitt's (1967) 16 Compliance-Gaining Strategies with Examples from a Hypothetical Compliance Situation

1. Promise

If you comply, I will reward you.
Example: You offer to increase Dick's allowance if he increases his studying.

2. Threat

If you do not comply, I will punish you.
Example: You forbid Dick to use the car if he does not increase his studying.

3. Expertise (Positive)

If you comply, you will be rewarded because of the "nature of things."
Example: You point out to Dick that if he gets good grades he will be able to get into a good college and get a good job.

4. Expertise (Negative)

If you do not comply, you will be punished because of the "nature of things."
Example: You point out to Dick that if he does not get good grades he will not be able to get into a good college or get a good job.

5. Liking

Actor is friendly and helpful to get target in "good frame of mind" before making request.
Example: You try to be as friendly as possible to get Dick in the "right frame of mind" before asking him to study.

6. Pregiving

Actor rewards target before requesting compliance.
Example: You raise Dick's allowance and tell him you now expect him to study.

7. Aversive Stimulation

Actor continuously punishes target, making cessation contingent on compliance.
Example: You forbid Dick to use the car and tell him he will not be able to drive until he studies more.

8. Debt

You owe me compliance because of past favors.
Example: You point out that you have sacrificed and saved for Dick's education and that he owes it to you to get good enough grades to get into a good college.

9. Moral Appeal

You are immoral if you do not comply.
Example: You tell Dick that it is morally wrong for him not to get as good grades as he can and that he should study more.

10. Self-Feeling (Positive)

You will feel better about yourself if you comply.
Example: You tell Dick he will feel proud if he gets himself to study more.

11. Self-Feeling (Negative)

You will feel worse about yourself if you do not comply.
Example: You tell Dick he will feel ashamed of himself if he gets bad grades.

12. Altercasting (Positive)

A person with "good" qualities would comply.
Example: You tell Dick that since he is a mature and intelligent boy he naturally will want to study more and get good grades.

(cont.)

TABLE 10.1. (continued)

13. Altercasting (Negative)	Only a person with "bad" qualities would not comply. *Example:* You tell Dick that only someone very childish does not study as he should.
14. Altruism	I need your compliance very badly, so do it for me. *Example:* You tell Dick that you really want him to get into a good college and that you would like him to study more as a personal favor to you.
15. Esteem (Positive)	People you value will think better of you if you comply. *Example:* You tell Dick that the whole family will be very proud of him if he gets good grades.
16. Esteem (Negative)	People you value will think worse of you if you do not comply. *Example:* You tell Dick that the whole family will be very disappointed in him if he gets poor grades.

Note. From "Dimensions of compliance-gaining behavior: An empirical analysis" by G. Marwell & D. R. Schmitt, 1967, *Sociometry, 30,* 350–364. Copyright 1967 by the American Sociological Association. Reprinted by permission.

attempting to convince a fiancé to relocate with her. In such a situation, the relational commitment reflects a high degree of intimacy, and the decision to move across country is relatively permanent and has long-term consequences. By contrast, a low intimacy, short-term scenario might depict a college student attempting to convince a classmate to join a study group. Miller et al. (1977) conducted a factor analysis of responses to scenarios like these and found different factor structures for each of their four scenarios, suggesting that strategy evaluation was situation specific. That is, they found that different combinations of message strategies were selected for use in each of the four hypothetical situations.

The typology developed by Marwell and Schmitt (1967) and adopted by Miller et al. (1977) was derived deductively from prior theorizing about power and control strategies. It was designed to reflect a range of strategies available to persuaders in interpersonal transactions. However, concerns about the representativeness of this typology fostered the development of an alternative list of compliance-gaining strategies. Operating from a framework that emphasizes the interpretative schemes that people bring to communicative situations, Wiseman and Schenck-Hamlin (1981) provided students with hypothetical influence situations and asked them to generate descriptions of the messages they would send to gain compliance from a person depicted in each scenario. These responses were then evaluated by researchers who codified them into a typology of compliance-gaining strategies (Table 10.2). Based primarily on its inductive rather than deductive derivation, Wiseman and Schenck-

TABLE 10.2. A List of Wiseman and Schenck-Hamlin's (1981) Compliance-Gaining Strategies and Examples of Each Strategy

1. Ingratiation	Actor's offer of goods, sentiments, or services precede the request for compliance. *Example:* "apple polishing" or "brown-nosing"
2. Promise	Actor promises goods, sentiments, or services in exchange for compliance. *Example:* If you comply, I'll help you later.
3. Debt	Actor recalls obligations owed him or her as a way of inducing the target to comply. *Example:* After all I've done for you . . .
4. Esteem	Target's compliance will result in automatic increase of self-worth. *Example:* Just think how good you will feel if you would do this.
5. Allurement	Target's reward arises from persons or conditions other than the actor. *Example:* If you comply, you'll have the respect of your friends.
6. Aversive stimulation	Actor continuously punishes target, making concession contingent on compliance. *Example:* Pouting, acting angry, or giving someone "the silent treatment."
7. Threat	Actor's proposed actions will have negative consequences for the target if he or she does not comply. *Example:* If you won't comply, I don't want to be your friend anymore.
8. Guilt	Target's failure to comply will result in automatic decrease in self-worth. *Example:* If you don't comply, you'll feel irresponsible.
9. Warning	The target's noncompliance could lead to circumstances in which other people become embarrassed, offended, or hurt. *Example:* If you don't comply, you'll make the boss unhappy.
10. Altruism	Actor requests the target to engage in behavior to benefit the actor. *Example:* It would help if you would comply.
11. Direct request	The actor simply asks the target to comply. *Example:* Will you please comply?
12. Explanation	Offer reasons for asking for the compliance. *Example:* I need your compliance because . . .
13. Hinting	Actor represents the situational context in such a way that the target is led to conclude the desired action or response. *Example:* Saying, "It sure is hot in here" rather than asking target to turn down the heat.

(cont.)

TABLE 10.2. (continued)

14. Deceit   Actor requests compliance by intentionally misrepresenting the characteristics of the desired response.
                  Example: Saying, "It's easy" when knowing it is not easy.

Note. From "A multidimensional scaling validation of an inductively-derived set of compliance-gaining strategies" by R. L. Wiseman & W. Schenk-Hamlin, 1981, *Communication Monographs, 48,* 252–270. Copyright 1981 by the Speech Communication Association. Adapted by permission.

Hamlin concluded that their typology was more generalizable, and hence superior, to the typology developed by Marwell and Schmitt.

Wiseman and Schenck-Hamlin's claim about the superiority of their inductively derived typology resides more on their philosophical approach to data collection than any empirical differences observed from the use of these typologies. For example, Boster, Stiff, and Reynolds (1985) found that the structural qualities of these typologies, and people's responses to them, were quite similar. Indeed, cursory inspection of these typologies reveals that the strategies in Wiseman and Schenck-Hamlin's inductively derived list overlap with more than 50% of those in Marwell and Schmitt's list. The complementary nature of these lists caused Boster et al. to conclude that "the 16 Marwell and Schmitt strategies could be combined with the 8 new strategies to form a 24 strategy list" (1985, p. 186).

Though questions about the structure and representativeness of these typologies are likely to remain, researchers have since followed the recommendations of Miller and his colleagues (1977) and examined aspects of compliance-gaining situations that affect people's evaluations of these strategies. Two models have been developed to explain how situational and individual difference factors affect people's likelihood-of-use ratings as they respond to hypothetical compliance situations. These models are described below.

The Expected Utility Model

The first published model in this literature adopted a subjective expected utility framework to explain strategy evaluation (Sillars, 1980). According to Sillars, when deciding whether to use a particular compliance-gaining strategy, people evaluate the acceptability of the strategy. This model posits that the acceptability (A) of any persuasive strategy is a function of the perceived value of compliance (PVC) (i.e., the importance of having the target perform the desired behavior); the perceived value of the relational costs and rewards associated with using a strategy

(*PVC/R*); and the expected probability that the strategy will be successful (*PVS*). These relationships are depicted in Equation 10.1.

$$A = f(PVC, PVC/R, PVS) \qquad (10.1)$$

This model highlights several factors that affect the evaluation of persuasive messages. First, it suggests that situations influence people's judgments about the appropriateness of message strategies such that the more important it is to have the target comply in the situation, the more likely people will find a strategy acceptable for use. The model also recognizes the importance of relational constraints on strategy selection. For example, the relational costs of coercive strategies may be sufficient to cause people in well-developed relationships to eschew coercion in favor of less costly or more rewarding strategies. However, people in less-developed relationships may perceive that there are fewer costs associated with the use of coercive strategies and, thus, may find them acceptable for use to gain compliance. Finally, the model emphasizes a critical feature of strategy evaluation, the likelihood that the strategy will produce compliance. Strategies that hold little promise for successful compliance are unlikely to be selected by persuaders.

To test this model, Sillars (1980) provided research participants with hypothetical scenarios in which the target of compliance was either a spouse or a new neighbor. In addition to standard likelihood-of-use ratings, Sillars asked respondents to rate the advantages and disadvantages of using particular strategies in terms of their persuasiveness and their likely effects on the relationship depicted in the scenario. Regression analyses of these evaluations supported the subjective expected utility framework for most strategies. In general, strategies that were perceived as more persuasive and less likely to adversely affect the relationship were rated as more likely to be used than strategies that were perceived as less persuasive and more costly to the relationship.

Although this model has received limited subsequent attention from persuasion scholars, these same issues were highlighted by Reardon (1981), who suggested that the appropriateness of a persuasive strategy is situationally dependent, and that strategy selection is affected by its perceived appropriateness and effectiveness.

The Ethical Threshold Model

An alternative model of message selection was developed by Hunter and Boster (1978, 1979, 1987). This model evolved out of a critical examination of factor-analytic studies of strategy selection ratings. Several prior investigations explored the dimensions that underlie people's ratings of compliance-gaining strategies. These investigations consistently found multiple dimensions of strategy evaluation.

> Marwell and Schmitt (1967) identify five dimensions, one for each type of interpersonal power (French & Raven, 1960). Miller et al. (1977) report eight dimensions, which they interpret as showing that compliance-gaining messages are chosen largely on situational bases. Kaminski, McDermott, and Boster (1977) report two dimensions, labeled positive message strategies and negative message strategies. Roloff and Barnicott (1978, 1979) report two dimensions, labeled pro-social and anti-social strategies. (Hunter & Boster, 1987, p. 63)

Through a series of complex statistical arguments, Hunter and Boster (1987) demonstrated that the factor-analytic findings of these studies were incorrect. Instead of the multiple dimensions found in prior research, Hunter and Boster argued that likelihood-of-use ratings formed a unidimensional factor model.[1] Evidence for their model came from a reanalysis of likelihood-of-use ratings from several prior studies. The conceptual implication of their reanalysis was that strategies could be arrayed on a single continuum.

Hunter and Boster (1978) argued that positive, prosocial strategies typically receive higher use ratings than negative, antisocial strategies. For example, messages reflecting a positive esteem strategy (i.e., you will feel better about yourself if you comply) should receive higher use ratings than messages that reflect a threatening strategy. Thus, at one end of the strategy continuum are positive, prosocial strategies that receive high use ratings. Anchoring the other end of the continuum are negative, antisocial strategies that receive low use ratings (Figure 10.1).

Hunter and Boster (1978) argued that the dividing point on this continuum is a person's *ethical threshold.* Above the threshold are strategies that persuaders deem acceptable for use in a particular compliance-gaining situation. Strategies residing below the ethical threshold are sufficiently negative that persuaders deem them unacceptable for use to gain compliance. An important feature of this model is that ethical thresholds vary from person to person and situation to situation. Thus, a strategy that may be unacceptable for use in one situation may lie above a person's ethical threshold in another situation. Moreover, strategies that are generally acceptable to one person may be unacceptable to another.

---

[1]Essentially, Hunter and Boster argued that the nonlinear regression of strategy use ratings onto the total strategy use score invalidated the findings of *linear* factor-analytic models. They demonstrated that likelihood-of-use ratings formed a Guttman simplex (1955) and actually reflected a unidimensional factor model.

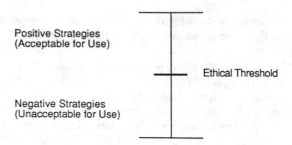

FIGURE 10.1. Ethical threshold continuum.

Given that a person's ethical threshold identifies which strategies are acceptable for use in compliance-gaining situations, an important concern is to identify the situational and individual difference factors that affect a person's ethical threshold. People with low ethical thresholds will rate more strategies as acceptable for use than people with higher ethical thresholds. Operationally, the ethical threshold is defined as the number of strategies a person finds acceptable for use in a particular situation. Hence, factors that affect strategy use determine ethical threshold.

Situational Predictors of Strategy Selection

Several situational factors have been investigated as possible determinants of strategy selection (for reviews, see Boster & Stiff, 1984; Cody & McLaughlin, 1985). Two factors that have received the most attention are the level of relational intimacy between the source and target of the compliance request and the perceived benefits from the compliance.

Relational intimacy has been the focus of many compliance-gaining investigations and perhaps the most accurate summary of these findings is that intimacy is positively correlated with the use of prosocial strategies, but that the size of this relationship is small (Fitzpatrick & Winke, 1979; Miller et al., 1977; Sillars, 1980; Williams & Boster, 1981). That is, relational intimacy may serve to raise a persuader's ethical threshold, but not by much. One explanation for the rather weak relationship between relational intimacy and message selection may be a methodological artifact of the strategy selection paradigm used in many of these studies. Cody and McLaughlin argue that the strategies people recall from nonintimate compliance situations may be qualitatively different than those recalled from intimate compliance-gaining situations (1985, p. 291). If so, then the evaluation of a list of strategies may not fully capture differences in strategy use between naturally occurring intimate and nonintimate compliance situations. Neverthe-less, existing data provide limited support for intimacy as an impor-tant determinant of a persuader's ethical threshold.

A second situational factor that has been the focus of several in-vestigations is *perceived benefit*. Boster and his colleagues (Boster & Stiff, 1984; Williams & Boster, 1981) were among the first researchers to investigate the predictive utility of this factor. They argued that situ-ations vary in the degree to which compliance benefits the persuader and/or target of the compliance-gaining message. For example, if you were trying to convince your roommate to quit smoking, the perceived benefit may be high for your roommate, but moderate or low for your-self. However, if you are asking your roommate for a $100 loan, the situation has considerable benefit for you and no benefit for your roommate.

Research on perceived benefit has produced a consistent pattern of findings (Boster & Stiff, 1984; Williams & Boster, 1981). When per-suaders perceive a situation has benefit for the target, they are more willing to use negative strategies to gain compliance. Moreover, when they perceive the situation has benefit for themselves, persuaders are also more willing to use negative strategies to gain compliance. Thus, both types of perceived benefit serve to lower a persuader's ethical threshold, though the effect of benefit-other appears to be stronger than the effect of benefit-self (Boster & Stiff, 1984). These findings are also consistent with Sillars' (1980) Expected Utility Model, which specifies that the perceived value of gaining the target's compliance affects the evaluation of compliance-gaining strategies.

Personality Predictors of Strategy Selection

In addition to situational factors, Boster and Hunter (1978) argued that individual difference factors may also affect a person's ethical threshold. Two personality factors that have received the most attention are Machiavellianism and dogmatism (for reviews, see Boster & Stiff, 1984; Seibold et al., 1985).

Machiavellianism is a personality construct developed by Christie and Geis (1970) to assess the manner in which people view their inter-actions with others. People with highly Machiavellian belief systems are cynical and believe that most people are unscrupulous. Armed with these negative belief systems, highly Machiavellian people should have lower ethical thresholds and rate more strategies as acceptable for use. Consistent with this hypothesis, several studies found a positive corre-lation between Machiavellianism and strategy selection (Boster & Hun-ter, 1978; Roloff & Barnicott, 1978), although these effects were small in size. Thus Machiavellianism appears to have a small effect on the ethical thresholds of persuaders.

A second personality variable that affects strategy selection is dogmatism. Highly dogmatic people tend to be closed-minded and exhibit limited flexibility in communicative situations. Studies have consistently found small positive relationship between dogmatism and message selection (Roloff & Barnicott, 1979; Williams & Boster, 1981). Like the Machiavellianism construct, dogmatism appears to lower a person's ethical threshold and results in greater selection of compliance-gaining strategies. That is, highly dogmatic people desiring compliance are more willing to use whatever strategies are available to them than less dogmatic people.

Evaluation of Strategy Selection Research

In summary, several studies provide evidence of a unidimensional model of strategy selection. Hunter and Boster (1987) argue that a person's ethical threshold separates strategies that are acceptable from those that are deemed unacceptable for use to gain compliance. Two personality factors, Machiavellianism and dogmatism, and one situational factor, perceived benefit, suggest that ethical thresholds differ across people and situations. Though it has received less attention from persuasion scholars, Sillars' (1980) Expected Utility Model offers an explanation of situational factors that affect the selection of compliance-gaining messages.

Although the models developed by Sillars (1980) and Hunter and Boster (1978, 1987) provided theoretical frameworks for investigating compliance-gaining message selection, limitations of the message selection research paradigm raised concerns about the validity of this line of research. In a recent review of this literature, Miller and his colleagues echoed these concerns and concluded that "most previous research on the selection of compliance-gaining strategies has used procedures that do not capture the interactive nature of compliance gaining" (G. R. Miller, Boster, Roloff, & Seibold, 1987, p. 103).

To support this conclusion, they (G. R. Miller et al., 1987, pp. 103–104) identified several important differences between the hypothetical selection of compliance gaining strategies and strategy use in naturally-occurring compliance transactions:

• First, participants in compliance-gaining studies may be more mindful or reflective about the nature of compliance gaining than are interactants in situated encounters.

• Second, information-processing demands are less formidable for research participants than for actual interactions. Participants in most studies are presented with fixed, static situations rather than dynamic, fluid ones.

•Third, research participants who select and/or compose compliance-gaining strategies may do so relatively unemotionally or may experience feelings unrelated to the communicative context described in the manipulation.

•Fourth, when evaluating lists of alternative strategies, respondents may report a preference for some they would not ordinarily enact.

•Fifth, research participants . . . do not expect to engage in actual persuasive transactions. Absence of anticipated interaction could influence the quality and type of strategy selected.

Though several authors have questioned the external validity of Marwell and Schmitt's (1967) strategy selection research paradigm (Boster et al., 1985; G. R. Miller et al., 1977), scant empirical evidence exists to assess the degree of correspondence between hypothetical message selection and actual message use. In a laboratory study of compliance-gaining behavior, for example, Boster and Stiff (1984) found that two situational variables, perceived benefit for self and other, affected the number of compliance-gaining messages sent by participants. Although these effects for perceived benefit were similar to those in a prior study using the message selection paradigm (cf. Williams & Boster, 1981), Boster and Stiff (1984) failed to find evidence of the complex message strategies identified by Marwell and Schmitt (1967) and Clark (1979). Boster and Stiff (1984) attributed this difference to the restrictiveness of their laboratory procedures and not to problems associated with the strategy typologies.

A subsequent study also failed to find evidence of the external validity of the strategy selection paradigm. Dillard (1988) asked participants to complete the standard message selection questionnaire containing two hypothetical compliance-gaining scenarios involving a spouse, lover, or close friend and the Wiseman and Schenck-Hamlin (1981) list of compliance-gaining strategies. Participants read the scenarios and indicated their willingness to use each strategy to gain compliance. Several weeks later, these same participants came to the lab with their spouse, lover, or friend, and engaged in a role-play situation in which they attempted to gain compliance from their partner. The strategies used in these role-play situations were identified and compared with strategies selected in their questionnaire responses to the hypothetical scenarios. Surprisingly, Dillard (1988) found very little correspondence between the strategies selected in response to the hypothetical compliance scenarios and those used in the role-play situations.

Though far from conclusive, the Boster and Stiff (1984) and Dillard (1988) studies suggest that there is merit to prior concerns about the generalizability of findings from studies using the message selection procedure.

As an alternative to the message selection research paradigm, constructivist researchers adopted message generation procedures to study compliance behavior. Instead of asking respondents to select the strategies they would use in particular situations, constructivist researchers ask respondents to write the types of things they would say to gain compliance in a hypothetical situation. These messages are evaluated and the strategies reflected in them are taken as evidence of compliance strategy use or message generation (e.g., see Clark, 1979; Delia & O'Keefe, 1979). There is evidence that this message generation procedure is more representative of actual compliance behavior than the message selection procedure. For example, Applegate (1982) found that the number of persuasive strategies people generated in response to a hypothetical situation was positively correlated with the number of strategies they employed in face-to-face persuasive situations ($r = .31$). In addition, the level of listener-adapted communication reflected in people's hypothetical messages was correlated with the level of listener-adapted communication in their face-to-face interaction ($r = .67$). Studies such as this (see also Applegate, 1980) provide evidence of the predictive validity of message generation procedures and alleviate some of the limitations inherent in message selection procedures. Nevertheless, the relative utility of message generation versus message production procedures has been the topic of considerable debate (for examples, see Boster, 1988; Burleson & Wilson, 1988; Burleson et al., 1988; Hunter, 1988; Seibold, 1988).

Thus, if message selection procedures do not reflect actual compliance behavior, one must ask: What do these responses reflect? One answer may lie in Hunter and Boster's (1987) suggestion that

> . . . the primary value of compliance-gaining message use judgments may not be as an overt indicator of compliance-gaining behavior. Rather, these responses may provide both a reliable and valid indicator of verbal aggression, argumentativeness, or some other trait. Such traits, in turn, may be predictors of overt compliance-gaining behavior. (p. 82)

However, one must question the utility of such an indirect measure of argumentativeness or verbal aggressiveness when direct measures of both constructs are readily available (see Infante, 1981; Infante & Rancer, 1982; Infante & Wigley, 1986). Instead of a global indication of argumentativeness or verbal aggressiveness, however, it is likely that strategy selection procedures reflect a situated judgment about a person's willingness to be verbally aggressive. That is, while Infante's measures of argumentativeness and verbal aggressiveness reflect a general tendency toward argumentativeness or verbal aggressiveness, message selection procedures may reflect a situationally determined willingness to be argumentative or verbally aggressive.

Whatever utility these perceptual judgments may have for persuasion scholars, they are no substitute for investigations of compliance-gaining behavior in naturally occurring persuasive situations. Indeed, "certain complex compliance gaining strategies (e.g., the bait and switch, low balling, the method of relevant scenarios, etc.) are difficult to put into a questionnaire format" (Boster et al., 1985, p. 186).

Though more than 40 articles and convention papers employing hypothetical compliance-gaining scenarios emerged within a few years of the Miller et al. (1977) investigation, researchers concerned about external validity soon abandoned the message selection paradigm. Recently, the compliance-gaining message selection literature has become a conceptual ghost town, as researchers adopted alternative methods that promised findings with greater correspondence to behavior in naturally-occurring compliance situations.

Two alternative avenues of research provide ample opportunity for scholars of interpersonal influence. One of these research traditions evolved contemporaneously with the message selection/message generation research. Studies of sequential request strategies emerged in social psychology in the mid-1970s and focus on compliance-gaining behavior. Recently, the study of sequential request strategies has captured the attention of communication scholars as well.

SEQUENTIAL REQUEST STRATEGIES

About the same time that Marwell and Schmitt (1967) published their seminal investigation of compliance-gaining message selection, Freedman and Fraser (1966) initiated a program of research on more complex compliance-gaining behavior. Unlike studies that employed hypothetical scenarios to stimulate evaluations of compliance-gaining messages, this line of research examined the effectiveness of complex compliance strategies and emphasized the study of actual compliance behavior. For the most part, studies on compliance-gaining behavior have investigated techniques that employ multiple messages and that are easily applied in everyday persuasive encounters. Three types of sequential request techniques—the foot-in-the-door, the door-in-the-face, and the low-ball techniques—are representative of this body of literature.

The Foot-in-the-Door Technique

In 1966, Freedman and Fraser published their seminal investigation of an influence strategy known as the foot-in-the-door technique (FITD). The FITD requires a persuader to send two sequential messages in order to gain compliance. The first message makes a request that is relatively innocuous and sufficiently small that most targets will agree to it. The second request, which often occurs several days after the initial request, can be made by another person and is much larger than the initial request. Persuaders using the FITD are interested in gaining compliance with the second, larger request. Presumably, persons agreeing to the initial small request will be more willing to comply with the second larger request.

Freedman and Fraser (1966) conducted two studies to assess the effect of compliance with an initial small request on compliance with a second larger request. In Study 1, they canvassed a residential neighborhood in Palo Alto, California and asked housewives if they would answer a brief survey about household products they use. After 3 days, these same housewives (experimental group), along with others who were not contacted during the initial phase of the study (control group), were contacted and asked if they would allow a team of researchers to spend two hours in their home cataloging the types of household products they had in their home. The pattern of compliance with this larger request was remarkable. Of those who agreed to participate in the survey three days earlier, 55% agreed to the larger request to have researchers in their home. Conversely, only 22% of the people who had not received the initial request agreed to the larger request.

In Study 2, Freedman and Fraser asked people to sign a petition or to place a small sign in the front window of their homes. The topic of the petition and sign was either safe driving or a "Keep California Beautiful" campaign. Once again, this initial request was sufficiently small that most people agreed to it (experimental group). Other residences were bypassed during the initial phase of this study. Those who did not receive the initial small request constituted the control group. Different researchers canvassed the neighborhood 2 weeks later and asked these same people if they would be willing to have a large sign promoting safe driving placed in their front yard. Once again, Freedman and Fraser found that those who complied with the initial small request were more likely to comply with the second larger request (54%) than control group subjects who did not receive the initial small request (16%). In both studies, large compliance effects were obtained when subjects were first asked to comply with a small initial request.

The FITD is analogous to a strategy employed by door-to-door salespeople who ask for a glass of water or to come in from the rain before attempting to sell their product. Salespeople in these situations may perceive that getting their persuasive target to do something for them may increase the likelihood that the target will comply with a subsequent request to purchase their product. People using this technique are only concerned with the initial request to the extent that it facilitates compliance with the second larger request.

Evidence for the FITD

Over 40 published articles have examined the FITD since Freedman and Fraser's (1966) seminal investigation. Recently, several meta-analytic reviews synthesized the findings of these studies (Beaman, Cole, Preston, Klentz, & Steblay, 1983; Dillard, 1991; Dillard, Hunter, & Burgoon, 1984; Fern, Monroe, & Avila, 1986). Findings from these reviews painted a consistent picture of the effectiveness of this technique, though each review highlighted separate subgroup analyses.

The overall effect of the FITD on compliance in prior studies was small; average effects range from $r = .09$ to $r = .12$ in the three meta-analyses (Table 10.3). However, subgroup analyses indicated that the FITD is more effective than one might conclude from these overall analyses. For example, two reviews included an analysis of "pure tests" of the FITD. Because the FITD requires an initial request that is sufficiently small that most people will comply with it, researchers have defined "pure tests" of this effect as those studies in which at least 80% of the participants complied with the initial request (Beaman et al., 1983; Fern et al., 1986). Among studies that met this 80% criterion, the FITD was somewhat more effective. The average effect was $r = .14$ in the Beaman et al. study and $r = .21$ in the Fern et al. (1986) study. In addition, Dillard et al. (1984) found that the FITD was only effective when the compliance request was prosocial and when targets were not offered incentives to comply ($r = .16$). In studies where the request was self-oriented or targets were offered incentives for compliance, the FITD effect was trivial.

These subgroup analyses suggest that when certain conditions are met, the FITD is an effective technique for gaining compliance. In summary, when the initial request is small enough to produce compliance from most targets, when the compliance requests are prosocial (vs. self-oriented), and when no incentives are provided for compliance, the FITD should increase compliance rates by about 20%.

TABLE 10.3. Summary of FITD Effects from Meta-Analytic Reviews

	Meta-analytic review		
	Dillard et al. (1984)	Beaman et al. (1983)	Fern et al. (1986)
Overall effect (r)	.11	.12	.09
Number of estimates	37	77	120
Effect from "pure tests" (80%) compliance with initial request	—	.14	.21
Effect from tests using prosocial appeal and no incentive to comply	.16	—	—

Theoretical Basis of the FITD

The most frequently cited theoretical explanation of the FITD effect is Self-Perception Theory (Bem, 1967, 1972). Recall from Chapter 4 of this volume that Bem's theory hypothesized that people look to their own behaviors for evidence of their underlying attitudes and beliefs. Applied to FITD studies, Self-Perception Theory predicts that when people comply with an initial small request, they conclude that their attitude toward the issue or the source of the compliance request must be favorable. After inferring that their attitudes are favorable toward the issue, the requestor, or both, people are more likely to comply with a second larger request.

Though the general pattern of compliance behavior in prior FITD studies is consistent with this interpretation, most studies failed to test directly the self-perception explanation. A recent study by Dillard (1990) is a rare exception. He argued that evidence of a self-perception explanation would be reflected in attitude change following compliance with the first request. He measured general attitudes toward the topic of the compliance request and toward several specific reasons for complying with the request. Analysis of the attitude data revealed that compliance with an initial request to support an environmental organization indicated more favorable attitudes toward the general issue of the environment, but less favorable attitudes toward several specific reasons for compliance (i.e., the source, emotional benefit, and appearances and obligations) (Dillard, 1990).

Dillard (1990) concluded that although a self-inference explanation was a viable account of his findings, the specific predictions of

Self-Perception Theory were not supported. Specifically, neither the size of the initial request nor actual compliance with the initial request (vs. simply agreeing to comply) predicted compliance with the larger second request.

Thus, although self-inference processes account for the attitude data, they were not the specific processes hypothesized by Self-Perception Theory. Dillard's finding that FITD strengthened some attitudes and weakened others suggests that additional theorizing about these self-inference processes may be necessary to fully explain the FITD phenomenon.

The Door-in-the-Face Technique

A companion to the FITD technique is the door-in-the-face technique (DITF). The DITF begins with an initial compliance request that is so large that it is rejected by most targets. After rejection of the initial request, the source proceeds with a second moderate request. The DITF is similar to the FITD in that both techniques are designed to increase compliance with the second of two sequential requests. However, instead of beginning with an initial small request and following it with a second larger request, the DITF begins with a very large initial request. Presumably, people who refuse an initial large request are more likely to comply with the moderate second request than people who only receive the moderate request.

The DITF is analogous to a strategy sometimes employed in negotiation sessions. Negotiators often begin with widely discrepant initial positions and reach consensus through a series of sequential concessions. For example, after college football players are drafted by National Football League (NFL) teams each spring, their agents sit down with team owners and begin contract negotiations. Player agents usually begin the negotiation process with a salary request that is unreasonably high. This request is routinely rejected and player agents respond with a more reasonable second request. Though this request–refusal process may occur several times, the concession made by the player's agent sets up an obligation for the NFL team to reciprocate with a concession of its own. Over time, the two sides reach agreement on the terms of the contract.

Cialdini and his colleagues (1975) were the first to investigate the effectiveness of the DITF. In the first of three studies, they asked some college students if they would be willing to work as counselors to juvenile delinquents for a period of at least two years. None of the students agreed to this initial request. Following their refusal, a second moderate request was made of these students; they were asked to act as chaperons for a group juvenile delinquents on a two-hour trip to the local zoo. Of the students who refused the large initial request, 50% agreed to the moderate second request. Conversely, less than 17% of the people in a control condition, who only received the moderate request, agreed to act as chaperons on the trip to the zoo (Cialdini et al., 1975). In this study, the DITF produced compliance rates that were three times higher than those obtained in the single request condition. Cialdini and his colleagues (1975) reported the findings from two additional studies that found the same patterns of compliance. They argued that the concession reflected in the size of the second smaller request establishes an obligation among targets who refused the initial request to make a concession of their own and agree with the second moderate request. No concession was made to people in the control group. They received a single moderate request and felt little obligation to comply with it.

Evidence of the DITF

Since the seminal investigations by Cialdini and his colleagues, at least 26 published articles have reported investigations of the DITF. Two meta-analytic reviews synthesized the findings of these studies (Dillard et al. 1984; Fern et al., 1986). Findings from these reviews painted a consistent picture of the effectiveness of this technique, though once again each review highlighted separate subgroup analyses. For example, Fern et al. found that the overall correlation between the use of DITF and compliance was small ($r = .07$), but subsequent analysis revealed that the timing of the second request had a significant effect on compliance rates. When there was no delay between refusal of the initial request and the second request, DITF had a positive effect on compliance ($r = .09$). However, when there was a delay between the first and second requests, the DITF technique had a *negative* effect on compliance ($r = -.08$). These findings suggest that the DITF may only be effective when the two requests occur in the same interaction.

The Dillard et al. (1984) review found that two factors maximized the effectiveness of this technique. They too found that the DITF was most effective when there was no delay between the two requests, as well as when the request was prosocial in nature ($r = .15$). When these conditions are met, DITF increases compliance rates by about 17%. However, DITF appears to be ineffective when a source's request is self-oriented, or when there is a delay between a target's refusal of the first request and the subsequent smaller request. Together these reviews provide compelling evidence of the effectiveness of this strategy. Although the overall correlations are small in size, these findings suggest that DITF is a reliable technique for significantly increasing the likelihood of a target's compliance.

Theoretical Basis of the DITF

The primary theoretical explanation of the DITF stems from Gould-ner's (1960) concept of the *norm of reciprocity*. This culturally accept-ed norm suggests that "You should give benefits to those who give you benefits" (Gouldner, 1960, p. 170). Cialdini et al. extended this dis-cussion by identifying the concept of reciprocal concessions, that is, "You should make concessions to those who make concessions to you" (1975, p. 206).

Applied to the DITF phenomenon, this norm suggests that

> . . . two conditions are necessary to activate the normative force that in-creases the likelihood of compliance to the second request . . . (1) the origi-nal appeal must be rejected and . . . (2) the target must perceive a concession on the part of the requestor. (Dillard et al., 1984, p. 464)

In two studies, Cialdini et al. (1975, Study 2 & Study 3) found that the success of the DITF technique requires that targets view the second smaller request as a concession from the source's original posi-tion. Consistent with this requirement, both meta-analytic reviews found that DITF is only effective when the second request follows immedi-ately after a target's refusal of the initial request. Indeed, a long delay between the two requests reduces the connection between the two re-quests and the likelihood that the target will perceive the second re-quest as a concession by the source.

Conceptual Integration of Sequential Compliance Techniques

Given the obvious similarities between these sequential request tech-niques, scholars have sought to find a single theoretical explanation of FITD and DITF phenomena. The separate explanations of the FITD and DITF (described above) are incompatible with one another. For example, Self-Perception Theory, which is frequently invoked to explain FITD, cannot account for the DITF effects. According to Self-Perception Theory, refusal of the initial request should cause targets of the DITF to infer that their attitudes toward the issue or source of the request are unfavorable, decreasing the likelihood of compliance with the second request. Similarly, the norm of reciprocal concessions, which has been invoked to explain the DITF phenomenon, cannot account for the effects of the FITD. Recall that the FITD requires a small initial request that is accepted by a target before a second larger request can be made. However, because no concession is made in the FITD, the norm of reciprocal concessions cannot explain its effectiveness.

Recently, several researchers have attempted to identify a theoretical process that will permit a conceptual integration of these techniques. One such explanation is the *availability hypothesis,* which suggests that availability of favorable information in a person's cognitive framework influences agreement with compliance requests (Tybout, Sternthal, & Calder, 1983). Applied to the FITD effect, the availability hypothesis suggests that compliance with an initial small request increases the amount of favorable information a target has available in memory to guide a response to the second larger request. This increased favorable information increases the likelihood of compliance with the second request. Applied to the DITF effect, the availability hypothesis suggests that the perception of a concession in the source's second smaller request is favorable information that targets use to make decisions about the compliance request. Thus, the greater the perceived concession, the more likely the target is to comply with the second request.

In assessing the viability of this explanation, Dillard (1991) concluded the following:

> Though conceptually elegant and empirically promising in its first tests (Tybout et al., 1983), the availability model does not comport well with the meta-analytic data. Fern et al. (1986) derive several hypotheses that are closely modeled on the reasoning of Tybout et al. (1983) . . . But, by ` my count only three of those seven hypotheses received support . . . In short, despite its hopeful beginning, the information availability perspective does not appear adequate to the task of providing a unified theoretical account of sequential-request phenomena. (p. 286).

Thus far, scholars have been unsuccessful in their search for a unifying theoretical process to explain the FITD and DITF. Although the search continues, it may be time to conclude that, although they are similar, these two sequential request strategies are driven by two theoretically distinct processes.

DITF and FITD are just two examples of sequential-request strategies for gaining compliance. Though these two techniques have received the most interest from persuasion scholars, other sequential-request strategies, such as low-ball procedures (Cialdini, Cacioppo, Bassett, & Miller, 1978), have proven effective for gaining compliance.

The Low-Ball Technique

The *low-ball technique* involves securing compliance from a target and then increasing the cost of performing the behavior by changing the request. The low-ball technique is a staple of salespeople, and it is especially prevalent among new-car dealers (Cialdini et al., 1978). This technique can take a number of forms. For example, new-car dealers often negotiate the price of a new car in combination with an offer to purchase a customer's used car. In these situations, the sales price of the new car may not be very attractive, but a generous offer for the customer's trade-in makes the total cost of purchasing the new car attractive. After the customer agrees to the new car sales price, the salesperson leaves the negotiation to seek a supervisor's approval of deal. Upon returning, the low-ball technique is enacted when the salesperson indicates that he or she has offered too much for the trade-in and that the supervisor has rejected the deal. The salesperson indicates that the company "would lose money" on the original deal and attempts to renegotiate the value of the customer's trade-in car. Typically, customers feel committed to their decision to purchase the new car and accept a lesser amount for the trade-in. Although the price of the new car has not changed, the total cost of the sale may be significantly greater than the original agreement.

Of course, there are a variety of ways to enact the low-ball technique. Several years ago my wife and I decided to buy a convertible sports car with a hard-top option. When we took delivery of the car several weeks later, we were told that the hard-top option had gone up in price. Although we had a written agreement, our salesman wanted us to pay an additional $700 for the car! Indeed, the salesman attempted to use a low-ball technique to increase his profit. He anticipated that after waiting several weeks for the car we would be so anxious to take delivery that we would agree to the price increase, or at least a portion of it. Although it was ultimately unsuccessful, this example reflects the variety of ways that a low-ball technique can be implemented.

Evidence for the Low-Ball Technique

Cialdini and his colleagues (1978) conducted three experiments that provided evidence of the effectiveness of the low-ball technique. In one study, undergraduate students were contacted by phone and asked if they were willing to participate in an experimental study in order to fulfill a requirement for their psychology class. Students in the control condition were told that the experiment was to take place at 7:00 A.M. before they were asked if they wanted to participate. Students in the low-ball condition were asked to participate, and if they said yes, they were told that the experiment was to take place at 7:00 A.M. and asked if they were still willing to participate.

Participants in the low-ball condition agreed to participate significantly more often (56%) than participants in the control condition (31%). More important, the behavioral commitment was similar across the two conditions; 95% of the participants in the low-ball condition and 79% in the control condition who agreed to participate actually showed up at 7:00 A.M. (Cialdini et al., 1978). Cialdini et al. reported the findings of two additional studies providing further evidence of the effectiveness of the low-ball technique.

Theoretical Basis for the Low-Ball Technique

In an attempt to explain the effectiveness of the low-ball technique, Cialdini and his colleagues tested the efficacy of dissonance, self-perception, and commitment explanations. In an experiment designed to separate these effects, Cialdini et al. (1978) found that the notion of *psychological commitment* was the most viable explanation for this effect. According to Kiseler (1971) commitment to a decision makes the decision more resistant to change. Applied to the low-ball technique, this formulation posits that once people agree to a request, they feel committed to their decision and are less likely to change it, even if the nature of the request changes. Applied in automobile sales situations, this explanation suggests that once people become psychologically committed to purchasing a car, they are unlikely to change their minds, even if the ultimate cost of the car is more than they originally agreed to pay.

I only applied the low-ball technique to automobile sales situations, but this technique has proven to be quite effective across a variety of compliance settings. There are similarities between the FITD and the low-ball technique, but Cialdini et al. (1978) drew important conceptual and empirical distinctions between these two sequential request strategies. Although the technical aspects and theoretical foundations of the FITD, DITF, and low-ball procedures differ, these techniques all reflect the influence that sequential compliance requests can have on the behavior of persuasive targets.

STUDIES OF COMPLIANCE-GAINING MESSAGE PRODUCTION

The contemporaneous research traditions of compliance-gaining message selection and compliance-gaining behavior provided useful knowledge about how people evaluate and effectively employ strategies for gaining compliance in interpersonal situations. Although these research traditions have been informative on the issues of message evaluation and effectiveness, they have offered little information about factors that affect the production of compliance messages. Recently, communication scholars have turned their attention toward understanding how these messages are produced. A discussion of the emerging tradition of research on message production is the focus of the remainder of this chapter.

Investigations of message production have examined how people form persuasive goals (Dillard, Segrin, & Hardin, 1989; B. J. O'Keefe & Shepherd, 1987; S. R. Wilson, 1990), what the effects of these persuasive goals are (Dillard et al., 1989), and how the functions of communication (B. J. O'Keefe, 1988, 1990; B. J. O'Keefe & McCornack, 1987) produce interpersonal influence messages. Each of these lines of research are examined below.

Multiple Goals in Interpersonal Influence

Much of the research on message production has been guided by a cognitive theoretical framework. This framework posits that people in interpersonal influence situations develop interaction goals, which lead to planning and selection of message strategies. Once developed, these plans are implemented as persuasive message appeals (Dillard, 1989). Because message production processes appear to be guided by the goals of persuaders, knowledge of how these goals are developed is essential to our understanding of the message production process.

Goal Formation

A Cognitive Rules Model has recently been introduced to describe the formation of interaction goals (S. R. Wilson, 1990). This model proposes that people possess cognitive rules for developing goals. These rules are stored in memory and are activated when there is a "match between the perceived features of the situation and the situational conditions represented in the rule" (S. R. Wilson, 1990, p. 82). The accessibility of a cognitive rule and its fit with the persuasive situation affect the production of persuasive goals. For example, S. R. Wilson found that "people were more willing to form supporting goals if a situational feature associated with those goals recently had been activated, making the relevant cognitive rules accessible" (1990, p. 97). The activation process described in the Cognitive Rules Model depicts people as parallel information processors. This suggests that rules for forming multiple persuasive goals can be simultaneously activated.

There are a number of different persuasive goals people bring to compliance situations (for descriptions, see Dillard, 1989; Rule, Bisanz, & Kohn, 1985). For example, a compliance situation may involve providing advice, asking a favor, or obtaining information. Communication scholars agree that people routinely form and manage multiple goals in persuasive situations. "In interpersonal influence attempts, the desire to bring about behavioral change in a target person is the primary goal" (Dillard et al., 1989, p. 20). However, other subsidiary goals, such as relational maintenance and impression management, are also apparent in interpersonal influence situations. Perhaps the best evidence of these secondary goals is the fact that people often avoid using coercive influence strategies, especially when more socially desirable strategies are judged to be equally effective. If these secondary goals did not exist, then people would routinely use the most forceful compliance strategy available to them, regardless of its impact on the target or reflection on the source.

Goal Identification

Studies conducted by Dillard et al. (1989) provide compelling evidence of primary and secondary goals in interpersonal influence situations. In one study they presented students with hypothetical compliance-gaining situations and Wiseman and Schenck-Hamlin's (1981) list of compliance-gaining strategies. These students were asked to imagine themselves in the compliance situation, indicate whether or not they would use each strategy in the situation, and provide a written justification for each decision. These written justifications were content analyzed and provided the basis for establishing the goals that determine strategy use.

This analysis revealed one primary and four secondary goals that were reflected in people's reasons for rejecting a message strategy (Table 10.4) (Dillard et al., 1989). The primary goal, *influence,* was the most frequently cited justification for message selection (44% of all justifications). However, four secondary goals—*identity, interaction, resource,* and *arousal,* were also reflected in the justifications people offered for their strategy selection. *Identity* goals reflect concerns about a person's internal moral standards and appeared in 34% of the justifications offered by respondents. *Interaction* goals reflect concerns about social appropriateness and impression management. These goals were present in 9% of the justifications. *Resource* goals are revealed through concerns about relational and personal costs/rewards associated with the compliance attempt. For example, threatening strategies may be avoided because they may damage the relationship and are incompatible with the resource goal of relational maintenance. These goals were apparent in 5% of the justifications. *Arousal* was the final secondary goal and was least frequently cited (1%) as a reason for not selecting particular compliance gaining strategies. In a second study, Dillard and his colleagues (1989) developed and validated self-report measures for each of these primary and secondary goals.

Goal Management

Primary and secondary goals are often incompatible with one another. In many influence situations, management of these competing goals requires the use of complex tactics that enable sources to gain compliance without harming themselves or their relationships. In this regard, the management of multiple goals reflects Sillars's (1980) concern about the perceived value of the relational costs and rewards associated with strategy use.

B. J. O'Keefe and Shepherd (1987) describe three strategies people use to manage the conflict created by incompatible primary and secondary goals. Their first goal management strategy, *selection,* allows people

TABLE 10.4. Justifications for Rejecting Message Strategies

Goal category	Frequency	Proportion	Exemplar statements
Influence	865	44%	It won't work. It's irrelevant.
Identity	672	34%	It's immoral. Not my style.
Interaction	180	9%	That would make me look bad. This is inappropriate for the situation.
Resource	98	5%	This would cost me our friendship.
Arousal	8	1%	This would make me apprehensive. Makes me too nervous.
Uncodable	136	7%	This is stupid. You must be kidding.
Total	1,959	100%	

Note. From "Primary and secondary goals in the production of interpersonal influence messages" by J. P. Dillard, C. Segrin, & J. M. Hardin, 1989, *Communication Monographs,* 56, 19–38. Copyright 1989 by the Speech Communication Association. Reprinted by permission.

to resolve this conflict by choosing between the conflicting goals. Applying the Dillard et al. (1989) distinction between primary and secondary goals, the selection strategy requires people to assign priority to either the primary goal of influence or to subsidiary goals such as relational maintenance and identity management. For example, if you wish to collect an overdue $50 loan from your roommate, your primary goal may be to reclaim the unpaid money. However, secondary goals of relational maintenance (you have to live with this person) and identity management (you don't want to appear cheap or petty) may affect the nature of your compliance request. To manage the apparent conflict between the primary and secondary goals you might adopt the selection strategy and give priority to either the primary or secondary goals. If priority is given to the primary goal you might produce a compliance message that reflects little concern about your own image or your relationship with your roommate, for example, "You still haven't repaid the $50 loan I gave you, and I want the money today." However, maintaining a favorable relationship with your roommate may be a higher priority than reclaiming the money you are owed. If priority is given to the secondary goals of relational maintenance and identity management, you might construct a more tactful message, even if it is less likely to cause your roommate to repay the loan, for example, "Did you repay the $50 I loaned you?"

The second strategy for managing conflicting goals is *separation*. O'Keefe and Shepherd argue that a separation strategy results in compliance messages that place priority on the primary goal and then address the secondary goals by elaborating messages with phrases that are designed to account for, minimize, or repair the negative characteristics of the primary message (1987, p. 401). Applied to the hypothetical loan situation, a separation strategy might involve a direct, forceful request to achieve the primary goal of loan repayment and another statement or phrase that explains why the money is important to you, for example, "You haven't repaid the $50 I loaned you and I need the money today. I'm sorry about being so direct, but I don't get paid until next week and I really need the money."

Integration is a third strategy for managing competing goals. Integration strategies resolve the competing demands of primary and secondary goals by redefining the persuasive situation (O'Keefe & Shepherd, 1987). Returning again to the hypothetical loan scenario, an integrative strategy might cause you to generate a message that redefines the loan obligation as a willingness for roommates to help one another. Such a message might permit you to request payment of the loan from your roommate without threatening the relationship, for example, "I am happy that we have the type of friendship that allows us to ask each other for help when we need it. And right now, I really need to ask for the $50 I loaned you a couple week ago. You see, I'm short on cash and don't get paid until next week."

In a study examining the use of these goal management strategies, B. J. O'Keefe and Shepherd found that the frequency of strategy use was unrelated to persuasive outcomes. However, greater use of integration strategies was associated with interpersonal success ratings. The more people used a integration management strategy, the more they were liked and perceived as competent by their interaction partners (1987, p. 415). These findings, and others like them (Bingham & Burleson, 1989; B. J. O'Keefe & McCornack, 1987) suggest that although the three goal management strategies may be equally effective for achieving the primary persuasive goal, use of an integration goal management strategy appears most effective for achieving secondary goals such as identity management and relational maintenance.

Goals and Persuasive Message Production

In an effort to link primary and secondary goals with the production of persuasive messages, Dillard and his colleagues asked research participants to recall and describe a recent interaction in which they attempted to influence someone with whom they were well acquainted. Participants were also asked to indicate how much planning and effort was involved in their influence attempt (Dillard et al., 1989, Study 3). Trained coders evaluated these influence descriptions to determine the level of directness, positiveness, and logic reflected in them. Participants also responded to measures of primary and secondary goals in influence situations (Dillard et al., 1989, Study 2). These scales assessed the influence, identity, interaction, relational resource, and arousal goals that people bring to interpersonal influence situations.

The goals that people reported in these influence situations were related to the characteristics of the messages they produced. Respondent concerns with primary goal of influence were positively related to their level of planning ($\beta = .29$), and effort ($\beta = .55$) of persuasive messages, as well as the logic and reasoning reflected in them ($\beta = .28$).[2] In addition, secondary goals were associated with planning and characteristics of persuasive messages. Identity goals were positively associated with both the level of planning ($\beta = .13$) and logic ($\beta = .15$), and negatively related to the directness of the message ($\beta = -.17$).

[2]Standardized beta-weights (β) are regression coefficients that reflect the relationship between an independent variable and a dependent variable, controlling for the effects of all other independent variables in the regression equation.

Interaction goals were positively related to planning ($\beta = .19$) and the level of positivity in the message ($\beta = .31$). Relational resource goals were positively associated with message positivity ($\beta = .22$). Finally, concerns about arousal management were negatively related to the directness ($\beta = -.14$), positivity ($\beta = -.24$), and logic ($\beta = -.19$) of message appeals.

The overall pattern of effects in these findings suggests an important relationship between goals and message production. The strongest relationships were observed between the primary goal, influence, and message production. However, significant relationships were also observed between secondary goals and characteristics of the persuasive messages. In addition, some goals created negative effects on message characteristics whereas other goals created positive effects, a finding that underscores the problem of goal management and the complexity of interpersonal influence attempts. For example, identity and interaction goals were positively associated with message positivity, but arousal management goals were negatively related with message positivity. Also, the primary goal of influence was positively associated with the logic of message appeals, but arousal management was negatively associated with message logic. Dillard and his colleagues (1989) offered the following conclusion about the influence of primary and secondary goals on message production:

> . . . the primary goal serves to initiate and maintain the social action, while the secondary goals act as a set of boundaries which delimit the verbal choices available to sources. (p. 32)

Message Design Logics and Message Production

In contrast with the cognitive rules and planning approach to message production, B. J. O'Keefe has introduced an alternative description of the message production process. Message production research based on rational goals analysis implies that people with similar goals will produce and enact similar persuasive messages. However, the findings of prior studies also suggest that differences exist among the messages produced by people holding similar interaction goals. To explain these effects, B. J. O'Keefe (1988) introduced the concept of *message design logics,* which reflect differences in fundamental premises people have about the nature and function of communication. Differences in these belief systems are reflected in three separate message design logics.

Expressive Design Logics

The most simple design logic one can possess is based on the premise that "language is a medium for expressing thoughts and feelings"

(B. J. O'Keefe, 1988, p. 84). People using this design logic fail to separate their thoughts and feelings from the messages they produce. These people are described as "dumpers" who openly express their thoughts and feelings and assume that others interact in the same fashion (B. J. O'Keefe, 1990).

Conventional Design Logics

People adopting conventional design logics view "communication as a game that is to be played cooperatively, according to socially conventional rules and procedures" (B. J. O'Keefe, 1988, p. 86). Conventional design logics view situational characteristics of communicative situations as fixed parameters that define rules of appropriate interaction.

Rhetorical Design Logics

People employing rhetorical design logics view communication as the "creation and negotiation of social selves and situations" (B. J. O'Keefe, 1988, p. 87). The primary function of messages is negotiation of a consensus about the social reality people find themselves in. Rather than reacting to prior situations, or viewing the situation as a fixed set of parameters, rhetoricals attempt to define the situation in a manner that is beneficial to the achievement of their goals.

Design Logics and Message Production

B. J. O'Keefe argues that these three design logics can be ordered on a developmental continuum. The expressive design logic is viewed as the least developed, while the rhetorical design logic is viewed as most cognitively developed. Using this developmental ranking, O'Keefe and McCornack (1987) assessed perceptions people have of messages that reflect these design logics. Their research participants rated messages with a rhetorical message design logic as more favorable and potentially more persuasive than messages that reflected conventional and expressive design logics. However, a subsequent study found that although messages with rhetorical design logics were perceived as more communicatively competent, they were not perceived as more effective than messages reflecting conventional and expressive design logics (Bingham & Burleson, 1989).

Together, these findings provide support for the preferential status given to rhetorical design logics. Presumably, people who employ these logics are likely to be judged as more competent communicators than people who use conventional and expressive design logics. These findings also suggest that persuaders who employ rhetorical design logics *may* be more influential in some persuasive situations.

Although these findings hold promise for the concept of message design logics, participants in all of these investigations were undergraduate students enrolled in communication courses. It should come as little surprise that students enrolled in courses designed to improve communication skills would perceive polished messages reflecting a rhetorical design logic to be more competent, satisfying, and successful than less developed messages indicative of an expressive design logic. Members of different social, cultural, and economic communities may place a higher value on messages that are more direct expressions of feelings and values. In other words, the perceptions of college students may differ considerably from the perceptions of people in other walks of life. Clearly, additional research on the robustness of these findings and the effects of message design logics is warranted.

SUMMARY

This chapter reviewed three distinct traditions of research on interpersonal influence. The compliance-gaining message selection research examined situational and personality factors that affect the ways in which people evaluate strategies for gaining compliance. Though few studies in this tradition examined communicative behavior, these studies provided a framework for understanding how people approach persuasive situations. A second tradition of research on interpersonal influence paralleled the growth of the message selection tradition. Studies of compliance-gaining behavior focused on the relative effectiveness of sequential request strategies for gaining compliance. Finally, an emerging tradition of research on message production has sought to examine factors that affect the production and implementation of persuasive message strategies. Though preliminary, these investigations suggest that people in similar situations are likely to differ in the goals they form and the messages they enact to achieve their persuasive objectives.

Models of Mass Media Influence

L OOKING AHEAD . . .

This chapter reviews three theories of persuasion that can effectively serve as the foundation for persuasion campaigns to affect political, health, and social behavior. The first theory I review is McGuire's (1964) Inoculation Theory, which has provided the foundation for political campaigns. Next, I discuss the implications of Social Learning Theory (Akers, Krohn, Lanza-Kaduci, & Radosevich, 1979; Bandura, 1977), which has been used to mold prosocial behavior in adolescents. Finally, I review the Health Belief Model (Becker, 1974), which explains the health behaviors of individuals and has been applied in health promotion campaigns.

During the past 30 years, the mass media, and television in particular, have become an essential conduit for the communicative messages of broad-based persuasive campaigns. Not long ago, voters relied on party labels for help in making their voting decisions. However, the nature of national politics has undergone dramatic change and party labels are not as informative or influential as they once were. In recent elections many voters "crossed over" and cast ballots for the nominee of an opposition party. This trend is evidenced by the label "Reagan Democrats;" which was developed to identify Democrats who voted for Reagan in the 1980 and 1984 elections. As the influence of political parties has declined, campaign organizations have found they are unable to communicate with voters without relying on the media (Arterton, 1984, p. 9). For example, Ross Perot's 1992 campaign for the

229

presidency involved very few personal appearances or speeches before live audiences. Instead, he relied on television newscasts, talk shows, and paid commercial announcements to explain his economic proposals to American voters.

Health promotion campaigns have found the mass media to be equally effective for persuasion. Antismoking, AIDS education, and driver safety campaigns routinely involve the heavy use of mass media to disseminate information and motivational messages. Slogans such as "AIDS: What you don't know can kill you" and "Don't drink and drive" have become etched in our memories as we have been repeatedly exposed to them over the course of several years.

Social influence campaigns are familiar to mass media consumers and persuasion scholars alike. Beginning with the propaganda research of the 1940s, persuasion research has examined the effectiveness of several theories that have been applied in mass media campaigns. In this chapter I describe three of these theories and examine their effectiveness in media campaigns. Although they are not "mass media" models, per se, each of these theories has been effectively employed in mediated persuasion campaigns.

INOCULATION THEORY

In the early 1960s, William McGuire developed a program of research that investigated resistance to persuasive messages. He was interested in understanding the psychological and cognitive processes that affect a person's willingness and motivation to resist arguments that attack widely held beliefs. McGuire called these types of beliefs *cultural truisms* because they are rarely challenged or given much thought.

A Biological Metaphor

McGuire (1961a, 1961b, 1964) described a technique for inducing resistance to persuasive attacks against cultural truisms. Inoculation Theory posits that promoting resistance to persuasion is analogous to inoculating the body against a virus. When people are inoculated against a virus, such as smallpox or the flu, the vaccine they receive contains a weak dosage of the virus. In response to the inoculation, the body's immune system creates antibodies to fight the virus. If the body's immune system is functioning properly, it will produce more than enough antibodies to kill the weak virus, leaving a reserve to resist any massive virus that may later attack the body.

Applied in persuasive situations, the inoculation metaphor suggests that because cultural truisms are widely believed they are rarely scrutinized or given much attention. Such beliefs are often vulnerable to persuasive attacks because people "have had little motivation or practice in developing supporting arguments to bolster [them] or in preparing refutations for the unsuspected counterarguments" (McGuire & Papageorgis, 1961, p. 327). McGuire's inoculation technique was designed to prepare people to resist attacks against cultural truisms. Similar to the biological process of inoculation, inoculation against persuasive arguments involves presenting people with weak arguments against a cultural belief and allowing them to develop arguments to refute these attacks. McGuire and Papageorgis proposed that "the 'supportive therapy' approach of pre-exposing a person to arguments in support of [a] belief has less immunizing effectiveness than the 'inoculation' procedure of pre-exposing them to weakened, defense stimulating forms of the counterarguments" (1961, p. 327). Presumably, after receiving weak counterarguments and developing a refutational defense of the cultural truism, people are better able and motivated to counterargue future attacks of their belief systems.

Persuasive Inoculation

The basic procedure for inoculating people against persuasive attacks involves providing them with an attack message containing weak arguments that opposes a particular belief. People are then given the opportunity to generate arguments to refute the arguments contained in the attack message. Sometimes, inoculation procedures involve presenting people with the refutational arguments (passive refutation) instead of asking them to generate their own refutational arguments (active refutation). For example, if you wanted to inoculate school children against likely persuasive appeals to try drugs, you might present them with a series of weak arguments supporting drug use, and then ask them to write an essay (active refutation) refuting the arguments advocating drug use that they had just heard. You could also inoculate students by presenting them with a weak message advocating drug use and then asking them to read a second message that refuted the arguments advocating drug use (passive refutation).

Once the inoculation procedure has been performed, people should be less susceptible to future arguments attacking their beliefs than people who do not receive the inoculation procedure. To test the effectiveness of this technique, researchers usually conduct an experiment in which an inoculation treatment (attack message followed by refutation message) is presented to people in the experimental group, while people in the control condition receive either a supportive message, or no message at all. After receiving these initial messages, people in the experimental and control groups are exposed to a message that attacks their beliefs about the issue in question. Following this second message, the attitudes or beliefs of experimental and control group participants are measured. If the attitudes or beliefs about the issue in question are more favorable among the experimental group than the control group, then the inoculation treatment is deemed effective for promoting resistance to a persuasive attack. Extending the example of promoting resistance to drugs, if children who receive the inoculation treatment are better able to resist subsequent invitations to use drugs than children who do not receive the inoculation treatment, then we can conclude that the inoculation treatment was effective.

Supporting Evidence

In an initial test of this technique, McGuire and Papageorgis (1961) examined beliefs about a number of cultural truisms such as, "Everyone should brush his [sic] teeth after every meal if possible," and "The effects of penicillin have been, almost without exception, of great benefit to mankind." For one belief, participants either read or generated a message supporting the belief statement (supportive message condition). For a second belief, participants read a weak attack against the belief statement and were asked to read (passive refutation condition) or write (active refutation condition) a message that refuted the attack on their belief.

Two days after these initial treatments, participants read essays that attacked the positions they had defended in the prior experimental session. After reading the essays, participants indicated the extent to which the belief statement was true or false. Findings revealed that the inoculation treatment was more effective than the supportive message in promoting resistance to persuasion. People who received the supportive message treatment, followed by the persuasive attack, were uncertain about whether the belief statement was true or false. However, when they received the inoculation treatment, people were more resistant to the subsequent persuasive attack and indicated greater agreement that the belief in question was true. In addition, McGuire and Papageorgis (1961) compared active and passive refutation inoculation procedures. When people read the refutational statement they were more resistant to subsequent persuasive attacks than when they generated their own refutational arguments. One explanation for this finding may be that students in this study had difficulty developing refutational arguments that were as strong as the arguments created by the experimenter in the passive refutation condition.

In addition to offering further evidence of the effectiveness of this technique (McGuire, 1961a), subsequent studies have extended the influence of inoculation treatments. For example, the combination of supportive and refutational treatments has been found to produce more resistance to persuasive attacks than the refutational treatment alone (McGuire, 1961b). In addition to promoting resistance to attacks against the cultural belief that was the focus of the inoculation treatment, Papageorgis and McGuire (1961) found that inoculation procedures also enhanced resistance to other, related beliefs.

In recent years, Inoculation Theory has been employed to promote resistance to beliefs that are not culturally accepted. However, a recent review of the literature concluded that inoculation treatments appear to be less effective for controversial topics than they are for cultural truisms (O'Keefe, 1990). Pfau (1992) argued that one difference between traditional inoculation studies and more recent investigations of supportive and refutational messages that involve more controversial topics is that traditional inoculation studies involved the use of *threat,* which is required for successful inoculation. He and his colleagues argued that "inoculation promotes resistance through the use of the impending attack, *employed in conjunction with* refutational preemption. The warning of an impending attack is designed to threaten the individual, triggering the motivation to bolster arguments supporting attitudes" (Pfau, Kenski, Nitz, & Sorenson, 1990, p. 28). Message treatments that do not threaten a person's belief system are unlikely to motivate people to generate arguments against the attack. Thus, the relatively small differences between supportive and refutational messages in many recent investigations may be due to the fact that the refutational messages in these studies failed to threaten the belief systems of message receivers.

Application of Inoculation Theory

Although most investigations of Inoculation Theory have been conducted in laboratory environments, inoculation treatments have recently become a central component in many naturally occurring persuasive campaigns. Extending the analysis that threat is an essential feature of effective inoculation treatments, Pfau and his colleagues have revitalized interest in Inoculation Theory by examining the effectiveness of inoculation treatments in political campaigns (Pfau & Burgoon, 1988; Pfau & Kenski, 1990; Pfau, Kenski, Nitz, & Sorenson, 1990), comparative advertising (Pfau, 1992), and campaigns designed to prevent the onset of smoking among adolescents (Pfau, Van Bockern, & Kang, 1992). In this section I examine how Inoculation Theory has been employed effectively in political and public health campaigns.

Inoculation against Political Attacks

Recent political campaigns for national, state, and local offices have become increasingly negative. Political campaigns must provide reasons for voting for a particular candidate, but they must also present reasons for voting against the opponent. As a result, the negative campaign, or attack politics, has become an essential feature of many campaign operations (Devlin, 1987, p. 7). Pfau and Kenski (1990) offer several reasons for the increased use of negative campaign advertising. For example, negative messages can be more influential than supportive messages. Negative messages are also cheaper to produce and can be aired effectively on radio, a low-cost medium. In addition, negative messages are often viewed as a counterweight against the influence of incumbency (p. 4).

The rapid growth of attack politics has sent candidates and campaign coordinators scrambling for effective defenses against negative campaign messages. Inoculation techniques provide an effective means for defending against the attacks of political candidates. Effective inoculation messages in political campaigns have two essential components. First, they must contain a preemptive refutation. That is, they must respond in advance to counterarguments that an opponent is likely to produce. Second, inoculation messages must contain a threat, a warning that an opponent is likely to launch a persuasive attack. The threat of an impending attack serves to motivate receivers to defend against the persuasive attack. Thus, effective inoculation (refutational) pretreatments warn of an impending threat which motivates receivers to develop arguments to bolster their position against subsequent attacks of their candidate (Pfau & Kenski, 1990, p. 75).

Two studies provide evidence of the effectiveness of inoculation techniques in political campaigns. A study of attitudes toward Bush and Dukakis in the 1988 presidential campaign involved direct mailing of political campaign messages and interview procedures to measure candidate preferences and voting intentions (Pfau et al., 1992). Three experimental conditions were created. Several days after responding to a telephone survey about their voting preferences, Bush and Dukakis supporters in the *inoculation condition* received an inoculation message in the mail. These messages warned that potentially persuasive attacks of their candidate were likely (threat component) and provided a refutation to these attacks (refutational component).

People in the *inoculation-plus-reinforcement condition* responded to the telephone survey, received an inoculation message, and a week later received another mailing that reinforced their candidate preference. Finally, people in the *post-hoc-refutation condition* responded to the telephone survey and later received a message that attacked the candidate they supported. A week later, these people were mailed a refutational message that responded to attacks against their candidate. Because this refutation occurred after the original attack message, it was labeled a *post-hoc* refutation.

Several days after the reinforcement and post-hoc refutations were mailed, researchers conducted interviews in the homes of the research participants. During these interviews, people in the inoculation and inoculation-plus-reinforcement conditions were presented with a message that attacked their candidate's position. Following this, participants completed a survey of their attitudes toward the candidate and indicated their likelihood of voting for the candidate. People in the post-hoc refutation condition had already received the attack message in the mail. These participants simply completed the attitude and voting preference survey.

Although party affiliation and treatment conditions interacted to affect posttest attitude and voting intentions, the general pattern of findings indicated strong support for the inoculation techniques. The effects for people with weak party affiliations were somewhat mixed, but the effects among people who clearly identified with one of the two political parties and among those with no party affiliation were consistently clear: The inoculation and inoculation-plus-reinforcement treatments were superior in deflecting the influence of an attack message to the post-hoc refutation treatment (Pfau et al., 1992).

A similar study found additional evidence of the effectiveness of inoculation treatments. Studying a campaign for a U.S. Senate seat, Pfau and Burgoon (1988) found that inoculation treatments increased resistance to attitude change following a persuasive attack. In discussing the implications of their findings, they concluded that,

> . . . inoculation deflects the persuasiveness of subsequent political attacks in a number of ways: undermining the potential influence of the source of political attacks, deflecting the specific content of political attacks, and reducing the likelihood that political attacks will influence receiver voting intention. (Pfau & Burgoon, 1988, pp. 105–106)

Inoculation against Smoking

Based on the success of these earlier studies, Pfau and colleagues (1992) endeavored to study this technique's effectiveness in adolescent smoking prevention programs. Students in 7th-grade health education classes were exposed to a videotaped message that was designed to help them resist peer pressure to smoke.

Consistent with other applications of Inoculation Theory, Pfau and his colleagues found that inoculation treatments were effective; however, these effects were limited to students with low self-esteem. Among low self-esteem adolescents, the inoculation pretreatment videos were effective, because they helped maintain negative attitudes toward smoking and increased the likelihood that a student would resist smoking (Pfau et al., 1992, p. 226). It is interesting that inoculation pretreatments were ineffective in promoting resistance among lower risk students with higher levels of self-esteem.

Summarizing Inoculation Findings

Early investigations of Inoculation Theory conducted by McGuire and his colleagues demonstrated the effectiveness of inoculation treatments in promoting resistance to persuasion. These investigations occurred in controlled laboratory settings and involved the use of cultural truisms, issues that are so widely believed that they are rarely questioned (e.g., "capitalism is good" or "patriotism is important"). Recently, inoculation treatments have also proved effective in promoting resistance to persuasion in naturally occurring persuasive campaigns. Applied in political, advertising, and public health campaigns, Pfau and his colleagues demonstrated that inoculation treatments that warn of an impending persuasive attack motivate receivers to resist a subsequent persuasive appeal. The breadth of this theory is evident in the variety of mass media persuasive campaigns that have effectively employed inoculation treatments.

SOCIAL LEARNING THEORY

"Social (or observational) Learning Theory is not specifically an account of learning from exposure to mass communication, but rather, is a general explanation of how people acquire new forms of behavior" (DeFleur & Ball-Rokeach, 1989, p. 212). Thus, like Inoculation Theory, Social Learning Theory (Bandura, 1977) was not developed as a mass media model of persuasion. Instead, it was developed as a general model of behavior acquisition and was subsequently applied in mass media campaigns.

Nevertheless, Social Learning Theory has been particularly relevant to the study of social influence via the mass media. Bandura noted that, "An influential source of social learning is the abundant and varied symbolic modeling provided by television, films, and other visual media" (1977, p. 39). Indeed, Social Learning Theory has become a staple of drug resistance and drunk driving campaigns. I begin the discussion of this theory by describing its major assumptions. After this, I examine tests of the theory and describe persuasive campaigns in which it has been effectively applied.

Social Learning

Before discussing the application of this theory in social influence campaigns, it is important to understand the fundamental assumptions of the theory and the predictions it makes about learning behavior. Most learning theories posit that behavior acquisition or change is a function of positive reinforcements that are provided when a desired behavior is produced and punishments that are experienced following undesirable behavior. Humans and animals learn behavior through the association of positive reinforcements with particular behaviors. For example, when parents teach their children to read, they routinely provide verbal praise when a word or phrase is properly pronounced. When a word or phrase is incorrectly pronounced, the error is noted and assistance is provided to help the child pronounce it correctly. Over time, the child learns the correct pronunciation because it has been associated with positive reinforcement. This learning process takes time and occurs "over a number of 'trials' in which the link between the stimuli and the response to be learned is reinforced" (DeFleur & Ball-Rokeach, 1989, p. 216).

Social Learning Theory (Bandura, 1977) differs from other learning theories in that it emphasizes the capacity of humans to learn through observation, instead of through direct experience of the positive and negative outcomes of trial and error.

> Observational learning is vital for both development and survival. Because mistakes can produce costly, or even fatal consequences, the prospects for survival would be slim indeed if one could learn only by suffering the consequences of trial and error. For this reason, one does not teach children to swim, adolescents to drive automobiles, and novice medical students to perform surgery by having them discover the appropriate behavior through the consequences of their successes and failures. The more costly and hazardous the possible mistakes, the heavier is the reliance on observational learning from competent examples. (Bandura, 1977, p. 12)

In addition to the advantages of observational learning over trial and error experience, some behaviors cannot be learned through trial and error alone. For example, a child's language acquisition and development is facilitated by adults and older children who constantly provide a model of developed communicative behavior for children to mimic. In other cases, observational learning provides the benefit of experience that cannot be acquired through trial and error. Though more rudimentary modes of learning are rooted in the positive and negative effects that behaviors produce, high-risk activities such as sky diving and bungee cord jumping may not afford participants the chance to recover from the negative effect of an error. In this regard, Social Learning Theory is tailor-made for persuasive campaigns that promote resistance to high-risk behaviors such as drug use and drunk driving.

Social Learning and Social Influence

The fundamental assumption of Social Learning Theory is that by observing others, people form an idea of how new behaviors are performed, and on later occasions this information serves as a guide for their own behavior (Bandura, 1977, p. 22). Observing the positive and negative consequences of a model's behavior serves several functions in the social learning process. First, this observation provides information about the consequences that are associated with particular behaviors. Thus, the *information function* allows people to develop and test hypotheses about which responses are most appropriate and most likely to be rewarded in particular situations. Second, observation of a model's behavior serves a *motivation function* by establishing a value for the desired behavior and an incentive to enact the behavior. Finally, observation serves a *reinforcement function* by strengthening the connection between behaviors and outcomes that have already been learned (Bandura, 1977, p. 17). It bears mentioning that this reinforcement function serves principally as an informative and motivational operation rather than as a mechanical response strengthener. The notion of "response strengthening" is, at best, a metaphor (Bandura, 1977, p. 21). Observational learning is effective to the extent that it causes people to anticipate the consequences of a particular behavior and establishes an incentive for learners to receive the positive consequences of behavior and avoid the negative ones.

There are several stages of effective modeling in mass media contexts. First, a target person *observes* a model engaging in a particular behavior. Second, the observer *identifies* with the model. Third, the observer *realizes* that the observed behavior will produce a desired result. Fourth, the observer *remembers* the actions of the model and *reproduces* the relevant behavior in a appropriate situations. Fifth, the modeled behavior is *reinforced*. Reinforcement increases the probability that the behavior will be enacted repeatedly (DeFleur & Ball-Rokeach, 1989, pp. 216–217).

Consistent with these stages of modeling, Bandura (1977) identified several factors that affect the extent to which people learn behavior through observation. For example, the rate and amount of observational learning is determined in part by the nature of the modeled behaviors; the more complex the behavior, the less likely it will be modeled effectively. In this regard, applications of Social Learning Theory in persuasive campaigns often include a skills training component. For example, researchers have found that skills training may be an essential component of effective drug resistance campaigns targeted at adolescents (Rohrbach, Graham, Hensen, & Flay, 1987).

In addition to observing and learning to perform a desired behavior, *differential reinforcement* serves to motivate people to enact the behavior they have learned. Differential reinforcement occurs when models are rewarded for performing desired behaviors and when they are punished or unrewarded for performing undesired behaviors. Over time, observers learn to match the performance of desired behaviors with the positive reinforcements and undesired behaviors with less favorable outcomes. This matching process motivates observers to enact desired behaviors once they have been acquired. In adolescent drug resistance campaigns, differential reinforcement increases the likelihood that teens will produce the resistance messages they have learned through modeling and practice. Bandura argued that the anticipated benefits of a particular behavior can strengthen what has been learned observationally by motivating people to rehearse modeled behavior that they value highly (1977, p. 37).

Supporting Evidence

Research has repeatedly found that children and adults acquire attitudes, emotional responses, and new styles of conduct through film and televised modeling (Bandura, 1973, 1977; Liebert, Neale, & Davidson, 1973). Recently, social learning models have been applied to investigations of adolescent drinking and driving (DiBlasio, 1986, 1987) and adolescent sexual behavior (DiBlasio & Benda, 1990). Based on a social learning model of deviant behavior (Akers et al., 1979), DiBlasio argued that "social behavior is understood through studying the impact of differential association with adults and peers, internalization of group norms (normative definitions), modeling, and the combination of positive and negative reinforcement (differential reinforcement)" (1986, p. 175).

Akers and his colleagues (1979) defined *differential association* as the approval levels of adults and peers for a particular behavior. For example, in his study of adolescent drunk driving, DiBlasio (1986) defined peer association as the frequency, duration, and intensity of interactions with peers who drive under the influence of alcohol (DUI), or who ride with someone who is under the influence of alcohol. *Group norms* reflect adherence to laws or a willingness to adhere to laws. In a study of adolescent drunk driving, group norms might reflect attitudes toward DUI laws and justification for occasional violation of DUI laws. Differential reinforcement actually reflects two theoretical factors. *Combined differential reinforcement* reflects the rewards, such as group acceptance and good feelings, derived from a particular behavior compared to the costs of performing the behavior. Adolescents may perceive that drinking and driving is fun and one way to gain acceptance from peers, but these benefits might be offset by the consequences of an accident or anticipated feelings of guilt. When perceived rewards outweigh anticipated costs, the behavior is more likely to be performed, and vice versa. *Differential social reinforcement* reflects the social praise and negative reactions of others. For adolescent drivers, praise from parents and peers for avoiding DUI combined with the negative reactions of peers and parents to DUI serves to reinforce adolescent decisions to abstain from drinking and driving. Finally, *modeling* occurs by observing others who either engage in or abstain from a particular behavior. In the case of adolescent drunk driving, television personalities who participate in DUI campaigns may serve as role models for adolescents. However, parents, relatives, and attractive friends also serve as important role models for adolescent drivers.

These five theoretical factors were hypothesized to affect the learning and performance of adolescent behavior (Akers et al., 1979) and several studies have examined their ability to predict the behavior of adolescents (DiBlasio, 1986, 1987; DiBlasio & Benda, 1990). A consistent pattern of findings emerges from investigations of this model (Table 11.1). In a study of adolescent drinking and driving, DiBlasio (1986) found that all five of the theoretical factors in the Akers et al. (1979) social learning model were significantly related to DUI and riding with drivers under the influence. Combined, these five theoretical factors accounted for 56% of the variance in adolescent DUI and 52% of the variance in riding with drivers under the influence. A subsequent study of adolescent sexual behavior produced similar results (DiBlasio & Benda, 1990). In this study, four theoretical factors were employed, and each factor was significantly related to sexual activity. Combined, these four factors accounted for 40% of the variance in the frequency of adolescent sexual intercourse.

DiBlasio concluded that these findings were consistent with prior studies that found peer groups are most influential for adolescents (Alexander & Campbell, 1966; Jessor & Jessor, 1977); that reinforcement

TABLE 11.1. Multiple Correlation Coefficients for the Theoretical Factors in the Social Learning Model

Theoretical predictors	Adolescent behavior		
	Study 1		Study 2
	DUI	Riding	Sex
1. Differential association	.66	.62	.54
2. Group norms	.52	.50	.41
3. Combined differential reinforcement	.44	.33	.50
4. Differential social reinforcement	.35	.30	NA
5. Modeling	.37	.44	.28
Total variance explained by theoretical factors	.56	.52	.40

Note. DUI = driving under the influence of alcohol, Riding = riding with person operating vehicle under the influence of alcohol, and Sex = sexual intercourse. Study 1 = DiBlasio (1986); Study 2 = DiBlasio & Benda (1990). NA = not available.

is an important determinant of behavior (Bandura, 1969; Wodarski & Bagarozzi, 1979); and that observation of adult and peer models contributes to DUI and riding with drivers under the influence (DiBlasio, 1986, p. 186). Findings from these studies provide strong evidence of social learning and its significant influence on behavior. Unlike learning by doing, which requires repeated experience by individuals, social learning occurs by observing others and the recognition of positive and negative reinforcements associated with their behavior (Bandura, 1977).

Application of Social Learning Theory

Regression models such as the ones developed by DiBlasio established the influence of social learning processes on the individual behavior of adolescents. The explanatory success of these models suggests that social learning processes may provide an excellent foundation for persuasive campaigns targeted at adolescents.

One important problem that adolescents experience is peer pressure to smoke. Over the years, a number of persuasive campaigns have been implemented to promote resistance to smoking. For the most part, these campaigns rely on school-based educational programs and mass media to affect adolescent smoking behavior (Flay, 1986, 1987). Adolescent smoking is a social phenomenon. More than one-third of the cigarettes smoked by adolescents are smoked in the presence of another teen, and over one-half are smoked in the presence of another teen or an adult (Biglan, McConnell, Severson, Bavry, & Ary, 1984). Given the social nature of adolescent smoking and the important influence of peer pressure, group norms, and social reinforcement in the regression models described above, social learning has served as a theoretical foundation for many smoking prevention campaigns.

One campaign tested the effectiveness of a refusal-skills training program for over 1,500 junior high and high school students. Mirroring the essential elements of Social Learning Theory, this program included instruction on specific skills for refusing cigarettes, modeling of effective refusals, behavioral rehearsal, teacher and peer reinforcement for refusal behavior, and practice (Biglan et al., 1987, p. 618). Videotaped presentations were used extensively to provide instruction on refusal skills and examples of effective refusals. Nine months after the intervention, adolescent smokers who received the refusal-skills program reported significantly less smoking and had significantly lower biological readings of smoking (carbon monoxide and saliva) than smokers in the control condition. However, students who were originally *nonsmokers* and who received the refusal-skills training reported significantly higher levels of smoking on the posttest than nonsmokers in the control condition, although the biochemical measures revealed no significant differences between these groups. Despite this finding, the overall results of this investigation indicate that a refusal-skills training program consistent with Social Learning Theory was effective in reducing smoking among adolescents.

Other skills training programs have proved equally effective in promoting long-term resistance to smoking among adolescents (Leupker, Johnson, Murray, & Pechacek, 1983; Schinke & Gilchrist, 1984). The resistance training program developed by Schinke and Gilchrist (1984) was effective in developing antismoking attitudes and encouraging nonsmoking. Leupker and his colleagues developed a resistance-skills training program that included videotaped presentations and interactive rehearsal of refusal strategies. In one experimental condition the resistance-skills program was taught by adults and in another condition it was taught by peer leaders. Self-report and biochemical measures of smoking revealed that the resistance training program taught by adults was initially effective, but over time, smoking rates approached the levels of students in a control group. When the resistance program was taught by peer leaders, significantly lower smoking rates prevailed for almost 2 years (Leupker et al., 1983, p. 61). Together, these investigations suggest that Social Learning Theory can be effectively applied in resistance campaigns provided that modeling, reinforcement, and rehearsal are integrated components of the resistance training program.

Summary of Social Learning Findings

Social Learning Theory distinguishes between acquisition and performance because people do not enact everything they learn. People are more likely to adopt modeled behavior if it results in outcomes they value (Bandura, 1977, p. 28). Reinforcement is essential to social learning because "anticipated benefits can strengthen retention of what has been learned observationally by motivating people to code and rehearse modeled behavior that they value highly" (Bandura, 1977, p. 37).

Social Learning Theory underscores human capacity to learn through observation and describes how people acquire integrated patterns of behavior without having to form them gradually by tedious trial and error (Bandura, 1977, p. 12). However, some behaviors, such as communicative strategies for refusing drugs, alcohol, and cigarettes, are sufficiently complex that they can only be acquired through modeling and rehearsal. Research has demonstrated the powerful influence of behavioral models portrayed in the mass media. When combined with interpersonal skills training, these models can effectively promote resistance to unwanted behavior.

THE HEALTH BELIEF MODEL

The Health Belief Model grew out of a set of problems that confronted the Public Health Service in the 1950s and early 1960s. In those days, public health programs focused on early detection and prevention of disease. In this regard, health behavior researchers sought to develop theories that would predict the health behaviors of individuals and explain their decisions to seek or avoid the screening and prevention services of public health agencies (Rosenstock, 1974).

Social psychologists in the School of Public Health at the University of Michigan were the first to model the influence of individual beliefs on health behavior. Influenced heavily by the work of Kurt Lewin, these researchers adopted the orientation that knowing the subjective perceptions of individuals is essential to understanding their behavior. This orientation produced a *value-expectancy explanation* of behavior, which posits that in uncertain situations behavior is determined by the value an individual assigns to a particular outcome and the expectation that the behavior will result in that outcome (Becker, Maiman, Kirscht, Haefner, & Drachman, 1977; Rosenstock, 1974). Applied in a health prevention context, this value-expectancy approach suggests that individual health behaviors are determined by the value an individual assigns to avoiding a particular disease and the likelihood that prevention behaviors will effectively ward off the disease. For example, the Surgeon General has recommended that in order to reduce the risk of heart disease, Americans should reduce the amount of fat in their diets. A value-expectancy explanation of individual behavior suggests that people will adhere to this recommendation if they wish to avoid heart disease *and* if they believe that a low-fat diet will reduce their risk of heart disease.

Over the years, value-expectancy models of health behavior evolved into what has become known as the Health Belief Model (HBM). Extensive reviews of this model are available in the literature (Becker, 1974; Janz & Becker, 1984), making another comprehensive review unnecessary. Instead, the remainder of this chapter describes the major components of the HBM, discusses investigations that provide support for the model, and examines the application of the HBM model in persuasive campaigns.

Components of the Model

Consistent with the view that explanations of human behavior reside in the perceptual judgments of individuals, the HBM posits that three perceptual variables combine to influence individual health behaviors. These perceptual factors are: perceived threat or susceptibility, perceived severity, and perceived efficacy (Rosenstock, 1974). *Perceived susceptibility* is the belief that an individual is vulnerable and therefore likely to contract the disease or adverse health condition. Extending the example of dietary recommendations for reducing the risk of heart disease, perceived susceptibility reflects an individual's assessment of his or her chances of developing heart disease later in life. Preventive health campaigns, intended to reduce the risk of future disease, are often ineffective because people's perceptions about their likelihood of developing the disease may be unreasonably low. This is especially true among adolescents, who often feel that they are invulnerable (DiBlasio, 1986) and therefore unlikely to contract prevalent sexually transmitted diseases such as AIDS and herpes. Indeed, creating a perception that people are "at risk" for contracting or developing disease is an essential step toward establishing their willingness to respond proactively.

Perceived severity reflects the beliefs people hold about the seriousness of a particular disease. Rosenstock (1974) argued that perceived severity includes emotional reactions people have about a disease as well as their cognitive reactions about the implications of the disease. During the mid-1980s, health care providers became concerned about contracting the AIDS virus from patients. Emotional reactions to the AIDS virus and knowledge of its clinical and psychosocial effects motivated the implementation of safety procedures for handling blood. These universal precautions for handling blood had previously been recommended to health care workers to prevent the spread of hepatitis. However, care providers exhibited relatively mild concern about the recommendations until the AIDS epidemic began. Ironically, the risk of acquiring HIV from a patient is substantially less than the risk of contracting hepatitis. Indeed, more than 200 health care workers die each year from complications associated with hepatitis contracted through their patients. By comparison, from the beginning of the AIDS epidemic through mid-1990, there were fewer than 30 documented cases of occupationally acquired HIV infection among health care workers (Gerberding, 1991).

Although the universal precautions recommended for safe handling of blood and other body fluids effectively reduced the risk of contracting both HIV and hepatitis, it was the perceived severity of the AIDS virus, not hepatitis, that motivated these changes (Gerberding, 1991). The fact that the AIDS virus motivated acceptance of these precautions underscores the influence of perceived severity on the health behaviors of health care workers. Clearly, the HIV infection is much more severe than hepatitis, though the latter is much more prevalent among health care providers.

The third essential component in the HBM is the *perceived efficacy* of the recommended behavior. Efficacy reflects the belief that a particular behavior will successfully achieve the desired outcome. For example, the efficacy of government recommendations to reduce the consumption of fat depends on a person's belief that a reduction in dietary fat can be reasonably achieved and that it can effectively reduce the likelihood of heart disease. Rosenstock (1974) identified two factors that contribute to perceived efficacy: *perceived benefits* of the behavior and *perceived barriers* to performing the behavior. Perceived benefits reflect beliefs that the behavior will be effective and perceived barriers reflect factors that inhibit the performance of the behavior. Combined, these perceptions affect the likelihood that a behavior can be effectively performed to reduce the perceived threat. For example, AIDS education programs have effectively created the perception that condoms can effectively reduce transmission of the AIDS virus. However, studies have found that many adolescents perceive that condoms decrease the enjoyment of sexual intercourse (Jemmott & Jemmott, 1991; Jemmott, Jemmott, Spears, Hewitt, & Cruz-Collins, 1992), and that these negative perceptions are associated with lower levels of condom use (Valdiserri, Arena, Proctor, & Bonati, 1989). These findings are consistent with the HBM, which posits that people conduct a cost–benefit analysis and will only enact a particular health behavior when its anticipated benefits outweigh its costs.

In addition to the perceptual factors, *cues to action* reflect triggering mechanisms in the model that motivate active consideration of the
recommended behavior. Although these cues have received less attention from researchers, they are essential to the model because perceived
health benefits could "reach quite considerable levels of intensity without
resulting in overt action unless some instigating event occurred to set
the process in motion" (Rosenstock, 1974, p. 5). These instigating cues
can be internal perceptions people form about the state of their own
health) (i.e., "I feel fat and sluggish, perhaps I should get more regular
exercise"), or they can be external prompts from mass media or friends
that draw attention to the problem and the recommended health behavior. For example, Magic Johnson's decision to publicize the fact that
he is HIV positive may serve as a motivating cue for adolescents and
young adults who already understand the benefits of "safe sex."

These three perceptual factors (susceptibility, severity, and efficacy)
are depicted in Figure 11.1. Also depicted in the figure are demographic variables, such as age, gender, and ethnicity, that affect the perceptions people form about their health belief situation. Thus, the upper
portion of the figure suggests that perceived severity and susceptibility
affect perceptions of threat posed by a particular disease, and that perceived threat affects the likelihood of adopting the recommended health
behavior. Also affecting the likelihood of adopting the recommended
behavior is the perceived efficacy of the behavior, that is, the perceived
benefits of the recommended behavior minus the perceived barriers to
enacting the behavior. All of these perceptual factors are affected by
demographic variables. Finally, the lower portion of the model depicts
the direct effects that cues to action have on the perceived threat of the
disease.

Supporting Evidence

Over the years a number of studies have directly tested the HBM. As
did tests of Social Learning Theory, most investigations of the HBM
employed regression models to assess the relative influence of the predictor variables on the adoption of recommended health behaviors. Using survey research methods to collect data, most tests of the HBM
focused on a particular health concern and measured the perceived variables, demographic characteristics, and enactment of the recommended preventive health behavior. Correlational analyses reflect the
relationship between each of these factors and adoption of recommended
health behaviors. For example, in a study of hypertension patients,
Kirscht and Rosenstock (1977) found that patient beliefs about their
susceptibility to the condition, the severity of the condition, and the

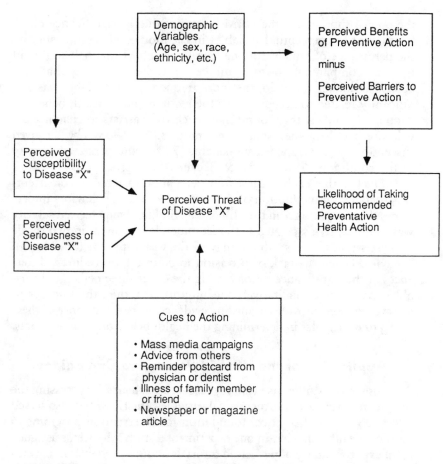

FIGURE 11.1. The original formulation of the Health Belief Model (HBM). From "A new approach to explaining sick role behavior" by M. H. Becker, R. H. Drachman, & J. P. Kirscht, 1974, *American Journal of Public Health, 64*, 205–216. Copyright 1974 by the American Public Health Association. Reprinted by permission.

perceived efficacy of treatment recommendations were all significantly associated with patient compliance with the recommended guidelines for treating hypertension. In addition, barriers to enacting the recommended behavior and several demographic characteristics were also associated with patient compliance.

Two extensive reviews of this literature (Becker, 1974; Janz & Becker, 1984) provide strong evidence of the validity of the HBM. Using a counting procedure (see Chapter 2, this volume), Janz and Becker conducted a quantitative summary of this literature. They determined the overall support for the HBM by computing a "significance ratio" for each of the perceptual variables in the model. This ratio reflected the percentage of studies finding significant effect for the variable in question compared to the total number of studies measuring that variable. The higher the ratio, the more frequently the variable was significantly related to acceptance of the recommended health behavior. Among all studies, they found that perceived barriers to enacting the behavior had the highest significance ratio (89%) followed by perceived susceptibility (81%), perceived benefits (78%), and perceived severity of the condition (65%) (Janz & Becker, 1984, p. 41).

The fact that each of these four perceptual variables is consistently associated with adoption of recommended health behaviors underscores their importance in the HBM. The finding that perceived severity was significantly associated with recommended behavior in two-thirds of these studies suggests that it may be the weakest predictor of health behavior. Given the lack of precision in counting procedures, differences in the significance ratios among the other three perceptual variables may not be qualitatively meaningful. Together, the findings of 46 investigations provide compelling evidence of the importance of these perceptual variables in determining the health behaviors of individuals.

Application of the HBM in Persuasive Campaigns

Although most studies used survey research strategies for assessing the relative importance of the theoretical variables, the HBM has also served effectively as the theoretical foundation for intervention programs to promote health behavior. In one experimental study, physicians assigned to an experimental group received tutorials about hypertension that emphasized the importance of perceptual components of the HBM (Inui, Yourtee, & Williamson, 1976). These tutorials stressed the effects of patient beliefs about susceptibility, severity, and the efficacy of treatment recommendations on patient compliance with physician recommendations for treating hypertension. Physicians in a control group did not receive the tutorial and were unaware that their patients' behaviors were monitored during the study. Among other findings, Inui and his colleagues found that patients of physicians in the experimental group maintained their medication regimen and controlled their blood pressure significantly better than patients of physicians in the control group. These findings suggest that training physicians about the importance of patient perceptions may effectively increase patient adoption of recommended health behaviors.

In another experimental study, Becker and his colleagues used components of the HBM to predict mothers' compliance with recommended prescriptions for their obese children (Becker et al., 1977). In addition, some mothers were exposed to either a high or low fear-arousing message (experimental groups) and others were assigned to a no-message control group. Follow-up physician visits provided information about their children's weight loss. Findings provided strong support for the HBM. Measures of perceived susceptibility, severity, benefits of compliance, and barriers to compliance were significantly correlated with childrens' weight loss. Children of mothers who were exposed to one of the fear-arousing messages about obesity exhibited significantly more weight loss over the course of the 8-week study than children of mothers in the control group, with the high fear message being more effective than the low fear message.

Taken together, these experimental studies provide evidence of the types of interventions that may "cue" people to adopt recommended health behaviors. Clearly, the measures of severity, susceptibility, benefits, and barriers reflect a "perceptual readiness" among research participants to adopt recommended health behaviors. The interventions included in these experiments reflect the sorts of interpersonal cues (physicians in the Inui et al., 1976, study) and mass media messages (fear-arousing messages in the Becker et al., 1977, study) that can effectively instigate people to enact health behaviors consistent with their health beliefs. In this regard, these experimental studies provide evidence that the HBM can serve effectively as the theoretical foundation for campaigns to promote public health.

Summarizing the HBM Literature

The HBM evolved out of a concern for promoting preventive health behaviors. Over the past 30 years, this model has been applied to adoption of health recovery behaviors as well. The model emphasizes the beliefs people have about their personal health and the likelihood that recommended behaviors will successfully contribute to their health. Regression models developed in over 40 studies provide compelling evidence about the predictive utility of personal health beliefs, hence, the validity of the HBM. Although experimental methods have only occasionally been used to investigate this model, two such studies provide insights about the types of interventions that can effectively cue people to act in accordance with their health beliefs. These studies suggest that the HBM can effectively provide the theoretical foundation for health promotion campaigns.

SUMMARY

This chapter examined three models of social influence that can be effectively applied in mass media campaigns. Research on Inoculation Theory documents the effectiveness of this technique for promoting resistance to persuasion. Recent field experiments document the effectiveness of this technique for promoting resistance to attack messages in political campaigns. Social Learning Theory reflects a general approach to persuasion that stems from observational learning. By observing the rewards and punishments that models receive for their behavior, people learn vicariously to enact socially desirable behaviors. For adolescents, social learning is a particularly effective method of acquiring behavior. The influence of peer and adult models provides one basis for developing programs to promote prosocial behavior in adolescents. Finally, the HBM reflects the importance of individual beliefs in the adoption of health behaviors. Evidence from numerous tests of the HBM provide clear evidence of the influence of these personal beliefs on individual health behavior. Experimental studies provide some suggestions about the types of interventions that serve to cue people to act on their beliefs, making this model particularly attractive for health promotion campaigns. Although none of the three models described in this chapter is inherently a mass media model of social influence, each can readily and successfully be applied in mediated campaigns of social influence. Given the multiplicative power of the media, these theories may ultimately prove to be more effectively applied in media campaigns than in interpersonal influence situations.

References

Ajzen, I. (1985). From intentions to actions: A theory of planned behavior. In J. Kuhland & J. Beckman (Eds.), *Action-control: From cognitions to behavior* (pp. 11–39). Heidelberg, Germany: Springer.

Ajzen, I., & Fishbein, M. (1977). Attitude behavior relations: A theoretical analysis and review of empirical research. *Psychological Bulletin, 84,* 888–918.

Ajzen, I., & Fishbein, M. (1980). *Understanding attitudes and predicting social behavior.* Englewood Cliffs, NJ: Prentice Hall.

Akers, R. L., Krohn, M. D., Lanza-Kaduci, L., & Radosevich, M. (1979). Social learning and deviant behavior: A specific test of a general theory. *American Sociological Review, 44,* 636–655.

Alexander, N. C., & Campbell, E. Q. (1966). Peer influence on alcohol drinking. *Journal of Studies on Alcohol, 28,* 444–453.

Allen, C., & Metoyer, P. (1987). Crimes of the occult. *Police,* 38–45.

Allen, M. (1991). Meta-analysis comparing the persuasiveness of one-sided and two-sided messages. *Western Journal of Speech Communication, 55,* 390–404.

Allen, M., Hale, J., Mongeau, P., Berkowits-Stafford, S., Stafford, S., Shanahan, W., Agee, P., Dillon, K., Jackson, R., & Ray, C. (1990). Testing a model of message sidedness: Three replications. *Communication Monographs, 57,* 274–291.

Allen M., Mabry, E. A., Banski, M., Stoneman, M., & Carter, P. (1990). A thoughtful appraisal of measuring cognition using the Role Category Questionnaire. *Communication Reports, 3,* 49–57.

Allen, M., & Stiff, J. B. (1989). Testing three models for the sleeper effect. *Western Journal of Speech Communication, 53,* 411–426.

Allport, G. W. (1935). Attitudes. In C. Murchison (Ed.), *A handbook of social psychology* (pp. 798–844). Worcester, MA: Clark University Press.

Anderson, N. H. (1959). Test of a model for opinion change. *Journal of Abnormal and Social Psychology, 59,* 371–381.

Anderson, N. H. (1971). Integration theory and attitude change. *Psychological Review, 78,* 171–206.

Anderson, N. H. (1981). *Foundations of information integration theory.* San Diego, CA: Academic Press.

Anderson, N. H., & Hovland, C. (1957). The representation of order effects in communication research. In C. Hovland (Ed.), *The order of presentation in persuasion* (pp. 158–169). New Haven, CT: Yale University Press.

Andreoli, V., & Worchel, S. (1978). Effects of media, communicator, and message position on attitude change. *Public Opinion Quarterly, 42,* 59–70.

Applegate, J. L. (1980). Person- and position-centered teacher communication in a day care center: A case study triangulating interview and naturalistic methods. *Studies in Symbolic Interaction, 3,* 59–96.

Applegate, J. L. (1982). The impact of construct system development on communication and impression formation in persuasive contexts. *Communication Monographs, 49,* 277–289.

Aronson, E. (1968). Dissonance theory: Progress and problems. In R. P. Abelson, E. Aronson, W. J. McGuire, T. M. Newcomb, M. J. Rosenberg, & P. H. Tannenbaum (Eds.), *Theories of cognitive consistency: A sourcebook* (pp. 5–27). Chicago: Rand McNally.

Aronson, E. (1984). *The social animal.* New York: W. H. Freeman.

Aronson, E., Turner, J. A., & Carlsmith, J. M. (1963). Communicator credibility and communication discrepancy determinants of opinion change. *Journal of Abnormal and Social Psychology, 67,* 31–36.

Arterton, F. C. (1984). *Media politics.* Lexington, MA: Lexington Books.

Asch, S. E. (1955). Opinions and social pressures. *Scientific American, 193,* 31–35.

Asch, S. E. (1956). Studies of independence and conformity: A minority of one against a unanimous majority. *Psychological Monographs, 70* (9, Whole No. 416).

Bacon, S. J. (1974). Arousal and the range of cue utilization. *Journal of Experimental Psychology, 102,* 81–87.

Bandura, A. (1969). *Principles of behavior modification.* New York: Holt, Rinehart, & Winston.

Bandura, A. (1973). *Aggression: A social learning analysis.* Englewood Cliffs, NJ: Prentice Hall.

Bandura, A. (1977). *Social learning theory.* Englewood Cliffs, NJ: Prentice Hall.

Bandura, A. (1982). Self-efficacy mechanism in human agency. *American Psychologist, 37,* 122–147.

Bandura, A., Adams, N. E., Hardy, A. B., & Howells, G. N. (1980). Tests of the generality of self-efficacy theory. *Cognitive Therapy and Research, 4,* 39–66.

Bargh, J. A., & Pratto, F. (1986). Individual construct accessibility and perceptual selection. *Journal of Experimental Social Psychology, 22,* 293–311.

Baron, P. H., Baron, R. S., & Roper, G. (1974). External validity and the risky shift: Empirical limits and theoretical implications. *Journal of Personality and Social Psychology, 30,* 95–103.

Baumhart, R. (1968). *An honest profit: What businessmen say about ethics in business.* New York: Holt, Rinehart, & Winston.

Beaman, A. L., Cole, C. M., Preston, M., Klentz, B., & Steblay, N. M. (1983).

Fifteen years of foot-in-the-door research: A meta-analysis. *Personality and Social Psychology Bulletin, 9,* 181–196.

Beatty, M. (1987). Erroneous assumptions underlying Burleson's critique. *Communication Quarterly, 35,* 329–333.

Beatty, M., & Payne, S. (1984). Loquacity and quantity of constructs as predictors of social perspective taking. *Communication Quarterly, 32,* 207–210.

Beatty, M., & Payne, S. (1985). Is construct differentiation loquacity?: A motivational perspective. *Human Communication Research, 11,* 605–612.

Beck, K. H., & Frankel, A. (1981). A conceptualization of threat communications and protective health behavior. *Social Psychology Quarterly, 44,* 204–217.

Becker, M. H. (1974). *The health belief model and personal health behavior.* Thorofare, NJ: Charles B. Slack.

Becker, M. H., Maiman, L. A., Kirscht, J. P., Haefner, D. P., & Drachman, R. H. (1977). The health belief model and prediction of dietary compliance: A field experiment. *Journal of Health and Social Behavior, 18,* 348–366.

Bem, D. J. (1967). Self-perception: An alternative interpretation of cognitive dissonance phenomena. *Psychological Review, 74,* 183–200.

Bem, D. J. (1972). Self-perception theory. In L. Berkowitz (Ed.), *Advances in experimental social psychology* (Vol. 6, pp. 1–62). New York: Academic Press.

Berlo, D. K., Lemert, J. B., & Mertz, R. J. (1969). Dimensions for evaluating the acceptability of message sources. *Public Opinion Quarterly, 33,* 563–576.

Berscheid, E. (1966). Opinion change and communicator–communicatee similarity and dissimilarity. *Journal of Personality and Social Psychology, 4,* 670–680.

Berscheid, E., & Walster, E. (1974). Physical attractiveness. In L. Berkowitz (Ed.), *Advances in experimental social psychology* (Vol. 7, pp. 157–215). San Diego, CA: Academic Press.

Bettinghaus, E. P., & Cody, M. J. (1987). *Persuasive communication.* New York: Holt, Rinehart, & Winston.

Bettinghaus, E. P., Miller, G. R., & Steinfatt, T. M. (1970). Source evaluation, syllogistic content, and judgments of logical validity by high- and low-dogmatic persons. *Journal of Personality and Social Psychology, 16,* 238–244.

Biglan, A., Glasgow, R., Ary, D., Thompson, R., Severson, H., Lichtenstein, E., Weissman, W., Faller, C., & Gallison, C. (1987). How generalizable are the effects of smoking prevention programs? Refusal skills, training, and parent messages in a teacher-administered program. *Journal of Behavioral Medicine, 10,* 613–628.

Biglan, A., McConnell, S., Severson, H. H., Bavry, J., & Ary, D. (1984). A situational analysis of adolescent smoking. *Journal of Behavioral Medicine, 7,* 109–114.

Bingham, S. G., & Burleson, B. R. (1989). Multiple effects of messages with multiple goals: Some perceived outcomes of responses to sexual harassment. *Human Communication Research, 16,* 184–216.

Bocher, S., & Insko, C. A. (1966). Communicator discrepancy, source credibility, and opinion change. *Journal of Personality and Social Psychology, 4,* 614–621.

Boster, F. J. (1988). Comments on the utility of compliance gaining message selection tasks. *Human Communication Research, 15,* 169–177.

Boster, F. J. (1990). Group argument, social pressure, and the making of group decisions. In J. A. Anderson (Ed.), *Communication yearbook 13* (pp. 303–312). Newbury Park, CA: Sage.

Boster, F. J., Fryrear, J. E., Mongeau, P. A., & Hunter, J. E. (1982). An unequal speaking linear discrepancy model: Implications for the polarity shift. In M. Burgoon (Ed.), *Communication yearbook 6* (pp. 395–418). Beverly Hills, CA: Sage.

Boster, F. J., & Hunter, J. E. (1978). *The effect of dimensions of Machiavellianism on compliance-gaining message selection.* Unpublished manuscript, Department of Communication, Arizona State University.

Boster, F. J., & Mayer, M. E. (1984). Choice shifts: Argument qualities or social comparisons. In R. N. Bostrom (Ed.), *Communication yearbook 8* (pp. 393–410). Beverly Hills, CA: Sage.

Boster, F. J., Mayer, M. E., Hunter, J. E., & Hale, J. L. (1980). Expanding the persuasive arguments explanation of the polarity shift: A linear discrepancy model. In D. Nimmo (Ed.), *Communication yearbook 4* (pp. 165–176). New Brunswick, NJ: Transaction Books.

Boster, F. J., & Mongeau, P. A. (1984). Fear-arousing persuasive messages. In R. N. Bostrom (Ed.), *Communication yearbook 8* (pp. 330–375). Beverly Hills, CA: Sage.

Boster, F. J., & Stiff, J. B. (1984). Compliance gaining message selection behavior. *Human Communication Research, 10,* 539–556.

Boster, F. J., Stiff, J. B., & Reynolds, R. A. (1985). Do persons respond differently to inductively-derived and deductively-derived lists of compliance gaining messages?: A reply to Wiseman and Schenck-Hamlin. *Western Journal of Speech Communication, 49,* 177–187.

Bowman, C. H., & Fishbein, M. (1978). Understanding public reactions to energy proposals: An application of the Fishbein model. *Journal of Applied Social Psychology, 8,* 319–340.

Brehm, J. W. (1966). *A theory of psychological reactance.* New York: Academic Press.

Brehm, J. W., & Cohen, A. R. (1962). *Explorations in cognitive dissonance.* New York: Wiley.

Brock, T. (1965). Communicator–recipient similarity and decision change. *Journal of Personality and Social Psychology, 1,* 650–654.

Brock, T. (1967). Communication discrepancy and intent to persuade as determinants of counterargument production. *Journal of Experimental Social Psychology, 3,* 296–309.

Buller, D. B. (1986). Distraction during persuasive communication: A meta-analytic review. *Communication Monographs, 53,* 91–114.

Buller, D. B., & Burgoon, J. K. (1986). The effects of vocalics and non-verbal sensitivity on compliance. *Human Communication Research, 13,* 126–144.

Burgoon, J. K., Burgoon, M., Miller, G. R., & Sunnafrank, M. (1981). Learning theory approaches to persuasion. *Human Communication Research, 7,* 161–179.

Burgoon, J. K., Stacks, D. W., & Burch, S. A. (1982). The role of rewards and violations of distancing expectations in achieving influence in small groups. *Communication, 11,* 114–128.

Burgoon, M. (1989). Messages and persuasive effects. In J. J. Bradac (Ed.), *Message effects in communication science* (pp. 129–164). Newbury Park, CA: Sage.

Burgoon, M., Cohen, M., Miller, M. D., & Montgomery, C. L. (1978). An empirical test of a model of resistance to persuasion. *Human Communication Research, 5,* 27–39.

Burleson B., Applegate, J., & Newwirth, C. (1981). Is cognitive complexity loquacity?: A reply to Powers, Jordan, and Street. *Human Communication Research, 7,* 212–215.

Burleson, B., Waltman, M., & Samter, W. (1987). More evidence that cognitive complexity is not loquacity: A reply to Beatty and Payne. *Communication Quarterly, 35,* 317–328.

Burleson, B. R., & Wilson, S. R. (1988). On the continued undesireability of item desireability: A reply to Boster, Hunter, and Seibold. *Human Communication Research, 15,* 178–191.

Burleson, B. R., Wilson, S. R., Waltman, M. S., Goering, E. M., Ely, T. K., & Whaley, R. B. (1988). Item desireability effects in compliance-gaining research: Seven studies documenting artifacts in the strategy selection procedure. *Human Communication Research, 14,* 429–486.

Byrne, D. (1971). *The attraction paradigm.* New York: Academic Press.

Cacioppo, J. T., & Petty, R. E. (1982). The need for cognition. *Journal of Personality and Social Psychology, 42,* 116–131.

Cacioppo, J. T., & Petty, R. E. (1984). The need for cognition: Relationship to attitudinal processes. In R. P. McGlynn, J. E. Maddux, C. D. Stoltenberg, & J. H. Harvey (Eds.), *Social perception in clinical and counseling psychology* (pp. 113–119). Lubbock, TX: Texas Tech Press.

Campbell, D. T., & Stanley, J. C. (1966). *Experimental and quasi-experimental designs for research.* Chicago: Rand McNally.

Chaiken, S. (1979). Communicator physical attractiveness and persuasion. *Journal of Personality and Social Psychology, 37,* 1387–1397.

Chaiken, S. (1980). Heuristic versus systematic information processing and the use of source versus message cues in persuasion. *Journal of Personality and Social Psychology, 39,* 752–766.

Chaiken, S. (1986). Physical appearance and social influence. In C. P. Herman, M. P. Zanna, & E. T. Higgins (Eds.), *Physical appearance, stigma, and social behavior: The Ontario Symposium* (Vol. 3, pp. 143–177). Hillsdale, NJ: Erlbaum.

Chaiken, S. (1987). The Heuristic Model of Persuasion. In M. P. Zanna, J.

M. Olson, & C. P. Herman (Eds.), *Social influence: The Ontario symposium* (Vol. 5, pp. 3–39). Hillsdale, NJ: Erlbaum.

Chaiken, S., & Eagly, A. H. (1976). Communicator modality as a determinant of message persuasiveness and message comprehensibility. *Journal of Personality and Social Psychology, 34,* 606–614.

Chaiken, S., & Eagly, A. H. (1983). Communication modality as a determinant of persuasion: The role of communicator salience. *Journal of Personality and Social Psychology, 45,* 241–256.

Christie, R., & Geis, F. L. (1970). *Studies in Machaivellianism.* New York: Academic Press.

Cialdini, R. B. (1987). Principles of compliance professionals: Psychologists of necessity. In M. P. Zanna, J. M. Olson, & C. P. Herman (Eds.), *Social influence: The Ontario symposium* (Vol. 5, pp. 165–184). Hillsdale, NJ: Erlbaum.

Cialdini, R. B., Cacioppo, J. T., Bassett, R., & Miller, J. A. (1978). Low-ball procedure for producing compliance: Commitment then cost. *Journal of Personality and Social Psychology, 36,* 463–476.

Cialdini, R. B., Levy, A., Herman, C. P., & Evenbeck, S. (1973). Attitudinal politics: The strategy of moderation. *Journal of Personality and Social Psychology, 25,* 100–108.

Cialdini, R. B., Levy, A., Herman, C. P., Kozlowski, L. T., & Petty, R. E. (1976). Elastic shifts of opinion: Determinants of direction and durability. *Journal of Personality and Social Psychology, 34,* 663–672.

Cialdini, R. B., & Petty, R. E. (1981). Anticipatory opinion effects. In R. E. Petty, T. M. Ostrom, & T. C. Brock (Eds.), *Cognitive responses in persuasion* (pp. 217–235). Hillsdale, NJ: Erlbaum.

Cialdini, R. B., Vincent, J. E., Lewis, S. K., Catalan, J., Wheeler, D., & Darby, B. L. (1975). Reciprocal concessions procedure for inducing compliance: The door-in-the-face technique. *Journal of Personality and Social Psychology, 31,* 206–215.

Clark, R. A. (1979). The impact of self interest and desire for liking on the selection of communicative strategies. *Communication Monographs, 46,* 257–273.

Cline, R. (1990). Small group communication in health care. In E. B. Ray & L. Donohew (Eds.), *Communication and health: Systems and applications* (pp. 69–91). Hillsdale, NJ: Erlbaum.

Cody, M. J., & McLaughlin, M. L. (1985). The situation as construct in interpersonal communication research. In M. Knapp & G. R. Miller (Eds.), *Handbook of interpersonal communication* (pp. 263–312). Beverly Hills, CA: Sage.

Cohen, A., Stotland, E., & Wolfe, D. (1955). An experimental investigation of need for cognition. *Journal of Abnormal and Social Psychology, 51,* 291–294.

Cohen, M. R. (1949). *Studies in philosophy and science.* New York: Holt.

Cook, D. T., & Campbell, D. T. (1979). *Quasi-experimentation: Design and analysis issues for field settings.* Chicago: Rand McNally.

Cook, T., Gruder, C., Hennigan, K., & Flay, B. (1979). History of the sleeper effect: Some logical pitfalls in accepting the null hypothesis. *Psychological Bulletin, 86,* 662–679.

Cooper, J., & Fazio, R. H. (1984). A new look at dissonance theory. In L. Berkowitz (Ed.), *Advances in experimental social psychology* (Vol. 17, pp. 229–266). New York: Academic Press.

Cooper, J., Zanna, M. P., & Taves, P. A. (1978). Arousal as a necessary condition for attitude change following induced compliance. *Journal of Personality and Social Psychology, 36,* 1101–1106.

Cronkhite, G., & Liska, J. (1976). A critique of factor analytic approaches to the study of credibility. *Communication Monographs, 43,* 91–107.

Cronkhite, G., & Liska, J (1980). The judgment of communicator acceptability. In M. E. Roloff & G. R. Miller (Eds.), *Persuasion: New directions in theory and research* (pp. 101–139). Beverly Hills, CA: Sage.

Croyle, D. T., & Cooper, J. (1983). Dissonance arousal: Physiological evidence. *Journal of Personality and Social Psychology, 45,* 782–791.

DeFleur, M. L., & Ball-Rokeach, S. (1989). *Theories of mass communication.* New York: Longman.

Delia, J. G., & Clark, R. A. (1977). Cognitive complexity, social perception, and the development of listener-adapted communication in six-, eight-, ten-, and twelve-year old boys. *Communication Monographs, 46,* 326–345.

Delia, J. G., & Crockett, W. H. (1973). Social schemas, cognitive complexity, and the learning of social structures. *Journal of Personality, 41,* 413–429.

Delia, J. G., Kline, S. L., & Burleson, B. R. (1979). The development of persuasive communication strategies in kindergartners through twelfth graders. *Communication Monographs, 46,* 274–281.

Delia, J. G., & O'Keefe, B. J. (1979). Constructivism: The development of communication in children. In E. Wartella (Ed.), *Children communicating* (pp. 157–185). Beverly Hills, CA: Sage.

Deutsch, M., & Gerard, H. B. (1955). A study of normative and informational social influence upon individual judgment. *Journal of Abnormal and Social Psychology, 51,* 629–636.

Devlin, L. P. (1987). *Political persuasion in presidential campaigns.* New Brunswick, NJ: Transaction Books.

DiBlasio, F. A. (1986). Drinking adolescents on the roads. *Journal of Youth and Adolescence, 15,* 173–188.

DiBlasio, F. A. (1987). Predriving riders and drinking drivers. *Journal of Studies on Alcohol, 49,* 11–15.

DiBlasio, F. A., & Benda, B. B. (1990). Adolescent sexual behavior: Multivariate analysis of a social learning model. *Journal of Adolescent Research, 5,* 449–466.

Dillard, J. P. (1988). Compliance gaining message selection: What is our dependent variable? *Communication Monographs, 55,* 162–183.

Dillard, J. P. (1989). Types of influence goals in personal relationships. *Journal of Social and Personal Relationships, 6,* 293–308.

Dillard, J. P. (1990). Self-inference and the foot-in-the-door technique. *Human Communication Research, 16,* 422–447.

Dillard, J. P. (1991). The current status of research on sequential-request compliance techniques. *Personality and Social Psychology Bulletin, 17,* 283–288.

Dillard, J. P. (in press). Rethinking the study of fear appeals. *Communication Theory.*

Dillard, J. P., Hunter, J. E., & Burgoon, M. (1984). Sequential-request persuasive strategies: Meta-analysis of foot-in-the-door and door-in-the-face. *Human Communication Research, 10,* 461–488.

Dillard, J. P., Segrin, C., & Hardin, J. M. (1989). Primary and secondary goals in the production of interpersonal influence messages. *Communication Monographs, 56,* 19–38.

Dion, K., Baron, R., & Miller, N. (1970). Why do groups make riskier decisions than individuals? In L. Berkowitz (Ed.), *Group processes* (pp. 227–299). New York: Academic Press.

Dulany, D. E. (1961). Hypotheses and habits in verbal "operant conditioning." *Journal of Abnormal and Social Psychology, 63,* 251–263.

Dulany, D. E. (1968). Awareness, rules, and propositional control: A confrontation with S-R behavior theory. In D. Horton & T. Dixon (Eds.), *Verbal behavior and S-R behavior theory* (pp. 340–387). Englewood Cliffs, NJ: Prentice Hall.

Eagly, A. H. (1974). Comprehensibility of persuasive arguments as a determinant of opinion change. *Journal of Personality and Social Psychology, 29,* 758–773.

Eagly, A. H. (1978). Sex differences in influenceablilty. *Psychological Bulletin, 85,* 86–116.

Eagly, A. H., & Carli, L. L. (1981). Sex of researchers and sex-typed communications as determinants of sex differences in influenceability: A meta-analysis of social influence studies. *Psychological Bulletin, 90,* 1–20.

Eagly, A. H., & Chaiken, S. (1976). Why would anyone say that? Causal attribution of statements about the Watergate scandal. *Sociometry, 39,* 236–243.

Eagly, A. H., Chaiken, S., & Wood, W. (1981). An attribution analysis of persuasion. In J. H. Harvey, W. J. Ickes, & R. F. Kidd (Eds.) *New directions in attribution research* (Vol. 3, pp. 37–62). Hillsdale, NJ: Erlbaum.

Eagly, A. H., & Warren, R. (1976). Intelligence, comprehension, and opinion change. *Journal of Personality, 44,* 226–242.

Eagly, A. H., Wood, W., & Chaiken, S. (1978). Causal inferences about communicators and their effect on opinion change. *Journal of Personality and Social Psychology, 36,* 424–435.

Edwards, K. (1990). The interplay of affect and cognition in attitude formation and change. *Journal of Personality and Social Psychology, 59,* 202–216.

Edwards, W. (1961). Behavioral decision theory. *Annual Review of Psychology, 12,* 473–498.

Fazio, R. H., Chen, J., McDonel, E. C., & Sherman, S. J. (1982). Attitude accessibility, attitude–behavior consistency, and the strength of the object-evaluation association. *Journal of Experimental Social Psychology, 18,* 339–357.

Fazio, R. H., Sanbonmatsu, D. M., Powell, M. C., & Kardes, F. R. (1986). On the automatic activation of attitudes. *Journal of Personality and Social Psychology, 50,* 229–238.

Fazio, R. H., & Williams, C. J. (1986). Attitude accessibility as a moderator of the attitude–perception and attitude–behavior relations: An investigation of the 1984 presidential election. *Journal of Personality and Social Psychology, 51,* 505–514.

Fazio, R. H., & Zanna, M. P. (1981). Direct experience and attitude–behavior consistency. In L. Berkowitz (Ed.), *Advances in experimental social psychology* (Vol. 14, pp. 161–202). New York: Academic Press.

Fazio, R. H., Zanna, M. P., & Cooper, J. (1977). Dissonance and self-perception: An interactive view of each theory's proper domain of application. *Journal of Experimental Social Psychology, 13,* 464–479.

Fern, E. F., Monroe, K. B., & Avila, R. A. (1986). Effectiveness of multiple request strategies: A synthesis of research results. *Journal of Marketing Research, 23,* 144–152.

Festinger, L. (1953). An analysis of compliant behavior. In M. Sherif & M. O. Wilson (Eds.), *Group relations at the crossroads* (pp. 232–256). New York: Harper & Brothers.

Festinger, L. (1954). A theory of social comparison processes. *Human Relations, 7,* 117–140.

Festinger, L. (1957). *A theory of cognitive dissonance.* Stanford, CA: Stanford University Press.

Festinger, L. (1964). Behavioral support for opinion change. *Public Opinion Quarterly, 28,* 404–417.

Festinger, L., & Carlsmith, J. M. (1959). Cognitive consequences of forced compliance. *Journal of Abnormal and Social Psychology, 58,* 203–210.

Festinger, L., & Maccoby, N. (1964). On resistance to persuasive communication. *Journal of Abnormal and Social Psychology, 68,* 359–366.

Fink, E. L., Kaplowitz, S. A., & Bauer, C. L. (1983). Positional discrepancy, psychological discrepancy, and attitude change: Experimental tests of some mathematical models. *Communication Monographs, 50,* 413–430.

Fishbein, M. (Ed.). (1967). *Readings in attitude theory and measurement.* New York: Wiley.

Fishbein, M., & Ajzen, I. (1975). *Belief, attitude, intention, and behavior.* Reading, MA: Addison-Wesley.

Fishbein, M., & Ajzen, I. (1980). Predicting and understanding consumer behavior: Attitude behavior correspondence. In I. Ajzen & M. Fishbein (Eds.), *Understanding attitudes and predicting social behavior* (pp. 148–172). Englewood Cliffs, NJ: Prentice Hall.

Fishbein, M., & Coombs, F. S. (1974). Basis for decision: An attitudinal analysis of voting behavior. *Journal of Applied Social Psychology, 4,* 95–124.

Fiske, S. T., & Taylor, S. E. (1991). *Social cognition* (2nd ed.). New York: McGraw-Hill.

Fitzpatrick, M. A., & Winke, J. (1979). You always hurt the one you love: Strategies and tactics in interpersonal conflict. *Communication Quarterly, 27,* 1–11.

Flay, B. R. (1986). Mass media linkages with school-based programs for drug abuse prevention. *Journal of School Health, 56,* 402–406.

Flay, B. R. (1987). Mass media and smoking cessation: A critical review. *American Journal of Public Health, 77,* 153–160.

Forsyth, D. R. (1983). *An introduction to group dynamics.* Monterey, CA: Brooks/Cole.

Freedman, J. L., & Fraser, S. (1966). Compliance without pressure: The foot-in-the-door technique. *Journal of Personality and Social Psychology, 4,* 195–202.

Freedman, J. L., & Sears, D. O. (1965). Selective exposure. In L. Berkowitz (Ed.), *Advances in experimental social psychology* (Vol. 2, pp. 58–98). New York: Academic Press.

French, J. P. R., Jr., & Raven, B. (1960). The bases of social power. In D. Cartwright & A. Zander (Eds.), *Group dynamics* (pp. 607–623). New York: Harper & Row.

Galanter, M. (1989). *Cults: Faith, healing, and coercion.* New York: Oxford University Press.

Gallup, G. H. (1977). *The Gallup Poll: Public opinion 72–77.* Wilmington, DE: Scholarly Resources.

Gerberding, J. L. (1991). Reducing occupational risk of HIV infection. *Hospital Practice, 26,* 103–118.

Gillig, P., & Greenwald, A. (1974). Is it time to lay the sleeper effect to rest? *Journal of Personality and Social Psychology, 29,* 132–139.

Glass, G. V., McGaw, B., & Smith, M. L. (1981). *Meta-analysis in social research.* Beverly Hills, CA: Sage.

Goethals, G. R., & Nelson, R. E. (1973). Similarity in the influence process: The belief–value distinction. *Journal of Personality and Social Psychology, 25,* 117–122.

Goldfarb, L., Gerrard, M., Gibbons, F. X., & Plante, T. (1988). Attitudes toward sex, arousal, and the retention of contraceptive information. *Journal of Personality and Social Psychology, 55,* 634–641.

Gouldner, A. W. (1960). The norm of reciprocity: A preliminary statement. *American Sociological Review, 25,* 161–178.

Greenwald, A. G. (1975). On the inconclusiveness of "crucial" cognitive tests of dissonance vs. self-perception theories. *Journal of Experimental and Social Psychology, 11,* 490–499.

Greenwald, A. G., Brock, T. C., & Ostrom, T. M. (1968). *Psychological foundations of attitudes.* New York: Academic Press.

Greenwald, A. G., & Ronis, D. L. (1978). Twenty years of cognitive dissonance: Case study of the evolution of a theory. *Psychological Review, 85,* 53–57.

Gruder, C., Cook, T., Hennigan, K., Flay, B., Alessis, C., & Halamaj, J. (1978). Empirical tests of the absolute sleeper effect predicted from the discounting cue hypothesis. *Journal of Personality and Social Psychology, 36,* 1061–1074.

Guttman, L. (1955). A generalized simplex for factor analysis. *Psychometrika, 20,* 173–192.

Haaland, G. A., & Venkatesen, M. (1968). Resistance to persuasive communications: An examination of the distraction hypothesis. *Journal of Personality and Social Psychology, 9*, 167–170.

Hale, J., Mongeau, P. A., & Thomas, R. M. (1991). Cognitive processing of one- and two-sided persuasive messages. *Western Journal of Speech Communication, 55*, 380–389.

Hample, D. (1977). Testing a model of value argument and evidence. *Communication Monographs, 44*, 106–120.

Hample, D. (1978). Predicting immediate belief change and adherence to argument claims. *Communication Monographs, 45*, 219–228.

Hample, D. (1979). Predicting belief change using a cognitive theory of argument and evidence. *Communication Monographs, 46*, 142–151.

Harkins, S. G., & Petty, R. E. (1981). The multiple source effect in persuasion: The effects of distraction. *Personality and Social Psychology Bulletin, 7*, 627–635.

Heider, F. (1946). Attitudes and cognitive organization. *Journal of Psychology, 21*, 107–112.

Herek, G. W. (1984a). Beyond "homophobia": A social psychological perspective on attitudes toward lesbians and gay men. *Journal of Homosexuality, 10*, 2–17.

Herek, G. W. (1984b). Attitudes toward lesbians and gay men: A factor analytic study. *Journal of Homosexuality, 10*, 39–51.

Herek, G. W. (1987). Can functions be measured?: A new perspective on the functional approach to attitudes. *Social Psychology Quarterly, 50*, 285–303.

Herek, G. W. (1988). Heterosexuals' attitudes toward lesbians and gay men: Correlates and gender differences. *Journal of Sex Research, 25*, 451–477.

Higgins, E. T., & King, G. A. (1981). Accessibility of social constructs: Information processing consequences of individual and contextual variability. In N. Cantor & J. Kihlstrom (Eds.), *Personality, cognition, and social interaction* (pp. 69–122). Hillsdale, NJ: Erlbaum.

Higgins, E. T., King, G. A., & Mavin, G. H. (1982). Individual construct accessibility and subjective impressions and recall. *Journal of Personality and Social Psychology, 43*, 35–47.

Hovland, C. I., Janis, I. L, & Kelley, H. H. (1953). *Communication and persuasion.* New Haven, CT: Yale University Press.

Hovland, C., Lumsdaine, A., & Sheffield, F. (1949). *Experiments in mass communication.* Princeton, NJ: Princeton University Press.

Hovland, C., & Pritzker, H. A. (1957). Extent of opinion change as a function of amount of change advocated. *Journal of Abnormal and Social Psychology, 54*, 257–261.

Hovland, C., & Weiss, W. (1951). The influence of source credibility on communication effectiveness. *Public Opinion Quarterly, 15*, 635–650.

Hunter, J. E. (1988). Failure of the social desireability response set hypothesis. *Human Communication Research, 15*, 162–168.

Hunter, J. E., & Boster, F. J. (1978, November). *An empathy model of compliance-gaining message strategy selection.* Paper presented at the annual meeting of the Speech Communication Association, Minneapolis, MN.

Hunter, J. E., & Boster, F. J. (1979, November). *Situational differences in the selection of compliance gaining messages.* Paper presented at the annual meeting of the Speech Communication Association, San Antonio, TX.

Hunter, J. E., & Boster, F. J. (1987). A model of compliance-gaining message selection. *Communication Monographs, 54,* 63–84.

Hunter, J. E., Danes, J. E., & Cohen, S. H. (1984). *Mathematical models of attitude change: Change in single attitudes and cognitive structure.* New York: Academic Press.

Hunter, J. E., Schmitt, F. L., & Jackson, G. B. (1982). *Meta-analysis: Cumulating research findings across studies.* Beverly Hills, CA: Sage.

Infante, D. A. (1981). Trait argumentativeness as a predictor of communicative behavior in situations requiring argument. *Central States Speech Journal, 32,* 265–272.

Infante, D. A., & Rancer, A. S. (1982). A conceptualization and measure of argumentativeness. *Journal of Personality Assessment, 46,* 72–80.

Infante, D. A., & Wigley, C. J. (1986). Verbal aggressiveness: An interpersonal model and measure. *Communication Monographs, 53,* 61–69.

Insko, C. A. (1967). *Theories of attitude change.* New York: Appleton Century-Crofts.

Insko, C. A., Turnbull, W., & Yandell, B. (1974). Facilitative and inhibiting effects of distraction on attitude change. *Sociometry, 37,* 508–528.

Inui, T. S., Yourtee, E. L., & Williamson, J. W. (1976). Improved outcomes in hypertension after physician tutorials. *Annals of Internal Medicine, 84,* 646–651.

Isenberg, D. J. (1986). Group polarization: A critical review and meta-analysis. *Journal of Personality and Social Psychology, 50,* 1141–1151.

Jaccard, J. J., Knox, R., & Brinberg, D. (1979). Prediction of behavior from beliefs: An extension and test of a subjective probability model. *Journal of Personality and Social Psychology, 37,* 1239–1248.

Jackson, S., & Allen, M. (1987, May). *Meta-analysis of the effectiveness of one-sided and two-sided argumentation.* Paper presented at the annual meeting of the International Communication Association, Montreal, Canada.

Jackson, S., & Jacobs, S. (1983). Generalizing about messages: Suggestions for design and analysis of experiments. *Human Communication Research, 9,* 169–191.

Jackson, S., O'Keefe, D. J., & Jacobs, S. (1988). The search for reliable generalizations about messages: A comparison of research strategies. *Human Communication Research, 15,* 127–142.

Janis, I. L. (1967). Effects of fear arousal on attitude change: Recent developments in theory and research. In L. Berkowitz (Ed.), *Advances in experimental social psychology* (Vol. 3, pp. 166–224). New York: Academic Press.

Janis, I. L., & Feshbach, S. (1953). Effects of fear arousing communications. *Journal of Abnormal and Social Psychology, 48,* 78–92.

Janis, I. L., & Frick, F. (1943). The relationship between attitudes toward conclusions and errors in judging logical validity of syllogisms. *Journal of Experimental Psychology, 33,* 73–77.

Janis, I. L., Kaye, D., & Kirschner, P. (1965). Facilitating effects of "eating-while-reading" on responsiveness to persuasive communications. *Journal of Personality and Social Psychology, 1,* 181–186.

Janis, I. L., & King, B. T. (1954). The influence of role-playing on opinion change. *Journal of Abnormal and Social Psychology, 49,* 211–218.

Janz, N. K., & Becker, M. H. (1984). The health belief model: A decade later. *Health Education Quarterly, 11,* 1–47.

Jemmott, J. B., III, Jemmott, L. S., Spears, H., Hewitt, N., & Cruz-Collins, M. (1992). Self-efficacy, hedonistic expectancies, and condum-use intentions among inner-city black adolescent women: A social cognitive approach to AIDS risk behavior. *Journal of Adolescent Health, 13,* 512–519.

Jemmott, L. S., & Jemmott, J. B., III (1991). Applying the theory of reasoned action to AIDS risk behavior: Condom use among black women. *Nursing Research, 40,* 228–234.

Jessor, R., & Jessor, S. L., (1977). *Problem behavior and psychosocial development: A longitudinal study of youth.* New York: Academic Press.

Johnson, B. T., & Eagly, A. H. (1989). Effects of involvement on persuasion: A meta-analysis. *Psychological Bulletin, 106,* 290–314.

Johnson, B. T., & Eagly, A. H. (1990). Involvement and persuasion: Types, traditions, and the evidence. *Psychological Bulletin, 107,* 375–384.

Kahneman, D. (1973). *Attention and effort.* Englewood Cliffs, NJ: Prentice Hall.

Kahneman, D., & Tversky, A. (1973). On the psychology of prediction. *Psychological Review, 80,* 237–251.

Kallgren, C. A., & Wood, W. (1986). Access to attitude-relevant information in memory as a determinant of attitude–behavior consistency. *Journal of Experimental Social Psychology, 22,* 328–338.

Kaminski, E. P., McDermott, S. T., & Boster, F. J. (1977, April). *The use of compliance-gaining strategies as a function of Machiavellianism and situation.* Paper presented at the annual meeting of the Central States Speech Association, Southfield, MI.

Katz, D. (1960). The functional approach to the study of attitudes. *Public Opinion Quarterly, 24,* 163–204.

Kelley, H. H. (1952). Two functions of reference groups. In G. E. Swanson, T. M. Newcomb, & E. L. Hartley (Eds.), *Readings in social psychology* (2nd ed., pp. 410–414). New York: Holt.

Kelley, H. H. (1967). Attribution theory in social psychology. In D. Levine (Ed.), *Nebraska symposium on motivation* (Vol. 15, pp. 192–238). Lincoln, NE: University of Nebraska Press.

Kelman, H. C. (1958). Compliance, identification, and internalization: Three processes of attitude change. *Journal of Conflict Resolution, 2,* 51–60.

Kelman, H. C. (1961). Processes of opinion change. *Public Opinion Quarterly, 25,* 57–78.

Kelman, H., & Hovland, C. (1953). Reinstatement of the communicator in delayed measurement of opinion change. *Journal of Abnormal and Social Psychology, 48,* 327–335.

Kerlinger, F. N. (1973). *Foundations of behavioral research.* New York: Holt, Rinehart, & Winston.

Kiesler, C., Collins, C. A., & Miller, N. (1983). *Attitude change: A critical analysis of theoretical approaches.* Malabar, FL: Robert E. Kreiger.

Kiesler, C. A. (1971). *The psychology of commitment: Experiments linking behavior to belief.* San Diego, CA: Academic Press.

Kim, M., & Hunter, J. E. (1993). Relationships among attitudes, behavioral intentions, and behavior: A meta-analysis of past research, part 2. *Communication Research, 20,* 331–364.

King, B. T., & Janis, I. L. (1956). Comparison of the effects of improvised versus non-improvised role playing in producing opinion changes. *Human Relations, 9,* 177–186.

Kirscht, J. P., & Rosenstock, I. M. (1977). Patient adherence to antihypertensive medical regimens. *Journal of Community Health, 3,* 115–124.

Kleinke, C. L. (1980). Interaction between gaze and legitimacy of request on compliance in a field setting. *Journal of Nonverbal Behavior, 5,* 3–12.

Kogan, N., & Wallach, M. A. (1967). Risky-shift phenomenon in small decision-making groups: A test of the information exchange hypothesis. *Journal of Experimental Social Psychology, 6,* 467–471.

Lamm, H., & Myers, D. G. (1978). Group-induced polarization of attitudes and behavior. In L. Berkowitz (Ed.), *Advances in experimental social psychology* (Vol. 11, pp. 145–195). New York: Academic Press.

LaPiere, R. T. (1934). Attitudes vs. actions. *Social Forces, 13,* 230–237.

Latane, B., & Darley, J. M. (1968). Group inhibition of bystander intervention in emergencies. *Journal of Personality and Social Psychology, 10,* 215–221.

Latane, B., & Darley, J. M. (1970). *The unresponsive bystander: Why doesn't he help?* New York: Appleton-Century-Crofts.

Latane, B., & Rodin, J. (1969). A lady in distress: Inhibiting effects of friends and strangers on bystander intervention. *Journal of Experimental Social Psychology, 5,* 189–202.

Lenihan, K. J. (1965). *Perceived climates as a barrier to housing desegregation.* Unpublished manuscript, Columbia University, Bureau of Applied Social Research, New York.

Leupker, R. V., Johnson, C. A., Murray, D. M, & Pechacek, T. F. (1983). Prevention of cigarette smoking: Three-year follow-up of an education program for youth. *Journal of Behavioral Medicine, 6,* 53–62.

Leventhal, H. (1970). Findings and theory in the study of fear communications. In L. Berkowitz (Ed.), *Advances in experimental social psychology* (Vol. 5, pp. 119–186). New York: Academic Press.

Lewin, K. (1935). *A dynamic theory of personality.* New York: McGraw-Hill.

Liebert, R. M., Neale, J. M., & Davidson, E. S. (1973). *The early window: Effects of television on children and youth.* New York: Pergamon Press.

Lumsdaine, A. A., & Janis, I. L. (1953). Resistance to "counter-propaganda" produced by one-sided and two-sided "propaganda" presentations. *Public Opinion Quarterly, 17,* 311–318.

MacHovec, F. J. (1989). *Cults and personality.* Springfield, IL: Charles C. Thomas.

Mackowiak, P. A., Wasserman, S. S., & Levine, M. M. (1992). A critical appraisal of 98.6 Degrees F, the upper limit of the normal body temperature, and other legacies of Carl Reinhold August Wunderlich. *Journal of the American Medical Association, 268,* 1578–1580.

Madden, T. J., Ellen, P. S., & Ajzen, I. (1992). A comparison of the theory of planned behavior and the theory of reasoned action. *Personality and Social Psychology Bulletin, 18,* 3–9.

Mandler, G. (1984). *Mind and body: Psychology of emotion and stress.* New York: W. W. Norton.

Marwell, G., & Schmitt, D. R. (1967). Dimensions of compliance-gaining behavior: An empirical analysis. *Sociometry, 30,* 350–364.

Matice, K. (1978). *The effect of source, class, dogmatism, and time on attitude change of police academy recruits.* Unpublished doctoral dissertation, University of Missouri, St. Louis.

Mayer, M. E. (1986). Explaining the choice shift: A comparison of competing effects-coded models. In M. L. McLaughlin (Ed.), *Communication yearbook 9* (pp. 297–314). Beverly Hills, CA: Sage.

McAlister, A. L., Perry, C., & Maccoby, N. (1979). Adolescent smoking: Onset and prevention. *Pediatrics, 63,* 650–658.

McCroskey, J. C. (1966). Scales for the measurement of ethos. *Speech Monographs, 33,* 65–72.

McCroskey, J. C. (1967). The effects of evidence in persuasive communication. *Western Speech, 31,* 189–199.

McCroskey, J. C. (1969). A summary of experimental research on the effects of evidence in persuasive communication. *Quarterly Journal of Speech, 55,* 169–176.

McGuire, W. J. (1960). A syllogistic analysis of cognitive relationships. In C. I. Hovland & M. J. Rosenberg (Eds.), *Attitude organization and change: An analysis of consistency among attitude components* (pp. 65–111). New Haven, CT: Yale University Press.

McGuire, W. J. (1961a). Persistence of resistance to persuasion induced by various types of persuasive defenses. *Journal of Abnormal and Social Psychology, 64,* 241–248.

McGuire, W. J. (1961b). The effectiveness of supportive and refutational defenses in immunizing and restoring beliefs against persuasion. *Sociometry, 24,* 184–197.

McGuire, W. J. (1964). Inducing resistance to persuasion: Some contemporary approaches. In L. Berkowitz (Ed.), *Advances in experimental social psychology* (Vol. 1, pp. 191–229). New York: Academic Press.

McGuire, W. J. (1966). Attitudes and opinions. *Annual Review of Psychology, 17,* 475–514.

McGuire, W. J. (1968). Personality and attitude change: An information processing theory. In A. G. Greenwald, T. C. Brock, & T. M. Ostrom (Eds.), *Psychological foundations of attitudes* (pp. 171–196). New York: Academic Press.

McGuire, W. J. (1969). The nature of attitudes and attitude change. In G. Lindzey & E. Aronson (Eds.), *Handbook of social psychology* (Vol. 3, pp. 136–314). Reading, MA: Addison-Wesley.

McGuire, W. J., & Papageorgis, D. (1961). The relative efficacy of various types of prior belief-defense in producing immunity against persuasion. *Journal of Abnormal and Social Psychology, 62,* 327–337.

McLaughlin, M. L., Cody, M. J., & Robey, C. S. (1980). Situational influences on the selection of strategies to resist compliance-gaining attempts. *Human Communication Research, 7,* 14–36.

McQuillen, J. S., & Higginbotham, D. C. (1986). Children's reasoning about compliance-resisting behaviors. In M. L. McLaughlin (Ed.), *Communication yearbook 9* (pp. 673–690). Beverly Hills, CA: Sage.

Meyers, R. A. (1989). Persuasive arguments theory: A test of assumptions. *Human Communication Research, 15,* 357–381.

Meyers, R. A., & Seibold, D. R. (1990). Perspectives on group argument: A critical review of persuasive arguments theory and an alternative structurational view. In J. A. Anderson (Ed.), *Communication yearbook 13* (pp. 268–302). Newbury Park, CA: Sage.

Millar, M. G., & Millar, K. U. (1990). Attitude change as a function of attitude type and argument type. *Journal of Personality and Social Psychology, 59,* 217–228.

Miller, G. R. (1963). Studies in the use of fear appeals: A summary and analysis. *Central States Speech Journal, 14,* 117–125.

Miller, G. R. (1967). A crucial problem in attitude research. *Quarterly Journal of Speech, 53,* 235–240.

Miller, G. R. (1973). Counterattitudinal advocacy: A current appraisal. In C. D. Mortensen & K. K. Sereno (Eds.), *Advances in communication research* (pp. 105–152). New York: Harper & Row.

Miller, G. R. (1980). On being persuaded: Some basic distinctions. In M. E. Roloff & G. R. Miller (Eds.), *Persuasion: New directions in theory and research* (pp. 11–28). Beverly Hills, CA: Sage.

Miller, G. R., Boster, F. J., Roloff, M., & Seibold, D. (1977). Compliance-gaining message strategies: A typology and some findings concerning effects of situational differences. *Communication Monographs, 44,* 37–51.

Miller, G. R., Boster, F. J., Roloff, M., & Seibold, D. (1987). MBRS rekindled: Some thoughts on compliance gaining in interpersonal settings. In M. E. Roloff & G. R. Miller (Eds.), *Interpersonal processes: New directions in communication research* (pp. 89–116). Newbury Park, CA: Sage.

Miller, G. R., & Burgoon, M. (1978). Persuasion research: Review and commentary. In B. D. Ruben (Ed.), *Communication yearbook 12* (pp. 29–47). New Brunswick, NJ: Transaction Books.

Miller, N. (1965). Involvement and dogmatism as inhibitors of attitude change. *Journal of Experimental Social Psychology, 1,* 121–132.

Mindred, P. W., & Cohen, J. B. (1979). Isolating attitudinal and normative influences in behavioral intentions models. *Journal of Marketing Research, 16,* 102–110.

Mindred, P. W., & Cohen, J. B. (1981). An examination of the Fishbein–Ajzen behavioral-intentions model's concepts and measures. *Journal of Experimental Social Psychology, 17,* 309–339.

Mongeau, P. A., & Stiff, J. B. (1993). Specifying causal relationships in the Elaboration Likelihood Model. *Communication Theory, 3,* 65–72.

Morley, D. D. (1988a). Meta-analytic techniques: When generalizing to message populations is not possible. *Human Communication Research, 15,* 112–126.

Morley, D. D. (1988b). Reply to Jackson, O'Keefe, and Jacobs. *Human Communication Research, 15,* 143–147.

Naisbitt, J. (1982). *Megatrends: Ten new directions transforming our lives.* New York: Warner Books.

National Gay Task Force. (1984). *Anti-gay/lesbian victimization.* Washington, DC: Author. (Available from National Gay and Lesbian Task Force, 1517 U Street NW, Washington, DC 20009).

Newcomb, T. (1953). An approach to the study of communicative acts. *Psychological Review, 60,* 393–404.

Newcomb, T. M., Turner, R. H., & Converse, P. E. (1965). *Social psychology.* New York: Holt, Rinehart, & Winston.

Norman, R. (1976). When what is said is important: A comparison of expert and attractive sources. *Journal of Experimental Social Psychology, 12,* 294–300.

O'Keefe, B. J. (1988). The logic of message design: Individual differences in reasoning about communication. *Communication Monographs, 55,* 80–103.

O'Keefe, B. J. (1990). The logic of regulative communication: Understanding the logic of message designs. In J. P. Dillard (Ed.), *Seeking compliance: The production of interpersonal influence messages* (pp. 87–106). Scottsdale, AZ: Gorsuch-Scarisbrick.

O'Keefe, B. J., & Delia, J. G. (1978). Construct comprehensiveness and cognitive complexity. *Perceptual and Motor Skills, 46,* 548–550.

O'Keefe, B. J., & McCornack, S. A. (1987). Message design logic and message goal structure: Effects on perceptions of message quality in regulative communication situations. *Human Communication Research, 14,* 68–92.

O'Keefe, B. J., & Shepherd, G. J. (1987). The pursuit of multiple objectives in face-to-face persuasive interactions: Effects of construct differentiation on message organization. *Communication Monographs, 54,* 396–419.

O'Keefe, D. J. (1990). *Persuasion: Theory and research.* Newbury Park, CA: Sage.

O'Keefe, D. J., & Delia, J. D. (1981). Construct differentiation and the relationship of attitudes and behavioral intentions. *Communication Monographs, 48,* 146–157.

O'Keefe, D. J., Jackson, S., & Jacobs, S. (1988). Reply to Morley. *Human Communication Research, 15,* 148–151.

Osterhouse, R. A., & Brock, T. C. (1970). Distraction increases yielding to propaganda by inhibiting counterarguing. *Journal of Personality and Social Psychology, 15,* 344–358.

Papageorgis, D., & McGuire, W. J. (1961). The generality of immunity to persuasion produced by pre-exposure to weakened counterarguments. *Journal of Abnormal and Social Psychology, 62,* 475–481.

Petty, R. E., & Cacioppo, J. T. (1981). *Attitudes and persuasion: Classic and contemporary approaches.* Dubuque, IA: Wm. C. Brown.

Petty, R. E., & Cacioppo, J. T. (1986). *Communication and persuasion: Central and peripheral routes to attitude change.* New York: Springer-Verlag.

Petty, R. E., & Cacioppo, J. T. (1990). Involvement vs. persuasion: Tradition vs. integration. *Psychological Bulletin, 107,* 367–374.

Petty, R. E., Cacioppo, J. T., & Goldman, R. (1981). Personal involvement as a determinant of argument based persuasion. *Journal of Personality and Social Psychology, 41,* 847–855.

Petty, R. E., Kasmer, J. E., Haugtvedt, C. P., & Cacioppo, J. T. (1987). Source and message factors in persuasion: A reply to Stiff's critique of the Elaboration Likelihood Model. *Communication Monographs, 54,* 233–249.

Petty, R. E., Ostrom, T. M., & Brock, T. C. (1981). *Cognitive responses in persuasion.* Hillsdale, NJ: Erlbaum.

Petty, R. E., Wells, G. L., & Brock, T. C. (1976). Distraction can enhance or reduce yielding to propaganda: Thought disruption versus effort justification. *Journal of Personality and Social Psychology, 34,* 874–888.

Pfau, M. (1992). The potential of inoculation in promoting resistance to the effectiveness of comparative advertising messages. *Communication Quarterly, 40,* 26–44.

Pfau, M., & Burgoon, M. (1988). Inoculation in political communication. *Human Communication Research, 15,* 91–111.

Pfau, M., & Kenski, H. C. (1990). *Attack politics: Strategy and defense.* New York: Praeger.

Pfau, M., Kenski, H. C., Nitz, M., & Sorenson, J. (1990). Efficacy of inoculation strategies in promoting resistance to political attack messages: Application to direct mail. *Communication Monographs, 57,* 25–43.

Pfau, M., Van Bockern, S., & Kang, J. G. (1992). Use of inoculation to promote resistance to smoking initiation among adolescents. *Communication Monographs, 59,* 213–230.

Powell, M. C., & Fazio, R. H. (1984). Attitude accessibility as a function of repeated attitude expression. *Personality and Social Psychology Bulletin, 10,* 139–148.

Powers, W., Jordan, W., & Street, R. (1979). Language indices in the measurement of cognitive complexity: Is complexity loquacity? *Human Communication Research, 6,* 69–73.

Reardon, K. K. (1981). *Persuasion: Theory and context.* Beverly Hills, CA: Sage.

Reinard, J. C. (1988). The empirical study of the persuasive effects of evidence: The status after fifty years of research. *Human Communication Research, 15,* 3–59.

Regan, D. T., & Fazio, R. H. (1977). On the consistency between attitudes and behavior: Look to the method of attitude formation. *Journal of Experimental Social Psychology, 13,* 28–45.

Reynolds, R. A., & Burgoon, M. (1983). Belief processing, reasoning, and evidence. In R. Bostrom (Ed.), *Communication yearbook 7* (pp. 83–104). Beverly Hills, CA: Sage.

Rhine, R. J., & Severance, L. J. (1970). Ego-involvement, discrepancy, source credibility, and attitude change. *Journal of Personality and Social Psychology, 16,* 175–190.

Rogers, R. W. (1975). A protection motivation theory of fear appeals and attitude change. *Journal of Psychology, 91,* 93–114.

Rogers, R. W. (1983). Cognitive and physiological processes in fear appeals and attitude change: A revised theory of protection motivation. In J. Cacioppo & R. Petty (Eds.), *Social psychophysiology* (pp. 153–176). New York: Guilford Press.

Rohrbach, L. A., Graham, J. W., Hansen, W. B., Flay, B. R., & Johnson, C. A. (1987). Evaluation of resistance skills training using multitrait-multimethod role play skill assessment. *Health Education Research, 2,* 401–407.

Rokeach, M. (1968). *Beliefs, attitudes and values: A theory of organization and change.* San Francisco: Jossey Bass.

Roloff, M., & Barnicott, E. F., Jr. (1978). The situational use of pro- and anti-social compliance-gaining strategies by high and low Machiavellians. In B. D. Ruben (Ed.), *Communication yearbook 2* (pp. 193–205). New Brunswick, NJ: Transaction Books.

Roloff, M., & Barnicott, E. F., Jr. (1979). The influence of dogmatism on the situational use of pro- and anti-social compliance gaining strategies. *Southern Speech Communication Journal, 45,* 37–54.

Ronis, D. L., & Greenwald, A. G. (1979). Dissonance theory revised again: Comment on the paper by Fazio, Zanna, and Cooper. *Journal of Experimental Social Psychology, 15,* 62–69.

Rosenstock, I. M. (1974). Historical origins of the health belief model. In M. H. Becker (Ed.), *The health belief model and personal health behavior* (pp. 1–8). Thorofare, NJ: Charles B. Slack.

Rule, B. G., Bisanz, G. L., & Kohn, M. (1985). Anatomy of a persuasion schema: Targets, goals, and strategies. *Journal of Personality and Social Psychology, 48,* 1127–1140.

Ryan, M. J. (1982). Behavioral intention formation: A structural equation analysis of attitudinal and social influence interdependency. *Journal of Consumer Research, 9,* 263–278.

Sadler, O., & Tesser, A. (1973). Some effects of salience and time upon interpersonal hostility and attraction during social isolation. *Sociometry, 36,* 99–112.

San Miguel, C. L., & Millham, J. (1976). The role of cognitive and situational variables in aggression toward homosexuals. *Journal of Homosexuality, 1,* 11–27.

Sarnoff, D. (1960). Reaction formation and cynicism. *Journal of Personality, 28,* 129–143.

Schachter, S., & Singer, J. E. (1962). Cognitive, social, and physiological determinants of emotional state. *Psychological Review, 65,* 121–128.

Schinke, S. P., & Gilchrist, L. D. (1984). Preventing cigarette smoking with youth. *Journal of Primary Prevention, 5,* 48–56.

Seibold, D. R. (1988). A response to "Item desireability in compliance-gaining research." *Human Communication Research, 15,* 152–161.

Seibold, D. R., Cantrill, J. G., & Meyers, R. A. (1985). Communication and interpersonal influence. In M. L. Knapp & G. R. Miller (Eds.), *Handbook of interpersonal communication* (pp. 551–611). Beverly Hills, CA: Sage.

Shannon, W. V. (1967). *The heir apparent: Robert Kennedy and the struggle for power.* New York: Macmillan.

Sheppard, B. H., Hartwick, J., & Warshaw, P. R. (1988). The theory of reasoned action: A meta-analysis of past research with recommendations for modifications and future research. *Journal of Consumer Research, 15,* 325–343.

Sherif, C. W., Sherif, M., & Nebergall, R. E. (1965). *Attitude and attitude change.* Philadelphia: W. B. Saunders.

Sherif, M., & Hovland, C. I. (1961). *Social judgment: Assimilation and contrast effects in communication and attitude change.* New Haven, CT: Yale University Press.

Sherif, M., & Sherif, C. W. (1956). *An outline of social psychology.* New York: Harper & Row.

Sherif, M., & Sherif, C. W. (1967). Attitude as the individual's own categories: The social judgment–involvement approach to attitude and attitude change. In C. W. Sherif & M. Sherif (Eds.), *Attitude, ego-involvement, and change* (pp. 105–139). New York: Wiley.

Sillars, A. L. (1980). The stranger and the spouse as target persons for compliance-gaining strategies: A subjective expected utility model. *Human Communication Research, 6,* 265–279.

Simons, H. W., Berkowitz, N. N., & Moyer, R. J. (1970). Similarity, credibility, and attitude change: A review and a theory. *Psychological Bulletin, 73,* 1–16.

Sivacek, J., & Crano, W. D. (1982). Vested interest as a moderator of attitude–behavior consistency. *Journal of Personality and Social Psychology, 43,* 210–221.

Smetana, J. G., & Adler, N. E. (1980). Fishbein's valence × expectancy model: An examination of some assumptions. *Personality and Social Psychology Bulletin, 6,* 89–96.

Smith, M. B., Bruner, J. S., & White, R. W. (1956). *Opinions and personality.* New York: Wiley.

Staats, C. K., & Staats, A. W. (1957). Meaning established by classical conditioning. *Journal of Experimental Psychology, 54,* 74–80.

Stiff, J. B. (1986). Cognitive processing of persuasive message cues: A meta-analytic review of the effects of supporting information on attitudes. *Communication Monographs, 53,* 75–89.

Stiff, J. B., & Boster, F. J. (1987). Cognitive processing: Additional thoughts and a reply to Petty, Kasmer, Haugtvedt, and Cacioppo. *Communication Monographs, 54,* 250–256.

Stiff, J. B., McCormack, M., Zook, E., Stein, T., & Henry, R. (1990). The effects of attitudes toward gay men and lesbians on learning about AIDS and HIV transmission. *Communication Research, 17,* 743–758.

Stoner, J. A. F. (1968). Risky and cautious shifts in group decisions: The influence of widely held values. *Journal of Experimental Social Psychology, 4,* 442–459.

Sutton, S. R. (1982). Fear-arousing communications: A critial examination of theory and research. In J. R. Eiser (Ed.), *Social psychology and behavioral medicine* (pp. 303–337). London: Wiley.

Sutton, S. R., & Eiser, J. R. (1984). The effect of fear-arousing communications on cigarette smoking: An expectancy-value approach. *Journal of Behavioral Medicine, 7,* 13–33.

Tannenbaum, P. H. (1953). *Attitudes toward source and concept as factors in attitude change through communications.* Unpublished doctoral dissertation, University of Illinois, Urbana.

Tedeschi, J. T., Schlenker, B. R., & Bonoma, T. V. (1971). Cognitive dissonance: Private ratiocination or public spectacle? *American Psychologist, 26,* 685–695.

Tellis, G. J. (1987). *Advertising, exposure, loyalty, and brand purchase: A two-stage model of choice* (Report No. 87-105). Cambridge, MA: Marketing Science Institute.

Tesser, A. (1978). Self-generated attitude change. In L. Berkowitz (Ed.), *Advances in experimental social psychology* (Vol. 11, pp. 289–338). New York: Academic Press.

Tesser, A., & Conlee, M. C. (1975). Some effects of time and thought on attitude polarization. *Journal of Personality and Social Psychology, 31,* 262–270.

Tesser, A., & Paulhus, D. L. (1976). Toward a causal model of love. *Journal of Personality and Social Psychology, 34,* 1095–1105.

Thurstone, L. L. (1928). Attitudes can be measured. *American Journal of Sociology, 33,* 529–544.

Thurstone, L. L. (1931). The measurement of social attitudes. *Journal of Abnormal and Social Psychology, 26,* 249–269.

Toulmin, S. (1964). *The uses of argument.* Cambridge: Cambridge University Press.

Triandis, H. C. (1971). *Attitudes and attitude change.* New York: Wiley.

Trodahl, V. C., & Powell, F. A. (1965). A short-form dogmatism scale for use in field studies. *Social Forces, 44,* 211–214.

Tversky, A., & Kahneman, D. (1974). Judgment under uncertainty: Heuristics and biases. *Science, 185,* 1124–1134.

Tversky, A., & Kahneman, D. (1982). Judgments of and by representativeness. In D. Kahneman, P. Slovic, & A. Tversky (Eds.), *Judgment under uncertainty: Heuristics and biases* (pp. 163–178). Cambridge: Cambridge University Press.

Tybout, A., Sternthal, B., & Calder, B. J. (1983). Information availability as a determinant of multiple request effectiveness. *Journal of Marketing Research, 20,* 280–290.

Vinokur, A., & Burnstein, E. (1974). Effects of partially shared persuasive arguments on group-induced shifts: A group problem-solving approach. *Journal of Personality and Social Psychology, 29,* 305–315.

Valdiserri, R. O., Arena, V. O., Proctor, D., & Bonati, F. A. (1989). The relationship between women's attitudes about condoms and their use: Implications for condom promotion campaigns. *American Journal of Public Health, 79,* 499–503.

Vohs, J. L., & Garrett, R. L., (1968). Resistance to persuasion: An integrative framework. *Public Opinion Quarterly, 32,* 445–452.

Warshaw, P. R. (1980). A new model for predicting behavioral intentions: An alternative to Fishbein. *Journal of Marketing Research, 17,* 153–172.

Wheatly, J. J., & Oshikawa, S. (1970). The relationship between anxiety and positive and negative advertising appeals. *Journal of Marketing Research, 7,* 85–89.

Whittaker, J. O. (1967). Resolution of the communication discrepancy issue in attitude change. In C. W. Sherif & M. Sherif (Eds.), *Attitude, ego-involvement, and change* (pp. 159–177). New York: Wiley.

Wicker, A. W. (1969). Attitudes versus actions: The relationship of verbal and overt behavioral responses to attitude objects. *Journal of Social Issues, 25,* 41-78.

Wicklund, R. A., & Brehm, J. W. (1976). *Perspectives on cognitive dissonance.* Hillsdale, NJ: Erlbaum.

Williams, D. L., & Boster, F. J. (1981, May). *The effects of beneficial situational characteristics, negativism, and dogmatism on compliance gaining message selection.* Paper presented at the annual meeting of the International Communication Association, Minneapolis, MN.

Willis, F. M., & Hamm, H. K. (1980). The case of interpersonal touch in securing compliance. *Journal of Nonverbal Behavior, 5,* 49–55.

Wilson, J. D. (1992, September 14). Gays under fire. *Newsweek,* pp. 35–40.

Wilson, S. R. (1990). Development and test of a cognitive rules model of interaction goals. *Communication Monographs, 57,* 83–103.

Wiseman, R. L., & Schenck-Hamlin, W. (1981). A multidimensional scaling validation of an inductively-derived set of compliance-gaining strategies. *Communication Monographs, 48,* 251–270.

Witte, K. (1992a). Putting the fear back into fear appeals: The extended parallel process model. *Communication Monographs, 59,* 329–349.

Witte, K. (1992b, November). *Fear control and danger control: An initial test of the extended parallel process model.* Paper presented at the annual meeting of the Speech Communication Association, Chicago.

Wodarski, J. & Bagarozzi, D. (1979). *Behavioral social work.* New York: Human Sciences Press.

Wood, W., & Eagly, A. H. (1981). Stages in the analysis of persuasive messages: The role of causal attributions and message comprehension. *Journal of Personality and Social Psychology, 40,* 246–259.

Woodall, W. G., & Burgoon, J. K. (1981). The effects of nonverbal synchrony on message comprehension and persuasiveness. *Journal of Nonverbal Behavior, 5,* 207–223.

Worchel, S., Andreoli, V., & Eason, J. (1975). Is the medium the message? A study of the effects of media, communicator, and message characteristics on attitude change. *Journal of Applied Social Psychology, 5,* 157–172.

Wyer, R. S. (1970). The quantitative prediction of belief and opinion change:

A further test of a subjective probability model. *Journal of Personality and Social Psychology, 16,* 559–570.

Wyer, R. S., & Goldberg, L. (1970). A probabilistic analysis of the relationships among beliefs and attitudes. *Psychological Review, 77,* 100–120.

Wyer, R. S., & Srull, T. K. (1981). Category accessibility: Some theoretical and empirical issues concerning the processing of social stimulus information. In E. T. Higgins, C. P. Herman, & M. P. Zanna (Eds.), *Social cognition: The Ontario Symposium* (Vol. 1, pp. 161–197). Hillsdale, NJ: Erlbaum.

Zanna, M. P., & Cooper, J. (1974). Dissonance and the pill: An attributional approach to studying the arousal properties of dissonance. *Journal of Personality and Social Psychology, 29,* 703–709.

Zimbardo, P. G. (1960). Involvement and communication discrepancy as determinants of opinion conformity. *Journal of Abnormal and Social Psychology, 60,* 86–94.

Zimbardo, P. G., & Ebbesen, E. B. (1970). Experimental modification of the relationship between effort, attitude, and behavior. *Journal of Personality and Social Psychology, 16,* 207–213.

Index